Joy and Hope

Pilgrim
Priest
&
Bishop

PAT POWER

**Foreword by
Bishop William Morris**

David Lovell Publishing
Melbourne Australia

Published in 2015 by
David Lovell Publishing
PO Box 44, Kew East
Victoria 3102 Australia
tel/fax +61 3 9859 0000
publisher@davidlovellpublishing.com

Front cover image: Graham Tidey/Fairfax Syndication
Typeset in 11.5/16 Adobe Garamond Pro
This edition printed through Ingram Spark

National Library of Australia Cataloguing-in-Publication data

Patrick P., 1942- author.
Joy and hope: pilgrim, priest and bishop / Pat Power.

ISBN: 9781863551588 (paperback)

Power, Patrick P., 1942- .Catholic Church – Bishops. Catholic Church.
Archdiocese of Canberra and Goulburn.   Clergy – Professional ethics.
Clergy – Conduct of life. Church work with people with
social disabilities – Australia. Pastoral counselling – Australia.
Pastoral theology – Australia.

262.12294

Foreword

Some time back I read Alyse Nelson's book, *Vital Voices: The Power of Women Leading Change around the World* (2102). It gave us strong women's voices, and showed how vital people's voices are when raised in support of justice, freedom and political rights, raised against domestic violence, raised in helping to rebuild hearts and minds by giving them faith again in humanity where hope has been lost. Voices raised in this way echo around the world, building bridges and planting the seeds of hope, powered by justice and peace and embracing respect and love for all life.

This book is the story of another vital voice proclaiming Good News, always with the hope of removing obstacles and changing attitudes which may be hiding the face of Christ. When our city streets were lit by only gas or kerosene-fed lamps, the lamplighter would walk the streets and with his long pole with its small flame at the top would light the lamps to illumine those streets. Like the lamplighters of old, the chapters of this book bring light to our path in the form of hope and joy, justice and peace, love and respect for all life.

This light, with its challenge, is spoken of by Pope Francis in his encyclical letter, *Laudato si'* ('On care for our common home'). It lights our way as the lit lamps brought light to our streets. The chapters show the importance of listening and hospitality, of asking questions, for wisdom shows that the answer is found in the mystery of the question and the search brings deeper understanding to life and relationships. Just as the glow from the lamps lit up the streets, so does the light from Bishop Pat Power's book give light to our path and hope for our journey.

Pope Francis writes in *Evangelii Gaudium*, 'Being church means being God's people, being God's leaven in the midst of humanity. The church must be a place of mercy freely given, where everyone can feel welcomed, loved, forgiven and encouraged to live the good life of the Gospel' (*EG* 114). 'I ask you to adopt in every activity that you undertake a missionary heart, [which] never closes itself off, never retreats into its own security, never opts for rigidity and defensiveness. It always does what good it can, even if in the process its shoes get soiled by the mud of the street' (*EG* 45).

The journey of this book shows the missionary heart of Pat Power. He did not retreat into his own security or opt for rigidity or defensiveness, but got his feet soiled in the mud of the street by walking as a pilgrim with his sisters and brothers, hand in hand in the journey of life. He gave them a voice that was filled with hope, and shared their tears and joys as he walked and celebrated with them as priest. As bishop, his words show that he lives to serve and reflects the thoughts of Pope Francis: '[The bishop] will sometimes go before his people, pointing the way and keeping their hope vibrant. At other times, he will simply be in their midst with his unassuming and merciful presence. Other times, he will have to walk after them, helping those who lag behind and – above all – allowing the flock to strike out on new paths. [He will] listen to everyone and not simply to those who would tell him what he would like to hear' (*EG* 31).

Faith is not a fixed standpoint, but rather a path on which every person, as well as the church as a whole, is on the way – pilgrims. Our task, the church's task, is to accompany people wisely, patiently, mercifully and with great compassion on this path, this process of growth. The journey this book of Bishop Pat Power takes us on does just that. It opens doors onto well-trodden paths and windows to gaze on old questions in new light and fresh questions that keep the rumour of God alive.

Bishop William Morris

Contents

Foreword Bishop William Morris   v

Introduction   vii

The quest for grace   1

See, judge and act: Reading the signs of the times   7

Chrism Mass 2011   19

Letter to Pope John Paul II   23

Letter to Pope Benedict XVI   25

Letter to Pope Francis   27

The selection of bishops   29

Pilgrims all   32

Listening to our people   39

A journey of discovery   42

An historic moment of grace   47

A time of grace   50

Pilgrims and healers   55

Marginalised people: In society and in the church   61

Rainbow sash   65

Women, homosexuals and the church   69

Keeping in touch with the people   71

Social policy connections   78

One hundred and fifty years of grace   87

Causeway's influence on my life as a priest   92

Remembrance ceremony   97

Real action on climate change   100

Conversation over a meat pie   102

Mary, our model   105

Galong Mass   108

Good Samaritan Sesquicentenary Mass   112

Goodbye to the Good Samaritans   118

St Clare's College   122

The value of a life 126

Further reflections on abortion 129

The Royal Commission 131

The Royal Commission revisited 133

Caught in the cross-fire 135

St Patrick: Champion of the oppressed 138

The Missionary Sisters of Service 144

Being a Catholic today 149

Welcome to Archbishop Christopher Prowse 152

Jerusalem 159

SIEV X 162

An appeal to President Bush 165

Breaking the silence 168

A hundred years of warfare 171

Three days in Dubrovnik 175

A short stay in Medjugorje 178

Pilgrimage to Santiago de Compostela 181

Lebanon: A personal encounter 189

East Timor 195

Funeral Mass for Pope John Paul II 200

Graham Greene 204

Bishop Geoffrey Robinson 208

Bishop Bill Morris 211

Gloria 213

Bridey 215

Carrying the Olympic torch 218

South Sydney Rabbitohs 220

Canberra Citizen of the Year 224

Retirement Mass: St Christopher's 226

Introduction

Just as I was leaving Rome in May 1975, having completed three years of post-graduate studies, Pope Paul VI issued an apostolic exhortation, *Gaudete in Domino* (*Rejoice in the Lord*). It was written in similar vein to Pope Francis' *Evangelii Gaudium* (*The Joy of the Gospel*) and not surprisingly, Francis draws on much of the positive spirit of Paul VI's writing.

Unfortunately, at about the same time as the publication of *Gaudete in Domino,* one of the Vatican congregations put out a paper on sexual ethics which was far from positive in its tone. Needless to say, all the media attention was focused on the latter document while Christian joy faded into the background. Sadly, that episode recurred all too often in various ways in the years following the Second Vatican Council, meaning that much of the hope and joy promised by Vatican II failed to materialise.

When I was retiring in mid-2012, I was often asked if I was going to publish some of the material I had produced over the years. As I now prepare to celebrate fifty years since my ordination to the priesthood, I have come to the conclusion that it is 'now or never'. I have never regarded myself as an academic, but I have been blessed with a pastoral heart which, I hope, has informed my ministry as a priest and bishop. I trust that will come through to those who read these pages.

At the time I was appointed bishop in 1986, many of the people closest to me told me not to turn away from being my real self. That advice in some ways was easy enough to adopt because I had been made auxiliary bishop in my home diocese of Canberra and Goulburn, and, surrounded by family and good friends, there were plenty of people to remind me of my humble origins if I became too big for my boots. On the other hand, becoming part of the national bishops' conference brings its pressures to conform to the party line and of course the pressure is even greater in relation to the central authority of the Vatican. Having said all that, my archbishop, Francis Carroll, was an excellent model for me as someone imbued with the teaching and spirit of Vatican II. He was supportive of my stances even when I might have gone further than he would have done personally.

As a bishop I have been in a position to give expression to much of the Vatican Council's call for the church to be engaged with other Christian churches, non-Christian faiths and the wider society. It has been a privileged place where I have learned so much from my sisters and brothers in all sections of the human family. Hopefully, too, I have been able to share with those outside the church something of the richness of the Christian tradition lived out in the Catholic Church.

Overall, I have enjoyed good relations with people in the media, which has enabled me to deliver a message beyond the confines of the Catholic Church. I tried to be available when requested to give comments or interviews. By and large, I was treated fairly and I do not recall ever being deliberately misrepresented. I think interviewers appreciated that I would not just give out the party line, but when I departed from that I tried to make a distinction between what was my personal view and what was official church teaching. A number of opinion pieces appear in these pages. Sometimes they were requested by newspapers or other publications; on other occasions they were accepted at my request. I found them a satisfactory medium as they were not subject to editing. Television was always a bit daunting especially when a ten or fifteen second 'grab' was all that would come out of a sometimes long interview. I found extended radio interviews probably the best way of communicating on air, especially if it was a direct broadcast, where the whole message was delivered. A long association with the Australian Catholic Social Welfare Commission meant that I was often called upon in the media to spell out Catholic social teaching on a whole range of issues affecting some of the most vulnerable people in society.

I hope my love for the church comes through in what I write. I have never doubted that the Catholic Church was where I was meant to be. But over fifty years of priesthood I have recognised that we are a church of sinners as well as a church of saints and that within each of us there is the saint and the sinner. The need for reform appears a number of times throughout what follows. I believe that any healthy organisation or individual needs to possess the ability to be self-critical.

This has become alarmingly true when almost daily our church is being justly criticised for its handling of the sexual abuse crisis. The Truth, Justice and Healing Council, set up by the bishops and religious leaders, spoke in an activity report in December 2014 of 'the impact of clericalism which can be understood as referring to approaches or practices involving ordained ministry geared to power over others, not service to others. Clericalism has been seen as a contributing factor to the way in which the church has responded to abuse claims and engaged with survivors.'

One of the most attractive images of the church to emerge from the Second Vatican Council is that of the *Pilgrim Church*. The notion of a people on the move, with a sense of adventure, supporting and encouraging one another, sometimes getting a bit lost or bloodied, sometimes questioning the path they have taken, but ultimately believing that Jesus is the way, the truth and the life, is an image that rings true for me. An earlier view that the church was changeless and unchanging stifled any questioning or ability even to contemplate change which may have been very much needed. Those who persevere with this book will understand how imbued I have become with what it means to be a pilgrim in so many ways.

There are many references in these pages to the place of women in the life of the church, but probably not enough. In so many instances where the presence of women in effective roles within the church is absent or diminished, the whole church is the poorer for it. There is no need here to anticipate what I have written along those lines except to say that it could have been spelt out even more strongly. Groups such as Women and the Australian Church (WATAC), Catalyst for Renewal and Australian Reforming Catholics are to be applauded for their tireless efforts to demonstrate the crying need for the gifts of women to be embraced. Religious sisters courageously witness to core Gospel values even when at times they must feel they are voices in the wilderness within the institutional church. Women's roles in family life, parish life, education, health care, social welfare all serve the total mission of the church, showing the face of Jesus to the world.

I have been blessed by the women in my life. I write and speak often of my dear mother, Olga, who taught me of the unconditional love of God. As well, my four younger sisters, Maria, Margaret, Loretta and Pauline, each in her own way reflecting my saintly mother's qualities, continue in adult life to share with me the joys and realities of family life as they support me in living out my vocation. Those who know me personally are aware that for many years I have been loved and sustained by Geraldine, my long-time friend and loyal confidant, especially since we began sharing our home in 2000 as I recovered from a serious car accident. I was pleased at the time of my retirement to have the opportunity in the media to speak publicly of Geraldine's significant part in my life.

My brother priests and deacons, many dear former parishioners and friends, as well as the religious sisters and brothers I write about, all help me to remain focused on Jesus and my vocation as his disciple. I apologise if I have not sufficiently highlighted their crucial role in my life's story.

There are a number of repetitions in the book. I deleted some but found it difficult to eliminate them all without damaging the integrity of the theme about which I was originally writing.

My friends sometimes tell me that I wear my heart on my sleeve and that I am too personal in the way that I speak and write. I hope that it is not a case of my ego getting in the way of the message I am trying to share.

Jubilee is a time for remembering, for looking back and giving thanks. As I celebrate my golden jubilee of ordination to the priesthood, I give thanks to God and to every person in my life who has helped me to see the face of Jesus and experience the love of God.

Pat Power

17 July 2015

The quest for grace

Given as an after-dinner talk at Manning Clark House, Canberra, 31 August 2004.

I think I had only one conversation with Manning Clark, even though I had long admired him as a great Australian. I spoke to him and Dymphna in 1990 after celebrating Mass for Malcolm Muggeridge who had died a little while previously. I commented then on the similarities I saw in the two great men. Prior to that I often saw Manning and Dymphna at the Manuka shops in the days when I was a young priest at St Christopher's in the late 1960s.

It turns out that the Clarks moved into this house in October 1953, just as I was finishing seven years of primary schooling at St Christopher's. It was Manning's dear friend, Archbishop Eris O'Brien, himself a distinguished Australian historian, who accepted me as a student for the priesthood in 1959 and ordained me to the priesthood in 1965.

When one of my seminary classmates, Paul McCabe, was sent to Rome in 1963 to complete his studies for the priesthood, I sensed that he was missing Australia. I sent him a copy of Manning Clark's *A Short History of Australia*. To this day, Paul is grateful to Manning and to me for helping him to remain in touch with his Australian roots.

In preparation for this talk, I read *The Quest for Grace*. I was referred to it by Jesuit priest, Chris Gleeson, in *Madonna* magazine: 'In his book, *The Quest for Grace*, the historian Manning Clark talks about the difference between life-straiteners and life-enlargers, between those people who have a very measured, narrow view of life and want to contain it, and those who love the banquet of life with a passion and want to share it with others.'

My own quest for grace begins quite differently to Manning Clark's, unfolds in other circumstances but in a perverse kind of way in 2004 identifies with much of Manning Clark at the end of his life. I suspect both of us moved a fair way on our pilgrimage of life and of faith.

Even as a young boy at St Christopher's I had thoughts of the priesthood, although I was far from sure that I had a calling from God. At school I made good friendships many of which still endure. The influence of the Good Samaritan Sisters was positive, even if I got more than my share of the cane. Incidentally, the Mother Superior of the founding community of sisters in 1928 was Mother Dympna. Her name is enshrined in the altar of St Christopher's Cathedral today.

Growing up in Queanbeyan, derisively or affectionately known as *Struggletown*, was formative. I had seen my father, as a Justice of the Peace and a member of the St Vincent de Paul Society, befriend and assist many of the 'New Australians', post-World War II refugees who had come to Queanbeyan in large numbers. Dad's contribution to the Catholic and the wider community was impressive, although at times it meant that my mother was left with greater burdens bringing up five children of whom I was the oldest with four younger sisters. Sometimes I clashed with my father (we were both hot-heads), but I learnt from him a sense of justice and the need to make the best of what you have. From my mother I learnt the unconditional love of God. At her funeral in 1995 (Dad had died in 1976), I said that it probably was not a good ecclesiological distinction to make but that I learnt from my father what it meant to be a good Catholic and from my mother what it meant to be a good Christian.

It snowed in Queanbeyan on 17 July 1965, the day I was ordained a priest. With my classmates at Springwood and Manly I had spent seven years studying philosophy, theology and many other things in preparation for priestly ministry. Significantly, our four years of theological training coincided with the four years of the Second Vatican Council.

The church and the world that we were to serve would be very different to what I had experienced in my childhood. The Second Vatican Council not only effected profound change within the church itself, but equipped it to contend with the changes that were taking place in society.

One of Pope John XXIII's hopes for the Council was for it to bring the

Catholic Church into the modern ecumenical movement. This movement is usually dated from 1910, the year of a significant missionary conference in Edinburgh where it was concluded that the Christian Church's missionary outreach would never be effective while the church was divided. Pope John's warm meetings with the Archbishop of Canterbury and with Orthodox leaders modeled the humble dialogue which he expected from his fellow Catholics.

Celebrating the liturgy in the vernacular enabled greater participation from all the faithful and challenged us Catholics to learn from our Protestant brethren their appreciation of the Scriptures and their love for hymn-singing.

Lay people were helped to appreciate the depth and the uniqueness of their own vocation; the universal call to holiness meant that sanctity was not the sole preserve of the clergy and religious; and the notion of collegiality was seen not just in terms of bishops in relation to each other and the Bishop of Rome but as promoting shared ministry and responsibility right down to the parish level. The dignity of conscience, promoted by the Council, and our freedom of choice enabled us to find God's will as a treasure within. The quest for grace and its attainment was open to us all.

To my mind, one of the Council's last documents, *The Pastoral Constitution on the Church in the Modern World,* is the most radical. It begins with these challenging words: 'The joys and the hopes, the griefs and anxieties of the people of this age, especially the poorest and most afflicted, these too must be the joys and the hopes, the griefs and anxieties of all the followers of Christ.' As the document unfolds, Christians are continually challenged to engage with the contemporary world. This has all sorts of implications locally, nationally and globally.

Dialogue was seen as one of the great gifts of the Second Vatican Council and one of the most important means of its implementation. In 1964, towards the end of the Council, Pope Paul VI wrote an encyclical, *Ecclesiam Suam,* on dialogue and renewal. Dialogue means coming down from a superior position, it means respecting the viewpoint of another, acknowledging that we don't have all the answers and showing a willingness to listen and to learn.

Much of what Manning Clark reacts against in *The Quest for Grace* is the church adopting a patronising attitude to individuals and to society and being out of touch with people's deepest human needs. He rightly points out that Jesus is found in real-life situations and often most dramatically in the poorest of the poor. He writes movingly of how as a teacher he learnt so much from his students both at high school and university.

As a young priest, I learnt a great deal from the people of Causeway, the students I tried to teach at Telopea Park, St Edmund's and St Clare's, the friends I made in the government hostels in Canberra and the young people in the Catholic youth movement. It was a time of hope and even though I often lacked the answers to the questions of my young friends somehow I always felt that together we were on a quest for grace.

These were the days of protest against Australia's involvement in the Vietnam War. I have to confess that at that time I didn't have a great deal of sympathy with the peace movement. I felt that an Australian presence in Vietnam was enabling the people of the South to resist the onslaught of communism and to enjoy the freedom of democracy. I now realise that things were not so simple. These days I still witness the pain of Vietnam veterans whose lives have been traumatised by their involvement in that war.

What transformation had taken place in my life between then and February 2003 when I had a very public disagreement with John Howard over the likelihood of Australia's being part of the invasion of Iraq? Had the quest for grace taken a different turn?

Becoming a bishop in 1986 was clearly a turning point in my life. While I had always hoped that God was calling me to the priesthood, I had no dreams of becoming a bishop. In 1985 I had happily returned to parish ministry as parish priest of my home town of Queanbeyan after an absence of nearly 13 years of study and administrative duties. Less than 15 months later I was asked by Archbishop Carroll to be his auxiliary bishop. While I knew that I was in contention for that appointment it wasn't an easy one to accept as I knew it would take me out of day-to-day contact with ordinary people, just when I was enjoying parish ministry once again.

Eighteen years later, I'm still struggling somewhat with the vocation of bishop. However, it has become clear to me that as a bishop I have the opportunity to be a voice for people who otherwise might be unheard.

For 15 years I served on the Australian Bishops' Committee for Social Welfare and for most of that time on the Australian Catholic Social Welfare Commission. That gave a wonderful opportunity for the church to be involved in shaping Australia's attitude to issues such as poverty, unemployment, family life and a whole range of social questions. Its role in the 1993 federal election regarding the GST was very significant.

In the 1990s I saw the need for the plight of the East Timorese people to be taken up by ordinary Australian people after a succession of governments of both persuasions had ignored the dire straits of the East Timorese. I am proud to have been part of that popular Australian support which eventually was so crucial in the liberation of East Timor.

Over time I have been asked to speak at rallies and in other forums in support of the rights of indigenous people, refugees and asylum seekers, and the Palestinian people in their struggle for survival. I was privileged to have been a speaker at the launch of the Sea of Hands in 1997 and to have crossed the Harbour Bridge in the 2000 reconciliation walk.

It has become clearer and clearer to me that we are all part of one human family and that until we recognise the dignity of every human person we have a myopic view of humanity.

On a number of occasions, I have stated that it would be much more productive for Australia to be fighting a war against poverty rather than sounding off about a war on terrorism. The Jubilee 2000 call for mitigation of the international debt on the world's poorest countries sought to allow those countries to attend to their basic needs rather than have their whole economies crippled by impossible debts. If our 'enemies' were able to see that the West really cared to the point of sharing some of our wealth and resources, giant steps for peace would be taken. Pope John Paul II frequently reminds us that there will be no true peace without underlying justice.

If any positive has emerged from the September 11 tragedy, it has been the realisation of the need for building up greater understanding between Christians and Muslims (and members of the other great world religions). Inter-religious dialogue can achieve a great deal in breaking down ignorance, prejudice and hostility. In simple terms, people cannot love and trust each other until they begin to know and understand one another. It is significant that Judaism, Christianity and Islam all recognise Abraham as their father in faith.

In the lead-up to the invasion of Iraq, I often posed the question: 'Is an Iraqi life of any less value than an Australian, a British or an American life?' Unfortunately, in the aftermath of the war none of the leaders of these three countries has been able to face up to the truth even though incontrovertible facts continue to emerge proving that we went into war under false premises. I was proud to add my public support to the 43 prominent Australians who called on our political leaders for truth in public life. I am sure that if Manning Clark were alive today his name would be there as well.

Just as war was about to break out in March 2003, I left for Spain with a friend to walk 300 km of the pilgrimage to Santiago de Compostela. In some ways I felt guilty in leaving at that stage, but I had just about exhausted myself in my opposition to the war, and the pilgrimage had been two years in the planning. As it turned out, we discovered that 91 per cent of the Spanish population was opposed to the war and we shared with most of our fellow pilgrims an abhorrence of war. In many ways it became a long walk for peace and our sixteen days on the track coincided with the worst of the fighting in Iraq. Earlier this year, I grieved in a special way for the 191victims of the train bombings in Madrid, knowing that 91 per cent of them most likely were opposed to Spain's involvement in the Iraq War.

As I read *The Quest for Grace*, I felt as if I was on pilgrimage with Manning Clark, barracking for the enlargers of life and shying away from the heart-dimmers and straiteners. I identified with his questioning and the humility of his search. On the pilgrimage to Santiago de Compostela, we never got too far off the track but there was always some anxiety about losing our way. But fundamentally we walked in trust and in hope, sometimes in pain, but with the support of our fellow pilgrims and the knowledge that God would see us through. I trust that my quest for grace and yours will continue in that vein.

See, judge and act
Reading the signs of the times

A talk given 24 March 2014 as the first of a year-long series in St Raphael's Parish, Cowra NSW, celebrating its 125th anniversary as a parish and the 75th anniversary of the parish church. The talk was repeated at Bathurst the following evening for Spirituality in the Pub.

This year you parishioners of Cowra are commemorating the 75 years since the opening of your parish church, St Raphael's. In 1956 a new church was opened in my home parish of Queanbeyan. It too was placed under the patronage of the Archangel Raphael. The parish priest responsible for St Raphael's, Queanbeyan, was Fr Michael Casey a very stern character who put the fear of God into the parishioners. He mellowed in his later years and I became quite close to him before his death.

I asked him what had inspired him to name the new church, St Raphael's. I was surprised by his reply. He reminded me that Raphael means 'God's healing' and he commented that we are all in need of healing. I must say that as a youngster, I did not see that aspect of Father Casey's vision. I would imagine that with Cowra's unique connection with World War II, St Raphael would have been frequently invoked as a source of healing during and in the aftermath of the war. Last year I was invited by the ecumenical Order of St Luke in Canberra to give the homily at their annual prayer service which focuses on some particular aspect of healing. I was asked to preach on the church itself in need of healing. At this moment in our history I think the reasons for that are fairly obvious.

I retired in mid-2012, and a few months later spent two weeks in Italy so that I was able to be in St Peter's Square on 11 October for the Mass which honoured the 50th anniversary of the opening of the Second Vatican Council. A few days earlier, I had been moved to tears in St Peter's Basilica as I prayed at the tomb of Pope John XXIII whose vision had given birth to Vatican II.

The Second Vatican Council and the Cardijn movement have been key influences in my life as a priest and bishop. I will return to the latter in a moment. My four years of theological study at St Patrick's College, Manly, between 1962 and 1965 coincided with the four sessions of the Second Vatican Council and 1965, the year of my ordination to the priesthood, marked the conclusion of the Council.

My early years in the priesthood were full of hope, thanks to Vatican II. I can honestly say that despite many disappointments in the church in subsequent years, I have never lost that sense of hope. Mass in the vernacular, greater participation in the liturgy, the vision of the church as the People of God rather than a hierarchical structure, the empowering of lay people, the recognition of human dignity and religious freedom, the richness of the ecumenical movement and the embracing of the realities of the modern world were all sources of great blessing as the message of the Gospel was able to be proclaimed in a way which fulfilled Pope John's vision of renewal. Catholics were challenged to live up to their name as being universal and all-embracing.

In those early years in the mid to late 1960s, I was introduced to the YCW, the Young Christian Workers movement. Its founder, Joseph Cardijn, was a Belgian priest who was challenged by young workers who were being exploited. He encouraged them to band together in a way which would empower them to take control of their lives and help their fellow workers to find the dignity to which we are all entitled.

As a chaplain to the YCW, I saw the importance of listening to young people, learning from them and helping them to reflect on life in the light of the Gospel. At their weekly meeting, the young people would share their experiences and help one another to discern what was happening and look for a course of action. Joseph Cardijn's method of *See, Judge and Act* was a great example to us all. I discovered the importance of all three steps. The temptation can be to rush to a particular course of action before recognising what the real issues are. The shared wisdom of the group was invaluable in judging what needed to be done and so too was the solidarity with the other members in embarking on a course of action. The gospel study was an important ingredient in asking the question of what would Jesus do in such a situation. The Cardijn method was dealing with real people in real life.

I remember too in those early years receiving good advice from one of my younger sisters who said, 'In your preaching, don't just be talking about things that happened thousands of years ago, but the things that are affecting people's lives today.' In recent times, as I read Pope Francis' apostolic exhortation, *The Joy of the Gospel*, I was particularly moved by what he wrote in relation to the homily. He wrote so beautifully on the challenge to preach the word of God in a way which would touch people's hearts and move them to respond with joy. 'The preacher needs to keep his ear to the people and to discover what it is the faithful need to hear. A preacher has to contemplate the word, but he also has to contemplate his people' (*EG* 154).

Seven years after ordination, I was sent to Rome by my archbishop to do a doctorate in Canon Law. I chose as the subject of my thesis the International Council of the Laity. It gave me the opportunity to study further the theology of the lay vocation and helped me to see that Vatican II had been heavily influenced by the Cardijn method of meeting people in the reality of their daily lives.

There was a happy chance meeting for me on 11 October 2012 as I made my way through thousands of people also attending the Vatican II anniversary Mass in St Peter's Square. I met up with Devett O'Brien, a young man from Brisbane who is the international secretary of the YCS, the student version of the YCW. I had previously seen the zeal with which Devett had promoted the Cardijn movement in many parts of Australia, including my own diocese of Canberra and Goulburn.

As Pope John XXIII officially convoked the Second Vatican Council on Christmas Day 1961, he urged his fellow Catholics 'to read the signs of the times'. The Pope showed great optimism as he said the Council would be 'a demonstration of the church, always living and always young, which feels the rhythm of the times'. He went on to state the hope 'of rebuilding that visible unity of all Christians which corresponds to the wishes of the Divine Redeemer'. Finally, he expressed the wish that in a world which is under constant threat of war all people of good will would be united in striving for peace.

At the opening of the Council on 11 October 1962, Pope John warned against the prophets of gloom, saying that, in the face of error, the church should make use of the medicine of mercy rather than severity. Its message should be life-giving, enlightened by the light of Christ. Much of this would find expression in the Council's *Pastoral Constitution on the Church in the Modern World*. Its opening words would herald its rich and challenging message: 'The joys and the hopes, the griefs and anxieties of the people of this age, particularly those who are in any way poor or afflicted, these too must the joys and the hopes, the griefs and anxieties of all the followers of Christ.' It would go on to speak of the importance of engagement with the modern world, the role of dialogue and a willingness on the part of the church to listen and to learn.

In many ways since becoming a bishop in 1986, I have struggled with the perception that the leadership of the church had moved away from the great opportunities given by Vatican II. But after the 50th anniversary Mass I wrote, 'As I left Rome, I felt privileged to have experienced an historic moment of grace on 11 October 2012 and I had hope in my heart for a new flowering of Vatican II which would more clearly enable the church to show its best self in witnessing to the love of God and showing the face of Jesus to a world hungering for meaning.' But, in the months that followed, I began to wonder how such hopes would come to fruition. Then out of the blue on 11 February last year, Pope Benedict announced that he was retiring. It was a courageous and noble gesture which in the election of Pope Francis would enable the church to begin to recapture much of the vision and power of the Second Vatican Council. It is amazing how many people have recognised Pope John XXIII in the person of Pope Francis.

At the beginning of this talk I spoke of the church itself being in need of healing. The horror of clerical sexual abuse which has become increasingly more apparent in recent years is one very obvious symptom but there are many others as well which need to be honestly confronted and dealt with. In 2010, I wrote for the *Canberra Times* a paper entitled *Much Needed Reform*. I have made that available to you tonight but will quote from some of it as well.

> In 1996, I gave a talk in which I expressed my hopes for the Catholic Church. They were that it would be
> — a more human church;
> — a humbler church;
> — a less clerical church;
> — a more inclusive church (and therefore more truly catholic);
> — a more open church;
> — a church which finds unity in diversity;
> — a church which discovers its whole tradition;
> — a church which reflects the person and values of Jesus.
>
> I have restated these hopes many times since, including at the Oceania Synod of Bishops in Rome in 1998 in the presence of Pope John Paul II, the future Pope Benedict XVI and my brother bishops. Surely such aspirations are even more pressing today.

Many Catholics believed that the church was becoming too comfortable, too respectable, yet up until the election of Pope Francis, they felt that nobody was listening to their concerns. Groups calling for reform are regularly dismissed as trouble-makers with little love for the church when in fact their hearts are breaking for the church which they see as drifting further away from the message of Jesus. Maybe it has taken the present crisis in the church to bring us all to our senses. Pope Francis' willingness to listen and his experience as a very human pastor give us all great hope, but even the Pope recognises the forces which are trying to maintain the status quo.

In 2010, I wrote that the reform needed by the church involved more than just 'tinkering around the edges'. Issues such as the authoritarian nature of the church, compulsory celibacy for the clergy, the participation of women in the church and the teaching on sexuality in all aspects cannot be brushed aside. Listening must be a key component of reform and at times that will involve listening to unpalatable truths. It means that all wisdom does not exclusively reside in the present all-male leadership in the church and that the voices of the faithful must be heard.

At Easter that year, I pointed out that it was largely Jesus' female disciples who stood by him at Calvary, that Mary Magdalene was the first witness to the resurrection and that she could legitimately be called an apostle in that she was sent to bring the good news to the other followers of Jesus. I wondered aloud if the church would be in its present state of crisis if women had been part of the decision-making in the life of the church.

At the Oceania Synod of Bishops in 1998, I spoke on marginalised people in society and in the church. I listed four groups of people as being on the margins of the church: divorced and remarried people; priests who have left the active ministry; homosexual people and women. At the final Synod Mass I happened to be sitting immediately behind the cardinals who headed the Vatican congregations. I asked myself two questions. First, where are the women in their lives, where are the young people in their lives, where is their contact with ordinary people in their joys and struggles? The second question I asked was how many of them aspired to the lofty position they hold in the ranks of the church. I am not suggesting that they all did but there is no doubt that the Vatican provides a happy hunting ground for careerists. But having got to the top, what satisfaction is there for them so removed from realities of pastoral life which can be so life-giving?

In my 26 years as a bishop, I sat through countless meetings where all the participants were men. I knew that the dynamic of those discussions would have been so much more balanced and productive with the input of women. Added to that, the issues being decided upon often had a major impact on women and children. I cringe when I think of popes, bishops and priests pontificating on sexual ethics without the wisdom and virtue of good women as instruments of the Holy Spirit in the whole process. To my mind, much of the future of the church depends on a far greater participation of women in the church. Pope Francis says as much: 'We need to create broader opportunities for a more incisive female presence in the church' (*EG* 103).

The election of Pope John XXIII and the unfolding of the Second

Vatican Council were often described in terms of the Good Pope opening the windows enabling the winds of the Spirit to blow through the church. Remarkably, since the election of Pope Francis just over a year ago, we have heard him so often described as a breath of fresh air. From the moment he stood on the balcony of St Peter's after his election, he put aside many of the formalities and engaged with everyone as a warm and loving pastor, asking for the prayers and blessings of the people before imparting his own. His choice of the name 'Francis' has been backed by his simple lifestyle, his willingness to meet with others in a down-to-earth manner and his refusal to be isolated from the sometimes harsh realities of life. On Holy Thursday he celebrated Mass not in St Peter's Basilica but in a young offenders' prison where he washed the feet of young women and Muslims. Earlier that day, he reminded a group of priests that as pastors they must be shepherds of their flocks and that they must be willing to embrace the smell of the sheep.

In November 2013 Pope Francis gave us the apostolic exhortation, *Evangelii Gaudium – The Joy of the Gospel*. It was his response to the Synod of Bishops which took place in Rome a year earlier and which discussed the New Evangelisation. In a review I was asked to write, I described it as the most enriching and life-giving papal document since Vatican II. For a number of years, I felt that there had been at many levels in the church a concerted effort to nullify or at least water down the great possibilities offered by the Second Vatican Council.

Now we are given by our Holy Father an unambiguous statement of the way forward for a church which had become bogged down in introspection and clericalism. The first great surprise was the fact that *The Joy of the Gospel* is so readable. I feel quite comfortable in giving it to people who are trying to make sense of life and wondering what the church has to offer them in their search. Right at the start Pope Francis tells them, 'The joy of the Gospel fills the hearts of all who encounter Jesus. Those who accept his offer of salvation are set free from sin, sorrow, inner emptiness and loneliness. With Christ, joy is constantly born anew' (*EG* 1). He goes on to quote Pope Paul VI in reminding us that no one is excluded from the joy brought by the Lord. I have often lamented that although the word 'catholic' means universal and all-embracing, sadly in practice it has often meant the opposite, where much energy has been channelled into saying who is in and who is out, who is right and who is wrong or who is worthy.

Earlier, I spoke of eight hopes I had for our church. It gave me great heart to read Pope Francis giving expression to those and similar aspirations for the future of the church. But he added another important hope, namely that the church would be truly missionary. He tells us that

> the Gospel joy which enlivens the community of disciples is a missionary joy ... Jesus felt it when he rejoiced in the Holy Spirit and praised the Father for revealing himself to the poor and to the little ones ... This joy is a sign that the Gospel has been proclaimed and is bearing fruit. Yet the drive to go forth and give, to go out from ourselves, to keep pressing forward in our sowing of the good seed, remains ever present ... God's word is unpredictable in its power. The Gospel speaks of a seed which, once sown, grows by itself even as the farmer sleeps. The church has to accept this unruly freedom of the word, which accomplishes what it wills in ways that surpass our calculations and ways of thinking (*EG* 21-22).

Whenever I see heroic acts of goodness, love and all kinds of virtue well beyond the confines of my own church and belief systems, I am reminded that God is at work in countless ways which we should not try to limit or restrict.

In 1990 Manning Clark, the great Australian historian and author, wrote *The Quest for Grace*. This moving account of his quest for grace articulates what many of us experience on our journey of life and of faith. I am sure that if he were alive today Manning Clark would be consoled by much of the message of Pope Francis who says unreservedly 'The joy of the Gospel is for all people: no one can be excluded.' (*EG* 23)

We often hear the question: 'Are we concerned with mission or maintenance?' Pope Francis answers that question decisively. 'I dream of a missionary option, that is, a missionary impulse capable of transforming everything, so that the church's customs, ways of doing things ... can be suitably channelled for the evangelisation of today's world rather than for her self-preservation ... making ordinary pastoral activity on every level more inclusive and open' (*EG* 27). 'An evangelising community gets involved by word and deed in people's daily lives; it bridges distances, it is willing to abase itself if necessary, and it embraces human life, touching the suffering flesh of Christ in others. Evangelisers thus take on the "smell of the sheep" and the sheep are willing to hear their voice' (*EG* 24).

The pope highlights the missionary possibilities of parish life: 'The parish is not an out-dated institution; precisely because it possesses great flexibility, it can assume different contours depending on the openness and missionary creativity of the pastor and the community ... In all its activities the parish encourages and trains its members to be evangelisers.' Pope John XXIII likened the parish to the village fountain where all could freely come and drink. Pope Francis' image of the parish is similar. 'It is a community of communities, a sanctuary where the thirsty come to drink in the midst of their journey, and a centre of constant missionary outreach' (*EG* 28).

Over the years, I have read and heard much of the church's 'preferential option for the poor'. I must say that it always embarrassed me because I saw so little evidence of it in practice. But our new pope, having placed himself under the patronage of the poor man St Francis, seriously challenges us to return to the simplicity and poverty of Jesus. He reminds us that 'The Saviour was born in a manger, in the midst of animals, like children of poor families; he was presented at the Temple along with two turtledoves, the offering made by those who could not afford a lamb; he was raised in a home of ordinary workers and worked with his own hands to earn his bread. When he began to preach the Kingdom, crowds of the dispossessed followed him, illustrating his words, "The Spirit of the Lord is upon me, because he has anointed me to preach good news to the poor"' (*EG* 197). 'This is why I want a church which is poor and for the poor. They have much to teach us. Not only do they share in the *sensus fidei*, but in their difficulties they know the suffering Christ. We need to let ourselves be evangelised by them' (*EG* 198).

Pope Francis harks back to a theme on which he regularly preached as Archbishop of Buenos Aires:

> I prefer a church which is bruised, hurting and dirty because it has
> been out on the streets, rather than a church which is unhealthy
> from being confined and from clinging to its own security. I do

not want a church which is concerned with being at the centre and then ends up by being caught up in a web of obsessions and procedures. If something should rightly disturb us and trouble our consciences, it is the fact that so many of our brothers and sisters are living without the strength, light and consolation born of friendship with Jesus Christ, without a community of faith to support them, without meaning and a goal in life. More than by fear of going astray, my hope is that we will be moved by the fear of being shut up within the structures which give us a false sense of security, within rules which make us harsh judges, within habits which make us feel safe, while at our door people are starving and Jesus does not tire of saying to us, "Give them something to eat"'(*EG* 49).

It only seems like yesterday that Catholics were considered suspect for speaking in such terms. Now we have a pope imploring us to live out the Gospel message by confronting the issues before us. But we are reminded that it is people rather than issues which should concern us.

I spoke earlier of the YCW method which urged young people to read the signs of the times. Pope Francis humbly and realistically recognises that he does not have all the answers but looks to local communities to search out, reflect on and take action in regard to the issues which are impinging on their people. It is not my place to spell out what are the issues facing this community. But, as I watch the evening news or read the newspaper, I am confronted with stories of the plight of refugees and asylum seekers, unemployment, homelessness, poverty in a multitude of forms, domestic violence, alcohol-induced violence, suicide especially among the young, mental illness, Aboriginal disadvantage, rural crises and drug addiction, as just some of the ills that are plaguing the Australian community. At the heart of these tragic stories is the loss of human dignity. Those of you who are attuned to the various forms of social media will be able to recognise there another set of challenges as well. Of course, there are also many good news stories but unfortunately they do not always attract the same publicity. Sometimes, we can be overwhelmed by the vastness and the complexity of the problems. But I am heartened by the slogan often used by development agencies which encourage us to think globally and act locally. My hope is that smaller communities are able to promote more personal contacts than are possible in bigger cities. Personal friendships, neighbourly concern and simple acts of kindness can be powerful antidotes to many of our contemporary evils.

Within our church communities, we need to ask how missionary and outward looking are we, how welcoming are we to newcomers, how joyful are our liturgies, how relevant are our homilies and how valued and engaged are our parishioners. Pope Francis has re-affirmed the Catholic Church's commitment to the ecumenical movement where we would recognise every baptised person as our sister or brother in Christ. He reminds us, as did Pope John XXIII, that what unites us as Christians is greater than what divides us. Throughout the apostolic exhortation, the Pope speaks of the imperative of dialogue on many different levels, ranging from the quest for world peace to harmony within family life. The Pope reminds us that the credibility of the Christian message is jeopardised while Christians remain divided and that we must never forget that with all Christians we are pilgrims journeying alongside one another. I have witnessed in the Diocese of Bathurst many splendid examples of ecumenical hospitality, combined witness and a real yearning for full Christian unity. I am reminded of an ecumenical principle which states that churches should only act separately in areas where they cannot conscientiously cooperate together. I suggest that the *See, Judge and Act* process is a valuable means of building up unity at many different levels.

In conclusion, let me say that I find the image of the pilgrim church a very attractive one. We are not standing still but are being constantly called to move forward, often re-adjusting to changing circumstances, sometimes falling over or getting a bit lost. Always we need Jesus and our fellow Christians as companions on the journey. Sometimes we find change difficult, but we are reminded by Cardinal John Henry Newman: 'In a higher order it is otherwise, but here below to live is to change and to be perfect is to have changed often.' I think too of the French philosopher, Charles Péguy, who writes of the church's struggle with relevance: 'At each new turn of the age, the church arrives a little late and a little breathless.'

In 2012, I saw two very enjoyable films. *The Way* is a lovely account of the pilgrimage to Santiago de Compostela in Spain. I had the good fortune of doing parts of that pilgrim walk in 2003 and 2008 and I am still up-lifted by the experience: the walking, my fellow-pilgrims, the local people, the sense of adventure, the time to reflect, the beautiful countryside, the bridges, the almost daily surprises and a sense of achievement at the end. It is a stunning expression of the pilgrim church as it brings together people of varying shades of faith and differing perspectives on life. The other film was *The Best Exotic Marigold Hotel*, the delightful story of a group of Eng-lish retirees who find themselves under false pretences in an Indian hotel which is pretty basic to say the least. When things become chaotic, which they often do, the unflappable young hotel owner has a reassuring line, 'Everything will be all right in the end, and if everything is not all right at the moment, it simply means that we have not yet reached the end.'

I leave the very last words to Pope Francis who gives expression to the deepest sentiments of my heart: 'We have a treasure of life and love which cannot deceive, and a message which cannot mislead or disappoint. It penetrates to the depths of our hearts, sustaining and ennobling us. It is a truth which is never out of date because it reaches that part of us which nothing else can reach. Our infinite sadness can only be cured by infinite love' (*EG* 265).

Chrism Mass 2011

Homily given at St Christopher's Cathedral, Canberra, during Holy Week, 18 April 2011, the 25th anniversary of the author's ordination as bishop.

When I made my First Holy Communion in St Christopher's on 24 April 1949 and when I was confirmed here on 3 May 1953, I never imagined that I would be ordained bishop in this cathedral church on 18 April 1986. I was confirmed by the first archbishop of Canberra and Goulburn, Terence McGuire, ordained priest by his immediate successor, Eris O'Brien, and I was secretary to the next three archbishops, Thomas Cahill, Edward Clancy and Francis Carroll before becoming auxiliary bishop to Archbishop Carroll and now to Archbishop Mark Coleridge. The night I was ordained bishop, Fr Joe Rheinberger in his speech of welcome pointed out that I was the fifth auxiliary bishop of Canberra and Goulburn and that my four predecessors were all present: Guilford Young, John Cullinane, John Aloysius Morgan and Patrick Dougherty.

I greatly appreciate Archbishop Mark's generosity in allowing me to be the principal celebrant at this Mass of the Chrism which focuses on the many blessings given to God's people through the ordained ministry. It is a privilege to celebrate this Mass with my brother priests and deacons, some of whom I have served with as a priest for almost 46 years. I can honestly say that there has not been a single day that I have not thanked God for the gift of the priesthood. There have been some difficult times but the grace of God has always been there, often coming through family, friends and colleagues. I resolved when I was appointed bishop that I would not lose touch with life at the 'grass roots'.

The Chrism Mass is a celebration of the whole people of God and tonight, as I look into the congregation, I see so many of you who have lived out your vocation in response to God's love in a way that has been a source of Good News to countless others. You have done that through your personal commitment, through family life, through parish life, through community life, through professional life, through political life and in numerous other arenas. You have been there for people who are poor, those who are struggling or less fortunate; you have cried out for justice on behalf of disadvantaged people and you have often done that in partnership with Christians of other churches, people of other faiths, and with people of good will. You have lived out the Second Vatican Council's call for the Church to be the Sacrament of Salvation to the whole world.

Professor Manning Clark lived just up the road from here and sometimes dropped into St Christopher's. He was not a Catholic and at times struggled with the whole notion of faith, but he was very much a searcher. He had enjoyed a warm friendship with his fellow historian, Eris O'Brien, even before both of them came to Canberra. In 1990, Manning Clark wrote his book, *The Quest for Grace*. It is the quest for grace which brings each one of us here this evening. Each person's life's journey and journey of faith has been different, but all have been under the influence of God's grace, even when we may not have recognised it. When I became bishop, I took as my motto *God is Love* because I had seen God's unconditional love so beautifully evident in the lives of the people I had been privileged to know and serve. Your quest for grace continues to inspire me in my ongoing journey.

The Gospel of this evening's Mass speaks to us of Jesus returning to his home town of Nazareth and going into the synagogue where he would have worshipped with Mary and Joseph as he was growing up. He applies to himself the words of the prophet Isaiah: 'The spirit of the Lord has been given to me, for he has anointed me. He has sent me to bring the good news to the poor, to proclaim liberty to captives and to the blind new sight, to set the down-trodden free, to proclaim the Lord's year of favour.' At the beginning of his public ministry, Jesus was proclaiming what his vocation was all about. In the three years of his public life, he consistently lived up to the promises he was making that day. He constantly sought to do the will of his Father and continually called his disciples into relationship with the Father under the influence of the Holy Spirit. Through his words and actions he gave comfort, healing, strength and hope to all with whom he came in contact. St Luke's Gospel, from which we read this evening, in a special way shows the compassionate heart of Jesus.

In the context of tonight's Chrism Mass, Jesus' challenge to us all in chapter six of Luke's Gospel is particularly relevant: 'Be compassionate as your Father is compassionate. Do not judge, and you will not be judged yourselves; do not condemn and you will not be condemned yourselves; grant pardon and you will be pardoned. Give and there will be gifts for you: a full measure, pressed down and shaken together, and running over, will be poured into your lap; because the amount you measure out is the amount you will be given back.'

The holy oils blessed and consecrated at this liturgy will be instruments of God's grace in the church's ministry of healing, in initiating new members into God's family and in consecrating for priestly ordination and in the sacrament of Confirmation. These are not some kind of magical rites but the powerful sacrament of Jesus' presence among us two thousand years after he walked this earth. We are all given the extraordinary privilege and responsibility of witnessing to Jesus' love, mercy and compassion as we seek to live as his disciples. In a very special way, the sacramental life of the church with the unique role of the ordained ministry makes Jesus present to today's world. Tonight, as bishops, priests, deacons and seminarians, we renew our commitment to our vocation, and we do so very much in solidarity with the whole People of God. Ours is a call to service in the mould of Jesus who came 'not to be served but to serve'.

If my joy is in all of you present tonight, my sorrow is in those who no longer feel at home in the life of the Catholic Church. In my ministry as bishop, I have tried to reach out those who are at the edges, both in the church and in the wider community. I don't think that any of us can be comfortable within the life of the church without asking what is causing so many of our sisters and brothers to walk away. So often I hear the heartfelt plea, 'I haven't abandoned the church, the church has abandoned me.' I appeal to every person here tonight to remain in communion with Pope

Benedict and our Bishop Mark as we pray in the Eucharistic Prayer. Just as earnestly I appeal for us all to be in communion with those who are struggling in their quest for grace. With the humility of Jesus, we need to listen to these sisters and brothers and to learn from what they have to tell us.

St Mary MacKillop is a great example to us of fidelity in the face of adversity and all kinds of disappointment. St Christopher, whose name literally means 'Christ-bearer', inspires us to show the face of Jesus in helping our church to be true to the best of the Catholic tradition. May this Holy Week and the great feast of Easter challenge us to be true to our calling to be faithful, hope-filled and loving disciples of Jesus.

Letter to Pope John Paul II

This letter was written to the Pope on the occasion of his visit to Canberra at the beginning of his 1986 visit to Australia. This and the following letters to Popes Benedict XVI and Francis are a plea for a reconsideration of the law of mandatory celibacy for priests. None of them received a personal reply.

His Holiness, Pope John Paul II
26 November 1986

Dear Holy Father,

I write to you regarding a group of people who are very close to my heart, namely, those priests who have left the active ministry. I am conscious that I am the youngest of the Australian bishops, but I believe that I am writing about an issue which is being neglected to the detriment of the men involved and the church as a whole.

It is not difficult to appreciate the problem you faced at the beginning of your pontificate with large numbers of priests applying for dispensations. Yet, I believe that the process has become so difficult that many very deserving cases are being refused or are being deferred indefinitely. As a canon lawyer, I believe that even cases which meet the 1980 criteria are being denied. Then there is a whole group of men who have not even applied for a dispensation because they believe that they have no hope of it being granted.

My concern extends to those priests who have been granted a dispensation and, although they have been laicised, are being denied the opportunity to participate fully in the life of the church as lay people. I know many excellent and loyal men whose talents are being wasted because of the restrictive terms of their rescripts of laicisation.

Just recently, I was approached by a parish priest concerned that one of his best parishioners, a former priest, was unable to be fully involved in the life of the parish. In the last week, I received a letter from a former priest in

Perth; he expressed sadness that he and a number of men in similar positions were being denied the opportunity to give their talents in the service of the church.

Going further, I believe there is a case for allowing some dispensed (and now married) priests to exercise, at least in a limited way, some of their priestly powers. Naturally, this would require close scrutiny, but it would be within the competence of the local bishop to exercise such vigilance. Many Catholics, priests and lay people, are critical of church laws prohibiting, in blanket fashion, the exercise of any church ministry by dispensed priests. I share that view.

It has caused me great sorrow to see many good priests leave the active ministry. In my ordination class of 1965, ten of the 26 ordained have left. I have always tried to maintain close contact with those men, both out of brotherly love and recognition of the years of dedication they have given to the church. I witnessed in many cases the great anguish through which many of them have passed in making their decisions.

Having been associated with the Canon Law Society of Australia and New Zealand and also the Australian Council of Priests for the past ten years, I know of their efforts to convey to the Holy See their concern about the issues I have raised. I should add that my fellow priests in both these bodies are totally loyal to the church.

In many ways, the people most affected by the church's present discipline in this matter are those who are most loyal and conscientious. It is not those who have taken the law into their own hands or who have left the Catholic Church who are being penalised, but rather those who have remained true to what the church demands of them.

I plead, Holy Father, for you to be a true father to our brothers in the priesthood who now find themselves in limbo. They need the same compassion which you have shown to other groups of wounded people in the world, and about which you wrote in *Dives in misericordia*.

Promising my prayers and pledging my loyalty, I remain
Yours sincerely in Christ,
Patrick Power,
Auxiliary Bishop, Archdiocese of Canberra and Goulburn

Letter to Pope Benedict XVI

His Holiness
Pope Benedict XVI
1 November 2010

Holy Father,

I write in desperation, in hope and in fear, for the church I love. While the Latin church continues to insist on compulsory celibacy for its clergy, the Catholic Church in Australia is witnessing a steady decline in both its faith practice and its credibility.

Much of this diminution is directly due to a severe shortage of clergy. In so many places, a single priest is trying to minister to a flock which was cared for by three or four priests one or two generations ago. It is no longer possible for him to have the close personal and pastoral contact so necessary for his ministry.

Despite good collaborative ministry with lay people and religious, the diminishing numbers of priests are under enormous pressure which is manifesting itself in poor health, a feeling of great frustration and sometimes depression.

At the moment, the Diocese of Wilcannia-Forbes is in a critical condition. This diocese covers 52 per cent of the area of the State of New South Wales and is larger than France. In church circles, there seems to be a grim resignation which would simply allow the diocese to die. Despite the importation of a number of foreign priests, priests from religious orders and other Australian dioceses, there are simply not enough priests to enable the diocese to function even at a minimal level.

Yet, in every parish of this historic diocese, there are suitable married men (*viri probati*) who could be ordained (after suitable formation) to serve their fellow parishioners.

The tragic fate of Wilcannia-Forbes will be successively experienced by the rest of the dioceses of Australia in the not too distant future. In my own archdiocese of Canberra and Goulburn, the health and morale issues earlier alluded to are very real. As auxiliary bishop, vicar for clergy and brother priest, I cannot remain passive or silent in the face of their predicament. While the church holds fast to its discipline of compulsory celibacy, there will be insufficient priests to proclaim the Gospel and to celebrate the sacraments.

At the time of the Synod of Bishops on the Eucharist, many priests pointed out that all the profound and beautiful proclamations on the church's richest gift sounded hollow when more and more people were being deprived of the Eucharist through a scarcity of priests. At last July's national convention of priests in Sydney, this point was frequently raised by the 250 priests present. These priests are faithful loyal pastors frustrated at seeing their church in a state of increasing decline.

My reading tells me that the situation in Australia is currently being experienced in many other parts of the world.

In 1986, the year I was ordained bishop, I wrote to Pope John Paul II on the occasion of his visit to Australia. I appealed to him to consider re-admitting to ministry many of the fine Catholic priests who had left active ministry in order to marry. I also asked him to consider the possibility of ordaining married men to the priesthood. In the years since that appeal the matter has become even more desperately urgent.

Holy Father, you have recently made strong statements and taken decisive action in the face of the reality of sexual abuse within the church. I appeal to you to act similarly in regard to the issues I am now raising with you. The church's continued silence and inaction in this area will have similar catastrophic consequences for the whole People of God and for our world for which we are called to be the 'sacrament of salvation'.

Holy Father, following the Year for Priests, I pray for understanding from you as our Universal Pastor.

Your brother in Jesus Christ
Patrick Power
Auxiliary Bishop
Archdiocese of Canberra and Goulburn, Australia

Letter to Pope Francis

Pope Francis
Bishop of Rome, Pastor of the Universal Church
Holy Thursday, 2 April 2015

Dear Pope Francis,

First, I offer my heart-felt best wishes on your election as pope just over two years ago and thank you for the Christ-like leadership which you have brought to the church and to the whole world. Everyone I speak to, inside and outside the church, is full of admiration for your down-to-earth goodness and your reflection of the love of God and the person of Jesus. I have particularly appreciated the way you have so clearly re-stated the teaching of the Second Vatican Council which still gives promise and hope to us all.

I was ordained to the priesthood in 1965 and in 1986 was ordained as auxiliary bishop of my home diocese of Canberra and Goulburn. I voluntarily retired in 2012, aged 70, to enable myself to be freed of bureaucratic duties and able to have a more pastoral ministry. All phases of my life as a priest and bishop have been very happy, for which I thank God and the people I have tried to serve.

For a long time, I have been convinced that many good Catholic men have a vocation to the ministerial priesthood but not to celibacy. Half of my ordination class of 1965 have left active ministry, nearly all have married and all have made significant contributions within and outside the church. They have remained very supportive of those of us who have remained in ministry and will share in our golden jubilee celebrations in a few months time.

When Pope John Paul II visited Australia in 1986, I wrote to him imploring him to consider restoring to ministry some of the many good men who had left to marry. I also asked him to give consideration to ordaining suitable married men (*viri probati*). I made further similar requests to him and also to Pope Benedict. I have also publicly spoken about the impoverishment of the Catholic Church in continuing to exclude such good men from ministry. As you may imagine, I have been in trouble with the Vatican at various levels for the stances I have taken.

Along with that, I have gone out of my way to give brotherly support to the men in that situation. I never refer to them as 'ex-priests' because I know that we never lose the character of ordination.

Since the great year of jubilee in 2000, I have been regularly meeting for a meal twice a year with an outstanding group of married priests and their wives. At one stage, I counted up about 40 of them in and around Canberra. They are a wonderful group and I am proud to be associated with them. They remain loyal to the church even though many feel hurt at their exclusion. When we recently met, they resolved to write to you. I willingly offered to introduce their letter with mine.

Please, dear Pope Francis, listen to the wisdom and goodness of these faithful members of the People of God. I thank you for listening to the cries of our heart.

May God continue to bless your inspirational leadership.

Yours sincerely in Christ,

(Bishop) Patrick Power

Canberra, Australia

The selection of bishops

A letter written to the Apostolic Nuncio and the Australian bishops, 1 October 2013. It was later published in *The Swag*, the publication of the National Council of Priests.

To the Apostolic Nuncio and the bishops of Australia
Dear brother Bishops
Re: The local church and the appointment of bishops

Both the election of Pope Francis and the appointment of Archbishop Paul Gallagher as Papal Nuncio to Australia have been seen as a source of great joy and hope for the universal church and those of us in Australia. The recent meeting of the pope with the nuncios from around the world gave me further reason for hope when Pope Francis expressed a desire for the selection of truly pastoral bishops for the local dioceses and called for respect for the needs and identity of the local churches.

Surely it behoves the bishops of Australia to do whatever is possible to see that the best possible candidates for the episcopate are brought to the attention of the nuncio and the people in Rome. If we sit on our hands and offer little or no advice, then there are hardly grounds for complaint when appointments are made which seemingly come out of the blue.

In these critical times for the Catholic Church in Australia, we need the best possible leaders to present the Gospel message to our own people and to the wider Australian society. Too often those chosen as bishops are 'safe' people who represent a particular view of church which does not always correspond with the teaching of the Second Vatican Council or the wishes or needs of the people they are being called to lead. Any advice proffered in relation to the selection of bishops must surely come out of a wide process of consultation and from bishops who truly listen to the people and are able to 'read the signs of the times'.

The powerful words and gestures of our new pope indicate that he wishes us to move away from the worst of clericalism and back to the person of Jesus. What sort of people then are we choosing as priests and what sort of priests are being appointed as bishops? Even though the Australian Confraternity of Catholic Clergy represents only a small number of Australia's clergy, their members have been disproportionately represented in episcopal appointments in recent years. On the other hand, the National Council of Priests is often regarded with suspicion even though its ranks contain arguably some of the most pastoral priests in our midst. The fact that they sometimes 'speak the truth in love' means that they are often seen as potential trouble with no place among Australia's bishops.

Those of you who have been around long enough will remember me questioning Archbishop Brambilla about the process of appointing bishops and failing to get a satisfactory response. The whole process shrouded in secrecy means that there is no real openness or accountability. Even among the bishops themselves, one wonders who has the real say in appointments. Is it the bishops who have the ear of the nuncio or those who are well connected in Rome?

In my 26 years of attending New South Wales bishops' meetings, I found that a potential candidate who did not fit into the sometimes narrow mindsets of the bishops discussing his merits was excluded. Added to that, there were many NSW appointments made of people whose qualities had never even been discussed.

It is my fervent hope that the expressed wishes of Pope Francis will come into effect in future appointments of bishops. If local churches at all levels (clergy, religious and laity) have no real say in the choice of their chief pastor, it will make it harder for the new bishops to lead their flocks. Having said that, I know that our priests and Catholic people are very accepting, but for many reasons their good will these days is being stretched to the limit.

What I have written should not in any way be seen as a veiled criticism of my new archbishop, Christopher Prowse. It was my hope that John

Woods, a priest of the archdiocese for 35 years, Canberra and Goulburn's vicar general and for the past 18 months its diocesan administrator would have been an excellent choice as archbishop. I have told that to Chris, but have also said that I believe Chris' genuine pastoral heart, his humility and spirit of compassion as well as his well documented stances in favour of our indigenous people, refugees and asylum seekers, the poor and the disadvantaged will make him a very effective chief pastor for Canberra and Goulburn. On his brief visit to Canberra, he has committed himself to being a good listener and has related well to the local media. His experience in ecumenical and inter-faith relations will also be invaluable.

Finally, I appeal to you all to give serious consideration to the matters I have raised at your next meeting, preferably during the session where the Apostolic Nuncio is present.

Dear brother bishops, please accept this letter in the spirit of love and concern with which it is written.

Yours sincerely in Christ the Good Shepherd,
Pat Power

Pilgrims all

An address given 2 May 2010, following the annual May Day Procession at the Redemptorist Monastery, Galong, NSW. It was given in the context of the Year for Priests.

Galong as a place of pilgrimage goes back a long way. Archbishop Polding was here in 1858, praying the Rosary on Rosary Hill and there were May processions around the monastery grounds in the 1930s well before the completion of the grotto in 1947. In its heyday there were 3000 pilgrims in attendance at this procession. Those of us here today are privileged to be walking in the footsteps of our fathers and mothers in faith. We do so honouring Mary, the mother of Jesus and our mother while reaching out to each other as sisters and brothers on a great faith journey.

Last year Pope Benedict called on the world's Catholics to observe a Year for Priests, beginning and ending on the Feast of the Sacred Heart in each year. Since that time the pope and many bishops, including Archbishop Mark, have written movingly about the role of the ordained priest in the life of our church today. On a local level, many parishes and other faith groups have honoured not only their own pastors, but priests across the nation and around the world. It is fitting that today we recognise this wonderful group of men who have served God and his people so generously as they have lived out a life-long commitment.

When Pope John XXIII announced in 1959 that he was going to call an ecumenical council which came to be known as the Second Vatican Council, it was just nine years after Pope Pius XII had declared Our Lady's Assumption into heaven as an article of faith. As preparations for the Council got under way, many people speculated that there may have been further titles given to Mary. In fact, rather than issuing a separate document on the

Blessed Virgin, the Council fathers decided to insert an important chapter into the Constitution on the Church: 'The Role of the Blessed Virgin Mary, Mother of God, in the Mystery of Christ and the Church'.

Part of the genius of Vatican II was to present the image of the pilgrim church, God's people on a journey. Our Lady is presented as an integral part of the People of God giving inspiration to her fellow pilgrims. 'Mary shines forth on earth, until the day of the Lord shall come, as a sign of sure hope and solace for the pilgrim people of God.' The Constitution speaks of Our Lady's unique role in God's plan of salvation and shows her consistently giving support to Jesus and to his disciples. She too was on a journey: 'She advanced in her pilgrimage of faith and loyally persevered in her union with her Son unto the cross.'

In a similar way, the Council placed ordained priests more clearly alongside their sisters and brothers in the People of God where all, through their baptism, are part of the priesthood of all the faithful. The Council quotes the First Letter of St Peter to describe membership in the priesthood of the faithful: 'You are a chosen race, a royal priesthood, a holy nation, God's own people.' In many ways, Vatican II's shift of emphasis gave theological justification to what had always been historically part of Catholic life in Australia. From its beginnings, Catholic lay people have borne their responsibilities for passing on the faith in Australia. In the earliest times of white settlement there were no priests here and when the priests did arrive they were welcomed by the original Catholics, mainly Irish and convicts. I find it fascinating to read of priests like Fr John Joseph Therry and other pioneering priests visiting towns and communities to be greeted by seemingly established groups of people waiting on them to celebrate Mass and the sacraments and to instruct the children. An admirable spirit of partnership which existed from those earliest times has been a hallmark of the relationship between priest and people in our still comparatively young nation.

During this Year for Priests we thank God for that healthy spirit of collaboration and mutual love and respect. In more recent times, I have been in awe of the relationship which has existed between the various ethnic communities and their chaplains, sharing in the joys, sorrows, hopes and challenges arising from life in Australia often very far from their country of origin. Their presence at Galong has been significant in recent years.

As newcomers to Australia appreciate more than the rest of us, being a pilgrim presents a whole raft of challenges. There is certainly a sense of adventure, lots of discoveries and surprises and a goal to be attained; there are friends and companions on the journey who enrich our pilgrimage; there are precious opportunities to be at one with nature and to appreciate the beauty of God's creation. But there is also a down side. In medieval times, pilgrimages were sometimes seen as a form of penance, with the harsh conditions and pain which are invariably part of the journey. In every age, there is uncertainty, the fear of getting lost, breaking a leg, being afflicted with blisters, falling by the wayside, meeting up with the wrong sort of people; then there are the self doubts which can make pilgrims wonder why they ever embarked on such a course in the first place. Yet a true pilgrimage is undertaken in a spirit of faith and reliance on God who is ever attentive and protective towards his wandering children, just as was the case with Moses and his people in the desert over three thousand years ago.

Every follower of Christ is called to be a 'companion on the journey' to his or her fellow pilgrims in the People of God, but the ordained priest has a privileged responsibility to walk beside his sisters and brothers in faith. He sometimes does this best when he is aware of his own humanity and limitations. The Dutch priest, Henri Nouwen, writes powerfully of priests as 'wounded healers'. Just as Jesus shared in our humanity with all its pains and sorrows, the priest as a good shepherd to his flock will be more effective the more he is able to identify with the struggles and pain of his people. During this Year for Priests, I suggest that there can be real mutuality as priests and people minister to each other as true brothers and sisters in Christ.

Compassion, encouragement and hope are three virtues that I believe are particularly relevant today. In a world where the difference between rich and poor, the haves and the have-nots, is becoming even greater, we all need to show a greater spirit of compassion, reflecting Jesus' identifying with the most vulnerable of people. Such identification with the hurts, needs and deprivation of others will involve us walking in the footsteps of Jesus who 'came not to be served but to serve'. It also means that we try to step into the shoes of our suffering sisters and brothers. With the publicity currently being given to sexual and other forms of abuse within the church, we should not back away from the horror and damage involved, often with lifelong consequences to the victims. They deserve to be heard and to be given justice and every possible form of reparation which will bring about their healing. At the same time, our faithful and dedicated priests need a great deal of encouragement to continue in their ministry with commitment and a love which reaches out to serve with wisdom, prudence and integrity.

In the New Testament, we encounter St Paul's companion, Barnabas, known as *son of encouragement*. We can all be Barnabas figures to each other. These are not easy times to be a Catholic, especially a Catholic priest. But they present wonderful opportunities to bring the message of Jesus to a world which desperately needs the good news Jesus has given us. We do not despair even if we are tempted to it. Rather we walk in hope, knowing that Jesus is faithful to his promise to be with us always even to the end of time. G. K. Chesterton tells us that the virtue of hope means nothing unless we possess it when the situation is humanly hopeless. I take this opportunity to thank the Redemptorists of Galong, priests and brothers, who for nearly one hundred years have been such inspiring ambassadors of hope, bringing compassion and encouragement to their brother priests and to the whole People of God.

In the special Eucharistic Prayer entitled *Jesus, Way to the Father* we pray for a strengthening of the bonds of communion between the pope, bishops, priests, deacons and all the holy people. We continue, 'Keep your church alert in faith to the signs of the times and eager to accept the challenge of the Gospel. Open our hearts to the needs of all humanity, so that sharing their grief and anguish, their joy and hope, we may faithfully bring them the good news of salvation and advance together on the way to your kingdom.'

If I have emphasised what the ordained priest shares with his people, I do not wish to play down his unique ministerial role. The priest who embraces his humanity as Jesus did, will break the bread of the Eucharist for his broken brothers and sisters, uniting them with the sacrifice of Jesus; he will minister to them the forgiving love of our Saviour in the sacrament of Reconciliation and he will bring them the healing love of Jesus through the Anointing of the Sick.

In proposing this Year for Priests, Pope Benedict offered St John Vianney, the Curé of Ars, as a model for priestly life. This humble priest's dedication to his vocation, his simplicity of life, his remarkable life of prayer and penance are nothing short of heroic. Yet, I believe it was his devotion to Our Lady which brought an important female perspective and gentleness into his life and ministry. When I was nominated as bishop in 1986, I received a very encouraging message from Cardinal James Freeman who had three years earlier retired as archbishop of Sydney. He gave me two pieces of advice: never lose touch with ordinary people and take every opportunity to promote devotion to Our Lady. In many ways, James Freeman was an Australian and more modern version of the Curé of Ars. He had a great love for priests and for the priesthood and was always very much in tune with his own humanity.

St John's Gospel depicts that very poignant scene where Jesus on the cross in his last moments of life entrusts his mother Mary and the apostle John to the care of each other. Pope John Paul II concluded each of his Holy Thursday letters to priests by commending them to Our Lady's love and care. He was taking up the more general teaching of Vatican II's *Constitution on the Church*: 'By her motherly love, Mary cares for the brethren of her Son who still journey on earth surrounded by dangers and difficulties, until they are led to their happy fatherland.'

Mary experienced the rigours of pilgrimage: hastening into the hill country of Judea to visit her cousin, Elizabeth, when they were both pregnant, travelling from Nazareth to Bethlehem where she would give birth to her divine son, escaping to Egypt with Joseph in order to protect the child Jesus from the treachery of Herod and travelling with Jesus for at least part of his public ministry. Her role in his first miracle at the wedding feast of Cana is in the forefront of the gospel account.

Two years ago during my long service leave, I had two months overseas on a kind of pilgrimage. I went to the lands of my ancestors in Lebanon and Ireland as well as spending time as a pilgrim in Lourdes and walking 650 km of the *Camino*, the pilgrim walk to Santiago de Compostela in Spain. I tried to relive some of that these past few days in the pilgrimage from Yass to this sacred shrine.

I planned it so that I would be in Lebanon on 29 February 2008, the day my late mother would have turned 100. As it turned out, my cousin that day took me about 100 km south of Beirut, and one of the places we visited was Mantara. A shrine in Mantara commemorates a legend that Mary waited there for Jesus while he was preaching in Sidon. Because Sidon was a pagan town, Mary as a devout Jewish woman could not accompany him. So she waited in Mantara through which Jesus would have to pass when returning to Galilee. I found the image of the waiting Mary as very touching. I thought of the patience of Mary the mother of Jesus and the patience of my own mother as well. I must confess that I was aware of my own lack of patience at times and prayed for the gift of waiting for things in God's time rather than my own. Legends aside, there are so many examples in the New Testament of Mary waiting on the Lord as she journeyed on her pilgrimage of faith.

Pope Paul VI in his 1974 apostolic exhortation, *Marialis Cultus*, gives a beautiful description of Our Lady's bond with her fellow pilgrims. Can I suggest during this Year for Priests that it be also applied to our priests as they live out their vocation inspired by the example of Mary, Mother of the Church.

> The Blessed Virgin Mary offers a calm vision and a reassuring word to the people of today, torn as they often are between anguish and hope, defeated by the sense of their own limitations, troubled in mind and divided in heart, uncertain before the riddle of death, oppressed by loneliness while yearning for companionship. She shows forth the victory of hope over anguish, of fellowship over solitude, of peace over anxiety, of joy and beauty over banality, of eternal visions over earthly ones, of life over death (*MC* 57).

I am sure that my brother priests would acknowledge that it is the closeness they experience with their people which gives validation to their God-given vocation. As I look back on nearly 45 years of priestly ministry,

I recognise how immensely I have been blessed by God. Those blessings have come through family, dear and loyal friends, my brother priests, dedicated religious, and good people, Catholic and non-Catholic alike, witnessing to the best of Christian and human values as part of the pilgrim church. I am often in awe of people in the face of tragedy and human suffering and I come away marvelling at the resilience of human nature and the grace of God. Each day I thank God for the grace of the priesthood and for all the wonderful people who have made my life such a blessed one.

As today's pilgrimage comes to a conclusion and as the end of this Year for Priests draws near, let us thank God for all our priests and entrust them to Our Lady's motherly care. We do so with Pope Benedict's affirming words to priests: 'Living witnesses of the power of God at work in human weakness, consecrated for the salvation of the world, you remain, my dear brothers, chosen by Christ himself in order to be, through him, salt of the earth and light of the world. I entrust you, with my blessing, to the Virgin Mary, Mother of Christ and of priests.'

Listening to our people

A response to Paul Collins and Frank Purcell, 26 June 2007, who
had written to the Australian bishops on a number of issues
relating to reform within the church.

Dear Paul and Frank,

I write in response to your letter of 18 June which I presume was sent
to the other Australian bishops as well. Both of you and the other signatories to the letter are people who have made significant contributions to the
church in Australia and I believe that the issues you raise are of concern to
the majority of practising Catholics around Australia. Daily, I hear people
express such concerns along with the frustration that their voices are being
ignored.

At the heart of the issue is the relationship of the local church to the
universal church. I nominated this as a possible subject for the last synod
held in Rome, but there was little support for my proposal. However, for a
number of years (some people would say since the beginning of Pope John
Paul II's pontificate in 1978) there has been a greater encroachment on the
life of the local church which has given the diocesan bishop and his collaborators little scope for effective leadership. I clearly recognise the need for
the local church to be in communion with the See of Peter but there needs
to be much more reciprocity in the relationship.

Circumstances vary enormously around the world and many of the
issues your letter raises will have differing consequences in other countries and cultures. That was apparent to me at the 1998 Oceania Synod of
Bishops when so many bishops of our region highlighted the particular
problems they were facing. Unless diocesan bishops are allowed to exercise
the powers intrinsic to their office, many urgent questions will be neglect-

ed. The ecumenical movement suggests that we should be seeking unity in diversity. Surely such wisdom needs to be applied to the church as a whole. The New Testament shows the first disciples' readiness to embrace such an approach.

Where there is the conviction that the Eucharist is at the heart of Catholic belief and practice, there must be questions asked about disciplinary laws in the church which have the net effect of denying many Catholics regular access to the Eucharist. This was the precise argument advanced by the National Council of Priests in Australia in the lead-up to the last Synod of Bishops which discussed the Eucharist. They argued that there is little sense in pointing to the centrality of the Eucharist when an increasing number of Catholics in many parts of the world are being deprived of the Eucharist because of the scarcity of priests.

On many occasions since my ordination as bishop in 1986, I have pleaded for consideration of the ordination of married men and the possibility of those who have married to be able to return to the active ministry. I wrote a letter to that effect to Pope John Paul when he visited Australia at the end of that year. In the ensuing twenty years, I have publicly canvassed such views on a number of occasions and I gave voice to them at the 1998 Oceania Synod. But, consistent with many papal and other Vatican pronouncements, there has been no acceptance of those views at that level. Yet invariably when I have made such statements, the overwhelming response I have received from ordinary Catholics has been one of support and a sense of urgency that the official church needs to act decisively to bring about reform.

In our own archdiocese, in line with the experience of other parts of Australia, parishes generally and priests personally are under added pressure with an increasing load being borne by a diminishing and ageing clergy. The irony is that in this archdiocese there are between thirty and forty priests who have married and thereby been debarred from active priestly ministry. Many of them and their families are active in parishes and other areas of church life, but they are unable to celebrate the Eucharist. There was a recent instance where a priest failed to arrive for Mass and a married priest and his wife sat rather helplessly in the congregation while an acolyte and other members of the parish attempted to lead a liturgy of the word with Holy Communion.

Of course, dioceses need to continue in their efforts to recruit men for the celibate priesthood but the limited response must say something in terms of a long-term solution. Many dioceses have recruited priests from overseas with mixed success. Some such priests have fitted very well into the life of the diocese while others have struggled with issues of culture, language and vision of church. In any case such solutions can only be partial and short-term.

Your point relating to the participation of women in the life of the church is crucial for a healthy, life-giving and nurturing church. While women's roles in the family, Catholic education and health-care are obvious, the opportunities for leadership in terms of the universal, diocesan and even parish church are extremely limited. The 1997 inquiry into the participation of women in the church in Australia brought out many of the gaps for which the whole church, and not just women, are the poorer. While I recognise the sensitivity to the question at the level of the Vatican, I am also aware that many loyal and committed Catholics want a more open and thorough examination of the issues around the ordination of women and the whole structure of the priesthood. A less clerical model of the priesthood is more in tune with 21st century societal values and arguably more faithful to the practice of the early Christian communities.

The opportunity which your letter gives for the whole people of God to claim a greater share of ownership in the life of the church in Australia is most welcome. I hope that the spirit of dialogue promoted by Pope Paul VI in his encyclical *Ecclesiam suam* and the spirit and teaching of the Second Vatican Council will be brought to bear on the discussions you seek to engender.

Yours sincerely,
(Bishop) Pat Power

A journey of discovery

An account of two months overseas travel during long service leave, given 2 May 2008

It has only been in the second half of my life that I have fully appreciated my Irish and Lebanese origins. Taking long-service leave in 2008 afforded me the opportunity to tap into some of my ancestral past as part of my own life's journey.

When I left Australia at the end of February 2008, I spent a week in Lebanon where I was generously cared for by Khalil Abukhalil. Khalil's grandfather, Boutros, and his brother, my grandfather, Nicholas, along with other extended family members migrated to Australia in the 1890s. Boutros returned to Lebanon, while Nicholas remained in Australia. It was wonderful for me to be able to meet a whole bunch of cousins, and to go back to the home village of Mashghara to see the family homes and to bless myself from the font from which my grandparents and their forebears were baptised. While in Lebanon, I met the Melkite and the Maronite patriarchs and enjoyed lots of warm Lebanese hospitality. Bishop Salim el Ghazal impressed me greatly. In his 70s now, he has won world acclaim for what he is doing for peace in promoting Christian-Muslim dialogue. I saw the scars of war in Beirut but I left there feeling much more hopeful for peace in this peace-loving country.

On the way to Lourdes, I had just enough time for an evening Mass in Notre Dame Cathedral in Paris before taking an overnight train (on which I was overcarried to Tarbes, fortunately only 25 km away). I was only meant to be a day and a half in Lourdes but it turned out to be a week while I recovered from the flu. During that time I was humbled by the care I received and I was able to experience the healing graces of that special place during its 150 years' celebrations.

The delay meant that I had to change some of my plans for the Santiago pilgrimage, starting at Pamplona rather than St Jean Pied de Port. As it was, I probably started a day too early, still not having fully recovered from the flu, and the first day's walking left me utterly exhausted. There was a tough climb up the Hill of Pardon, but the walk down on a rough stony track was the real killer. Dehydrated and with not an ounce of energy left, I had to ask a lift from a kind married couple for the last few hundred metres to the pilgrim refuge. Lying in bed that night I wondered how I would cope with the almost 700 km ahead of me. But the next day, I was able to resume the *camino* with a less than 20 km walk and I did the same the next day. After that I got stronger and more confident, but for the whole journey I was deeply dependent on God for strength and courage. Added to that was the joy of being with my fellow pilgrims. Normally, I walked alone but would meet up with others at night in the refuges where there was always a lot to share.

I didn't broadcast being a bishop but in conversation when people began asking what I did I would acknowledge what I was about. I became something of a father figure to the younger pilgrims, very occasionally as a father confessor, but for the most part it was a case of them looking after the old man for whom they felt the need to care. In my nature it is sometimes easier for me to give rather than to receive but I learned to graciously accept the kindnesses of my fellow pilgrims. In fact one young fellow gave me a lecture on the need to do just that. I shared in some basic but tasty meals cooked by my young friends, but at least I insisted on doing the washing up!

I carried 12 kilos in the backpack. Sometimes early in the piece it felt like a ton and my shoulders ached but there were times especially towards the end when I hardly noticed I was carrying it. I walked on average 25 km a day through some spectacular countryside, beautiful and green, and further decorated with yellow and purple bushes, with rosemary and lavender among the vegetation. The last 100 km of the walk is through eucalypt forest, the first smell of which was quite special for an Australian as was the smoke coming out of a house on a cold wet day. I was fascinated by the storks nesting in the church bell-towers, impressed by the eagles soaring above, delighted by the twittering of little birds and entertained by the hooting of owls which I never sighted. There were lots of dogs but for the most part I gave them a wide berth, especially the savage ones. One day I saw some squirrels but they were too quick for me to photograph. What I did get great satisfaction in photographing was a great variety of bridges whose architecture constantly charmed me.

For most of the *camino*, I was blessed with unseasonably warm weather, with the temperature sometimes in the high twenties. But I also walked through snow and rain and some really strong winds on a couple of days when I felt for the pilgrims on bikes. In the latter part of the walk, at one stage I walked 96 km in three days of beautiful weather, knowing that the rain was coming and wishing not to spend too much time in it. It proved to be a wise decision.

It is just over 700 km from Pamplona to Santiago, but at one point I took the bus for 50 km to Burgos in order to be there for Easter. However, I walked every kilometre of the rest of the way and a bit more when I occasionally got lost by not paying enough attention to the yellow arrows which are faithful waymarkers. The local people too are great the way they put you back on track when you stray. It was snowing lightly when I went to bed in Burgos on Holy Saturday night and when I got up in the morning all the parked cars were covered in snow. When I came out of Mass on Easter Sunday morning it was snowing quite steadily but I set out on my day's walking hoping and praying it wouldn't get any heavier. Fortunately, it didn't.

The time for reflection on the *camino* was a real gift. It is hard to sum it all up, but it was for me the opportunity to thank God for the blessings of my life up to the present, to ask for guidance for the future, to pray for family and friends and to rejoice in friends made along the way. I didn't manage to get to Mass every day (but always made it on Sundays) and when churches were closed I would say an Our Father as I went by. I said the rosary each day as I walked and there was always plenty to talk to God about and the environment in which to do some listening.

The final stages of the pilgrimage were marked by heavy rain which caused some local flooding, but there was always a hot shower at the refuge and usually some way of getting clothes dry. Everyone puts up with hardships (including snoring in the refuges) with good grace and a sense of humour. I was spared the blisters which afflicted so many others.

I arrived in Santiago on Sunday 13 April just in time for the Pilgrims' Mass and had the joy of seeing the *botafumeiro*, the giant censer, in action. After Mass I went to the pilgrims' office to receive the *compostela*, the certificate of completion, and there made arrangements to concelebrate the Pilgrims' Mass the next day. They made quite a fuss of me, suggesting that I be the principal celebrant with the Mass in Latin, but I said I was quite happy to concelebrate. The Pilgrim Masses are bitter-sweet occasions: the opportunity to meet up with dear friends made along the way but also the farewells which are so final. I had to fight back the tears each time.

On the whole journey I found myself associating mostly with the German pilgrims while sharing special moments with people of 18 nationalities, but not a single Australian, although I did hear reports of some sightings at times. (There is a bit of a bush telegraph among the pilgrims, especially with modern technology, but I stuck to my resolve not to have a mobile phone.) It isn't hard to imagine the joy I felt at hearing the very distinctive voice of an Australian pilgrim who had registered just after me at the pilgrims' office. He had taken a different route to most of us, walking about 1000 km from Seville. That merged with the route taken by Tony Kevin and described in his informative book, *Walking the Camino*, which Jim my Aussie friend had read. I have also been able to report to Neil Harrigan that the Australian fifty cent coin planted by him on top of the meter box in the pilgrims' office is still there.

I began my journey in Lebanon getting in touch with my Lebanese roots and I ended in Ireland visiting the land of my father's ancestors. That part was never going to be quite as satisfying as Lebanon, given that there are no known relatives in Ireland. Morgan Power and Bridgette Byrne were transported to Botany Bay in 1796 and 1802 and the best efforts of our family historian, Bill Power, have failed to get back into Ireland because of the lack of records. But it was very special to visit Roundwood in County Wicklow and Trim in County Meath where Morgan and Bridgette came from and to stand on the waterfront in Cobh, the spectacular harbour in

Cork from which they both sailed in what must have been dreadful and fearsome circumstances.

I didn't do a lot of sight-seeing but got to see Powerscourt, Glendalough monastery and Avoca of Ballykissangel fame, all in County Wicklow, and in the area called on my Australian cousin, Loretta Power, who is heroically living in a community with handicapped people. In County Meath I was drawn by the magic of the Hill of Tara and Newgrange which has a 6000 year history. The Rock of Cashel and lots of old castles made me realise the antiquity of Ireland and I felt privileged to walk in the footsteps of St Patrick at Tara and to drink from the Holy Well which may have slaked his thirst. I saw two magnificent Pugin cathedrals in Enniscorthy and in Cobh.

In Dublin itself I was given splendid hospitality by Fr Mark Noonan and the community of All Hallows College which trained many Irish priests for missionary service abroad, not least Australia. It is now transformed, educating lay people to take their place in today's church and world in a manner which I found to be truly edifying and the source of great hope. I was given some insights into Celtic spirituality at All Hallows and visiting the Mercy Sisters in Baggot Street and praying at the tomb of Catherine McAuley all gave me a taste of the faith of our fathers and mothers.

It turns out that St James' Gate in Dublin is next to the Guinness' Brewery and Irish pilgrims to Santiago de Compostela often get their pilgrim passport (*credencial*) stamped there as the first step of their journey. I was given this significant information just as I was about to return to Australia and as chance would have it I had just one space left in my *credencial* for a stamp. I hurried down to Guinness' and, with mission accomplished, thanked God for a two month journey which covered thousands of kilometres and an inner journey which cannot be measured.

And it is good to be back in Australia.

An historic moment of grace

**Celebrating in Rome the 50th anniversary of the opening of the
Second Vatican Council, 11 October 2012**

Planning a two week holiday in Italy, I had overlooked the fact that 11
October would mark the 50th anniversary of the opening of the Second
Vatican Council. So on that day I travelled by train from Spoleto in Umbria
to Rome for the historic occasion which was marked by a Mass celebrated
in St Peter's Square by Pope Benedict XVI with hundreds of bishops, many
of whom were present in Rome for the Synod of Bishops. Australia was represented by Archbishop Denis Hart, President of the Australian Catholic
Bishops Conference, and Cardinal George Pell, Archbishop Timothy Cos-
telloe and Bishop Christopher Prowse who were participating in the Synod.

The only clerical attire I had was a blue clerical shirt, so I did not concelebrate but happily sat among the People of God for the celebration of the
Mass. Archbishop Denis Hart had kindly arranged a ticket for me. A week
earlier, I had prayed at the tomb of Pope John XXIII in St Peter's Basilica
and was moved to tears as I contemplated the great contribution he and the
Second Vatican Council had made to the life of the church and its impact
on the contemporary world.

Prior to the Mass, I had a chance meeting with Australian, Devett
O'Brien, International Secretary of the Young Christian Students move-
ment. That meeting reminded me of the influence on Vatican II of Joseph
Cardijn, founder of the Young Christian Workers. The YCW method of
See, Judge and Act is very much in harmony with John XXIII's call for us all
to 'read the signs of the times'.

Pope Benedict used the 50th anniversary of Vatican II as the occasion
for the inauguration of the Year of Faith. During his homily he called for a

renewed study of the Council documents to better understand Vatican II's significance for today.

Present at the Mass and given prominence close to the Pope were the Archbishop of Canterbury, Rowan Williams, and the Orthodox Patriarch of Constantinople, Bartholomew I.

The previous day, Archbishop Rowan Williams, a few months prior to his retirement, became the first Archbishop of Canterbury to address a Synod of Bishops in Rome. In a major speech, he spoke of Vatican II's crucial impact on the ecumenical movement and of the opportunity it gave to the church to bring the message of Christ to the contemporary world in a way which made sense to believers and unbelievers alike. 'Today especially we cannot forget that great gathering which did so much for the health of the church and helped the church to recover so much of the energy needed to proclaim the Good News of Jesus Christ effectively in our age.'

At the end of the Mass, Patriarch Bartholomew, speaking in fluent Italian, reflected in detail on the Vatican Council's impact on the life of the church and of the world.

On the train trip from Spoleto to Rome and back, I read from the newly published book, *Speak with the Heart*, containing some of the reflected wisdom of recently deceased Cardinal Carlo Maria Martini. Although not treating directly of Vatican II, the book is taken from a series in which the cardinal is writing in an Italian secular newspaper addressing the questions posed by the readers. They are touching examples of Vatican II's plea for the church to be in conversation with today's world with all its complex questions.

During the Mass, I was conscious of the parts played at the Council by Australian bishops, Thomas Cahill, Guilford Young, Francis Rush and others, and what they did subsequently to help implement Vatican II as part of the life of the church in Australia. I recalled, too, Kevin Barry-Cotter, at that time a student priest in Rome, and many others who had witnessed the historic events of 11 October 1962. Kevin is in the course of writing for *Catholic Voice* a series of personal reflections on those momentous happenings. A young Wagga priest, Francis Carroll, was also absorbed in it all.

As I left Rome, I felt privileged to have experienced an historic moment of grace on 11 October 2012 and I had hope in my heart for a new flowering of Vatican II which would more clearly enable the church to be its best self in witnessing to the love of God and showing the face of Jesus to a world hungering for meaning.

A time of grace

A reflection on forty years of ordained ministry, July 2005.

The children I confirm are at a delightful age, mostly coming towards the end of their primary schooling. They have lots of questions: 'How do you become a bishop? Why did you become a priest? What is it like being a priest?' and many others, sometimes quite personal and insightful enquiries.

It is forty years since Albert Havas and I were ordained to the priesthood by Archbishop Eris O'Brien in St Raphael's Church, Queanbeyan, on 17 July 1965.

Sometimes I hear or read of people never doubting that they would achieve their dream or accomplish what they wanted in life. The first thoughts of the priesthood came to me as a seven-year-old, making my first Holy Communion in St Christopher's, Canberra. The desire to be a priest never really left me but I knew it was a vocation and I was far from certain that it was God's plan for me.

Growing up in a committed Catholic family meant that I was given a beautiful experience of God's unconditional love by my mother. From my father I gained a sense of justice, what it meant to be a Catholic (in pre-Vatican II ways) and the ability to make the best of what I had. My four younger sisters put up with me when I was over-protective (bossy!) and especially in my growing years were a softening influence on me. Ours wasn't a perfect family but I grew up in an atmosphere of security and love.

My schoolboy friendships at St Christopher's, St Edmund's, Canberra, and Chevalier College, Bowral, were significant then and many still endure. I will always be grateful to my teachers – the Sisters of the Good Samaritan, the Christian Brothers and the Missionaries of the Sacred Heart. In different ways without knowing it, they nurtured my faith and my vocation to the priesthood.

To be honest, the seven years in the seminary from 1959 to 1965 were difficult years. I found the isolation hard to take and much of the formation seemed to be removed from the realities of life, but we were given a good grounding in philosophy, theology, scripture, canon law, church history and a smattering of languages. I could just about read the New Testament in Greek by the time I had finished. I often say that the three things that got me through the seminary were the desire to be a priest, the great companionship of my classmates and the holidays (twice a year).

At the end of 1965, still only 23, I took up a temporary appointment at Braidwood. I was touched by the way I was welcomed into people's homes and their lives. I still have dear friends from those days.

Early in 1966, I began five happy years as junior curate in St Christopher's Parish amidst many families I had known since primary school. For most of that time I was chaplain of Catholic Girls' High School, Griffith (now St Clare's), 'scripture teacher' at Telopea Park, and for just over three years live-in chaplain at St Edmund's. I was also chaplain of the Young Christian Workers (YCW), and chaplain to many of the commonwealth hostels, housing young public servants from interstate. I enjoyed the interaction with the young people, not always able to answer their questions but being prepared to journey with them in their ups and downs.

Regular parish duties such as celebration of Mass, hearing confessions, celebrating weddings and baptisms, visiting people in their homes (particularly in my beloved Causeway) and giving instructions to prospective converts were always grace-filled moments. I am still not a person who is innately self-confident, but I always felt assured that God was with me in my priestly life. Hearing confessions was for me arguably the time when I most experienced the nearness of God. It was humbling to have people often much older and holier than myself confessing in a way which showed great insight and humility. And when people made a 'confession of conversion' after a long time or a major lapse, God's love and forgiveness were almost palpable.

The two years in Goulburn from 1971-72 were in much the same vein as St Christopher's and just as happy. In fact, as I look back, those first seven years were the most satisfying in my forty years as a priest, mainly because I was engaged almost totally in pastoral life, without much of the burden of administration.

Archbishop Cahill 'twisted my arm' to undertake three years of study in Canon Law at Propaganda Fide College in Rome from 1972 to 1975. But it was a great experience living in a missionary college, studying under Spanish and Italian professors who gave me a broader and more human understanding of law, and with the opportunity to see some of the rest of the world.

From 1975 to 1985 I was secretary to three archbishops and worked on the Marriage Tribunal with people seeking an annulment after the break-down of their marriage. While I still missed parish life, it was a privilege to work with Archbishops Cahill, Clancy and Carroll and the secretary's position put me in close relationship with the priests of the archdiocese. I don't know a diocese which has a better spirit than Canberra and Goulburn's and I believe that is largely due to the great spirit which exists among our priests. They have been and continue to be dear brothers to me.

Working on the tribunal was in many ways like hearing confessions. So often I was touched by people's heroism in facing marital difficulties, their loyalty to the church and the trust they placed in me in revealing some of their deepest secrets and pain. Again, I learnt so much from them.

My joy was great in returning to parish life in 1985 when I became parish priest of my home town of Queanbeyan. I had a fair bit of catching up to do after 13 years 'away' but everyone was patient and there was never any sense of 'a prophet not being accepted in his home town'. Mother Teresa visited her community in Queanbeyan a week after I arrived and meeting her is one of the highlights of my life.

It wasn't easy acceding to Archbishop Carroll's request to be his auxiliary bishop in 1986, even though I realised I was in contention for the position. Saying yes would mean saying goodbye forever to parish life, but I did so because I have always tried to do what God wanted of me and I had such an admiration of Archbishop Carroll as a truly pastoral and holy bishop.

In the 19 years I have been bishop, I have tried to retain my priestly heart and not lose touch with my human roots. At times, I have felt the tension of trying to be faithful to the teaching and discipline of the church and responding to people's very real pastoral needs. For me the bottom line has been trying to be true to myself and to God. Fifteen years on the Bishops' Committee for Social Welfare helped me to see some of the problems and injustices experienced by many Australians and the church's social teaching as a Christ-like response. As a bishop, I have had wonderful ecumenical experiences and I see many of my sisters and brothers in other churches as much-loved fellow pilgrims.

Being a bishop has also afforded me the opportunity of being a voice for many who would otherwise be left unheard. I've been privileged to speak on behalf of the unborn, the old and the dying, mentally ill people, those in prison, the East Timorese people seeking independence, Aboriginal people looking for justice and reconciliation, refugees and asylum seekers. I've tried to advocate for individuals 'in strife' and simply listen to people, even when I've had no answer to their problems.

At the 1998 Oceania Synod of Bishops in Rome, I spoke on 'Marginalised People in Society and in the Church'. The four groups I named as being marginalised in the church were priests who have left the active ministry, the divorced and remarried, homosexual people, and women. I gave my speech in the presence of Pope John Paul II, the Vatican cardinals (including the present pope) and our own Australian bishops. I was pleased to be able to say in their presence much of what I had been saying in my previous 12 years as bishop. I still see the Second Vatican Council as giving all of us in the church the means of witnessing to Jesus' mission in today's world.

The past ten years or more have seen the church facing up to revelations of sexual abuse. It has been a painful time, mainly for victims themselves, but also their families and indeed the whole church family. I have tried to be available to and to listen to victims and I have also tried to be supportive of perpetrators, some of whom have been my friends. With the other bishops I have worked on procedures enabling victims to find healing and protocols to promote protective behaviour in our pastoral relationships. In these painful circumstances our priests and religious need more than ever the friendship, affirmation and support of their people. As a bishop, I am in a good position to offer such support. As I write this I realise I probably haven't done enough of it.

As a priest and bishop, I have often stood beside and prayed with people in all kinds of tragic situations. So often I am in awe at their ability to cope with such painful realities. I find myself in those moments marvelling at two things – the resilience of human nature and the grace of God.

As I look back over the past forty years, I see it as a time of grace when every day I have thanked God for the gift of the priesthood and for the wonderful people who have given joy to my life.

Pilgrims and healers

An after-dinner talk given for the ACT chapter of the Australian Health and Welfare Chaplains Association, Canberra, 16 November 2006.

> *To act justly, to love tenderly and to walk humbly with your God.*
>
> Micah 6:8

Some of you may have read Morris West's 1990 novel, *Lazarus*. It is the story of a fictional pope, but one with striking resemblance to the pope of the day, John Paul II. Based on Morris West's own experience of open heart surgery, the pope of the story finds himself facing the same potential life-threatening operation. In the whole fearful process, he gets in touch with his own humanity at all kinds of new levels. Used to being the one in control and having all the answers, he now finds everything turned upside down. Things are no longer black and white; he is utterly dependent on the hospital staff and finds the need for continual comfort and reassurance. He discovers a deeper and more human side of his personality.

It is a time for reflection as well and the pope resolves that if he survives the ordeal he will bring a more human dimension to his pontificate. He does in fact come through the operation, but finds putting his good resolutions into effect is somewhat problematic because his closest advisers and collaborators have not undergone his life-changing experience and are still stuck in their old ways. But that is a story for you to explore further if you take up the novel.

The point that I am wishing to make is that unless and until we face our own vulnerability and mortality, we are probably not best equipped to be ministering to others. An essential part of any life training is to be on the other side of the power equation: to do our time as patient, student, client, as the one in need of healing, guidance and help.

I never felt that my first seven years in the priesthood as junior curate carried very much power and authority. But when, at the end of that period, my archbishop sent me to Rome, to study in a foreign language with people from a whole range of cultures and backgrounds, many of whom appeared to be much brighter than I and coping much better, I began to understand what it meant to be powerless. I hope that some of those painful lessons helped to shape my character.

I think it was Henri Nouwen who introduced the notion of *the wounded healer* in his book of that title. Spare us the priests, doctors, nurses, pastoral care and aid workers who are so focused on their job that they lack insight into their own humanity. How can they minister to other people's deepest needs when they are out of touch with their own? We need, occasionally at least, to weep, to bleed, to stumble and even to be out of control.

In the latter part of his life, Henri Nouwen became part of a L'Arche community founded by that most wonderful human being, Jean Vanier. Vanier speaks and writes so movingly of how we are to relate to the most vulnerable of people, those who are handicapped. There is no hint of superiority in such relationships; simply a recognition of the innate dignity of every human being and the very special gifts of those who might be seen by some as lacking in one way or another. Clearly, Jean Vanier is a student of life who learns something new and refreshing each day of his community living. At the same time there is a basic realism and honesty in acknowledging that at times life is not pretty and each day brings new challenges.

Vanier wrote the foreword to Sheila Cassidy's book, *Sharing the Darkness: The Spirituality of Caring*. His words say much about his own and the author's values and spirituality.

> I find this book very beautiful because it is about people in their utter poverty, littleness and vulnerability; not about those who pretend to be big and strong, who are successful and winning prizes, but who are also hiding their fears and vulnerability behind masks. This book is about people who are very earthy and very vulnerable;

people who no longer wear masks because they do not even have the energy to maintain them. It is also about the people who truly care about those who have become vulnerable and who are dying. These carers are experiencing their own deepest fears. They themselves have become very vulnerable. They no longer hide behind masks of medical technique or of well-set formulas. So often they feel empty-handed and powerless. They let themselves be touched and their hearts be opened. Not only are they competent which all doctors and nurses must be, but they are also compassionate.

The prophet Micah's challenge *to act justly, to love tenderly and to walk humbly with our God* is a lofty aspiration for those called to pastoral care.

A sense of justice will dictate that every person is treated with the dignity which befits a child of God. It will acknowledge that people are more important than things and systems and that people are not to be used even for the good of another. Justice demands that every person be seen as equal in dignity and rights. It reminds us that we are all responsible for each other and that we must work for social conditions that ensure every person and every group in society are able to have their needs met and realise their potential. Every group must take into account the rights and aspirations of other groups, and of the well-being of the whole human family. The principle of subsidiarity teaches that responsibility should be kept as close as possible to the grass-roots. The people or groups most directly affected by a decision or a policy should have a key decision-making role. Human life is to be seen as sacred. Human beings are part of God's creation and are called to act as stewards safeguarding the integrity of creation. I have taken these principles from the mandate of the Australian Catholic Social Justice Council. I suggest that many of them will find resonance with you in your chaplaincy vocation. I stress again the point that I tried to make earlier, namely, that those of us exercising power should tread lightly in our relationships with others.

Social justice dictates that inclusiveness be a vital ingredient in pastoral care. It was refreshing to read Anglican priest David Oliphant's letter in the *Canberra Times* in which he demonstrated how people of differing religious persuasions need to work together in harmony for the good of all concerned. Our world is in crisis at the moment precisely because different groups of people are failing in understanding the needs of others and are not prepared for the dialogue necessary to bring people together. Chaplaincy offers a wonderful opportunity for many barriers of division to be crossed in a way which will bring out the best of human behaviour. For Christians, much of that will be motivated by our following of Jesus, but we recognise that people of other beliefs will be similarly impelled by their own ideals.

It seems to me that religion deserves all the bad press it gets when it retreats into a narrowness which is inwardly focused and which is incapable of healthy self-criticism. Those of us involved in the ecumenical and interfaith movement can testify to the enrichment of our own personal faith as we have been privileged to learn from other traditions and practices. I believe that chaplaincy at its best will recognise and respect the individual beliefs of the people who are being ministered to and help to bring to all an understanding of the unconditional love of God.

I am fond of quoting the opening words of the Second Vatican Council's *Pastoral Constitution on the Church in the Modern World.* 'The joys and the hopes, the griefs and anxieties of the people of this age, particularly those who are in any way poor or afflicted, these too must be the joys and the hopes, the griefs and anxieties of all the followers of Christ.' When the church is able to engage with contemporary society in such a manner then it is truly showing the face of Christ to the world. I suggest that those of you engaged in chaplaincy are in a privileged position to give such witness.

There have been times in the church's history when it has considered itself to be above the law. In such times, accountability was not high on the priorities of church leaders. Like it or not, this is no longer the case. Yet we should surely welcome the opportunity to give account of our stewardship.

Jesuit priest, Frank Brennan in his book, *Acting on Conscience,* offers some advice which can be modified to fit the situation of chaplaincy.

> We need appropriate checks and balances on state power and on
> the rhetoric of our mass media and elected politicians. We need
> a tradition of civic discourse respectful of the views of all people,

including those with passionately held religious views. We need a commitment to mutual tolerance accommodating the utterances and actions of others who think differently from the majority. We need to have a special care for the most vulnerable in our diverse society without unduly curbing the liberty and opportunities for those less vulnerable and those with few or no religious sensibilities. We need to prize individual conscience. We need to value the dissenter. With appropriate checks and balances, and respect for the argued positions of our fellow citizens (even if those positions are premised on religious or other world views foreign to us), we can work together for laws and policies that provide the social order necessary for all citizens to achieve their human flourishing, despite their contentious and argumentative differences.

I often say how much more peaceful life would be without difficult people. How often we yearn for schools without pupils, hospitals without patients and families without kids! Yet the challenge is consistently to be prepared to meet people 'where they are at' and empower them to be their best selves in whatever their life's circumstances.

Finally, we never lose sight of the fact that much of what we are about is a work in progress. We only have to look back on our lives to see the extraordinary changes which have taken place in society and within our own selves. I love the notion of the *pilgrim church*, God's people always on the journey. Because we have not reached our destination, sometimes we become weary, sometimes we stumble and fall, other times we lose our way; we can wonder if it is all worth while and whether we will ever reach our journey's end. But each new day gives us the opportunity for a new beginning and so often we are uplifted by our companions on the journey. As Christians, we take heart that ultimately it is Jesus who is our inspiration and goal. It is his, not our task, to which we are committed. Last year, when I reflected on forty years as a priest, the thing that struck me most forcibly was the way I had been privileged to walk with people at times in seemingly hopeless situations. The fact that so often they not only survived but even grew through such ordeals could only be explained by the incredible resilience of human nature and the grace of God. I know that as chaplains and pastoral carers that has been your experience and privilege as well.

I began with Morris West. I conclude with him, this time towards the end of his life in *A View from the Ridge*.

> The strongest compulsion to belief is not reason, but need. We cannot endure to live in a mad universe. We are compelled, for our own sanity, to make sense of it. Sooner or later we are forced either to blasphemy or to the pilgrim search for the source of light – the shrine where creative love resides. This opening of the Self to the Other, the Creature to the Creator, is the first step along the winding road, the first qualification for the promised gift: 'Seek and you shall find, knock and the door shall be opened to you.'

Marginalised people
In society and in the church

Address to the Oceania Synod of Bishops, Vatican Synod Hall, November-December 1998.

If we are to walk the way of Jesus, as the theme of this Synod suggests, we must walk with the poor, we must tell the truth on behalf of poor and powerless people, we must attempt to share something of their life as Jesus did.

The *Instrumentum Laboris* for the Synod reminds us that we bear witness to Jesus and the Gospel not just by words but 'by charity and justice, by solidarity with the poor, the marginalised, the oppressed.'

Some of the principal groups of such people in Australia are:

Mentally ill people – no longer in institutions, but at times coping poorly in boarding houses or just wandering the streets.

Prisoners – out of sight and out of mind, frequently considered as deserving of all they get, having no real human rights.

AIDS victims – still often feared and judged harshly.

Drug addicts – sometimes perceived simply as a threat to others' lives and property, but feared rather than helped.

Unemployed people – who lack the resources to live decently and are often without hope.

Aboriginal people – while some of their rights are beginning to be recognised, they are still likely to be among our poorest people, who leave school earliest, die youngest and have a much higher chance of going to prison.

Victims of sexual abuse – still, in many cases, suffering alone and in silence.

Young people – especially those who do not conform. Suicide is a major cause of young deaths in Australia.

Disabled people – who still suffer discrimination.

Older persons – who are not always valued.

Refugees – who do not always find a welcome in Australia.

Single parents – who have a daunting task and are frequently the subject of prejudice.

Poor people – who are often forgotten by those more fortunate and blamed for their poverty.

While individuals and groups within the church are committed to marginalised people in Australia, for the most part such people do not see the institutional church sympathetic towards them or standing at their side. Very few of the poorest Catholics feel at home in our churches. I feel embarrassed at hearing of the church's 'preferential option for the poor' when I see so little evidence of it. At the same time I am proud of the work of the Australian Catholic Social Welfare Commission, the Australian Catholic Social Justice Council, the St Vincent de Paul Society, the L'Arche communities and many other wonderful groups working at a local level.

A friend of mine replied in these terms to my request for help in preparation for the Synod:

The Gospel of love is an invitation to mutual acceptance and non-judgement. The church, however, in some of its practices, appears to express the exact opposite. Many people in the broader community see the expressed values of the church as being inconsistent with many of its actions and pronouncements. This is a very real difficulty for the church in terms of its credibility in the wider community. Some members of the church community and hierarchy appear to act quite cruelly towards people such as single parents, homosexuals, divorced and remarried couples, former priests and religious. This incongruity between stated values and practice is a major issue in our church and one that needs attention.

My own experience fully supports the observations of my friend. I must add that many Catholic women feel marginalised by the church. The non-inclusive language of the Catechism, the Sacramentary and the Lectionary continues to hurt and offend them as does the seemingly deaf reaction to their pleas for change. Many women and men believe that the church will continue to be impoverished and only half-graced and half-alive while women are prevented from bringing their particular gifts to the church and are deprived of any significant voice. I share those views. This very Synod is lacking because the participation of women is so restricted.

The *Instrumentum Laboris* (#7) reminds us that

> The Gospel is a call to conversion, first of all a call addressed to the church herself, to all her members and communities. It is a call away from being exclusively inward-looking and preoccupied with her own needs, towards becoming outward looking and responding to the needs of others. It is in fact a radical call to holiness … It is a call to reconciliation, to renewal and reform of life in Jesus Christ and to greater fidelity to his Spirit.

As church, we must be prepared to meet people 'where they are at' and to enter into genuine dialogue with them. My own experience in meeting with a group of homosexual Catholics earlier this year gave me new insights into their lives and struggles, and, I hope, helped them remain within the church. I experience the same dynamic in my relations with Epiphany, a group of priests who have left the active ministry.

Walking with the poor, living with their ambiguity and un-certainties, being truly catholic and inclusive are just some of the challenges we face as church if we are to be true to the Gospel. As well, we need to be a humbler church, a less clerical church, a more forgiving church. We should minister to whole persons, and not just to their intellects if we are to offer them a true experience of God as revealed in Jesus.

The *Instrumentum Laboris* (#51) tells us, 'The church and her members are drawn into the communion of life and love of the Trinity as a people brought into unity, through the unity of the Father, the Son and the Holy Spirit. This sharing in the community of Trinitarian life is the basis for all Christian relationships and the foundation of all Christian communities.'

Jean Vanier and the assistants in the L'Arche communities recognise how handicapped people lead them to the person of Jesus. A priest friend tells me how his fellow members of Alcoholics Anonymous have taught him more about spirituality than he ever learnt in the seminary. It is the poorest among us who are graced to draw the rest of us into closer communion with God.

As church entering the new millennium, we must find new ways of embracing those people closer to the heart of Jesus so that authentically we may 'walk his way, tell his truth and live his life'.

Rainbow sash

**Background to the homily given in St Christopher's Cathedral,
Canberra, on Trinity Sunday, 7 June 1998, when a number of
people requesting Holy Communion sought acceptance for
homosexual people; and subsequent follow-up.**

*On Pentecost Sunday (31 May) 1998, a group of protestors wearing rainbow
sashes presented for Holy Communion at St Patrick's Cathedral, Melbourne, at
a Confirmation Mass celebrated by Archbishop George Pell. They claimed that
their homosexual lifestyle should not prevent them from receiving Holy Communion. The Archbishop refused and at the end of Mass scolded them for what
they had done. This brought applause from the congregation. Needless to say,
the would-be communicants were further alienated.*

*During the following week, Archbishop Carroll received a communiqué
saying that a similar group would present themselves at the 11.00 am Mass at St
Christopher's Cathedral, Canberra, on the following Sunday (Trinity Sunday).
As it happened, Archbishop Carroll had two other Masses that Sunday, so I
agreed to be the celebrant.*

*Twelve people wearing rainbow sashes sat in the front seats of the cathe-
dral, joined by a number of other supporters. At the beginning of the Mass, I
welcomed them and said that I would try to address their concerns in the second
part of the homily from which I now quote.*

This morning we have with us here people who are wearing rainbow sashes.
You may have heard on the news that these are a group of homosexual people and their supporters and they ask to be given Holy Communion as a
sign of the church's acceptance of a homosexual lifestyle.

Can I say to you people, with great pain, that I cannot give you Holy Communion because what you are asking runs contrary to the church's understanding of God's law in relation to human sexuality. For that eason, I ask you to refrain from seeking Holy Communion for surely Holy Communion is a time of sacred encounter with God and not a time for confrontation.

Yet I think our friends are asking for more than that as well. They say they are asking for dialogue, for understanding, for justice and for a willingness to learn from their experience. I think that as a group of God's people we must embrace that and we must accept the plea they are making towards us this morning. I sincerely welcome that and I am quite prepared to talk with you outside the church this morning and to continue the dialogue in some way in the future if you believe that it will be productive. I invite you parishioners too to do the same, and to have that same spirit of welcome towards our brothers and sisters here with us this morning.

I have to admit that at times the church's teaching on human sexuality has been overly negative and there have been times when it has been out of touch with human reality. On the other hand, I am painfully aware of the sexual revolution and I am not just talking about within homosexual relations, but, generally, that the sexual revolution we have all experienced has had some disastrous effects on countless people, both as individuals and in society as a whole.

However, the presence of the Rainbow Sash people here today reminds us that together we need to find new and better ways for the church to enunciate its teaching on sexual morality. I recognise the pain of you homosexual people here today, as I recognise the pain too of other groups of Catholics: of Catholics in irregular marriages, of some of my dear friends who have the left the active ministry in the priesthood. I am very much involved in the ecumenical movement and I experience pain at not being able to share Holy Communion with my sisters and brothers who belong to other Churches. I see the pain of the family whose mother I buried from this church just last Wednesday. We know that at times, probably most times, we cannot take away another person's pain, but we can be there to give them support, encouragement and hope.

Let me conclude with a prayer which gives expression to all that.

Jesus, you are the fullness of God's love for us. Draw us into wholeness that our potential might be realised. Be with us, Lord, as we struggle to keep all things in balance in the feverish activity in which we are so often engaged. Thank you for the fullness of life which you lavish upon us and for the abundance of colour, activity and joy that we experience.

As we strive to become fully alive as Christians, may we be open to the needs of others. May we never be content with complacency but continue to be open in the knowledge that you are our friend. May we constantly be your light to those who are struggling with life's problems and your warmth to those who are lonely. Amen

Only one person wearing a rainbow sash presented for Communion and he happily accepted a blessing when I told him I could not accede to his request for Holy Communion.

After Mass, even though there was drizzling rain, a large number of the congregation greeted the Rainbow Sash people. There were some very moving scenes of welcome and reconciliation. One gay person told me that it was the closest he had felt to the church for a long time. I repeated my invitation to meet further down the track and that invitation has been acted upon in various ways since. The Canberra Times *responded with a balanced editorial the following Tuesday.*

When someone wrote to the Canberra Times *suggesting that the protestors were not practising Catholics, I replied that I believed they were and went on to say:*

To have refused them Holy Communion is one of the hardest things I have had to do in my 33 years as a priest. It is to their credit that they responded to my invitation to dialogue and I applaud the many other parishioners who met with them after Mass.

If our Church is to be truly catholic we need to find new and better ways of embracing groups and individuals who are alienated from us. Reconciliation can take many forms.

The events of that weekend marked a new beginning in my understanding of the struggles of minority groups in our church and in the wider society. Since then many times I have met personally and corresponded with gay people and their families and friends. I feel very much at home with them and I believe they recognise me as their ally and trusted friend.

The Tablet (20 June 1998) reported:

A spokesman for the Rainbow Sash homosexual group, Michael Kelly, paid tribute to 'the way in which Pat Power has welcomed gay people and even the Rainbow Sash into the church'. In this way, he said the bishop had encouraged 'warmth and acceptance rather than misunderstanding and anger. What he has done has expressed the heart of Jesus.'

Women, homosexuals and the church

A reflection written for the September 1999 issue of *Catholic Voice*, Archdiocese of Canberra and Goulburn.

During the launch of the *Report on the Participation of Women in the Catholic Church in Australia*, there was a moving appeal for the whole church to enrich itself by drawing on women's wisdom, distinctive talents and experience.

Hearing these words, I was reminded that the following evening I was due to meet some homosexual Catholics as part of a dialogue to which I had committed myself at the time the Rainbow Sash people attended Mass at St Christopher's Cathedral. On that occasion they made a plea for understanding, dialogue and a willingness for the church to listen to and to learn from their experience.

During the homily I affirmed their requests. Subsequently I wrote to the *Canberra Times*: 'To have refused them Holy Communion is one of the hardest things I have ever had to do in my 33 years as a priest. It is to their credit that they responded to my invitation to dialogue and I applaud the many parishioners who met with them after Mass. If our church is to be truly Catholic we need to find new and better ways of embracing groups and individuals who are alienated from us. Reconciliation can take many forms.'

At the end of last year at the Oceania Synod of Bishops in Rome, I included homosexual Catholics in speaking of marginalised people in society and in the church.

Before the pope and my brother bishops, I stated that my experience earlier in the year had given me new insights into their lives and struggles and, hopefully, had helped them remain within the church.

Both of these events have brought some very moving responses – from gay people themselves, from their parents and from 'ordinary' people in the church and in the wider community. Many people have written and spoken of their pain, anger and sense of rejection by the church.

In the overview of the *Report on the Participation of Women in the Church* we read: 'Pain, alienation and often anger resulted from a strong sense of women's marginalisation, struggles, disenfranchisement, power-lessness, irrelevance and a lack of acknowledgement within the church.' Most homosexuals would say 'Amen' to that in their situation.

A man previously unknown to me wrote in these terms: 'I am unsure as to what the church had to say to me as man who is gay (apart from being objectively disordered and intrinsically evil). I am unsure of the church's capacity to deal with the mystery of gay people, which I believe is of God. I believe that I am essentially good; the gay people I know are essentially good. The love and compassion I am privileged to share in and witness is profoundly of God.'

Many of the voices in the Women's Report called for a new expression of the church's teaching on sexuality taking into account the experiences of women.

The homosexual people with whom I am in dialogue make a similar appeal. They, along with the women, see the whole issue of sexuality impinging on wider issues in the church. In some ways, they are calling on all of us to 'come out', to engage in a conversation, even though it means being prepared to step into an uncomfortable space.

Such dialogue will reveal the special gifts of gay people and the unique contribution they can make to the life of the church and wider society.

American Jesuit John Powell says that good communication involves listening and speaking honestly and kindly. Surely such openness is not beyond us as we prepare to accept Pope John Paul's challenge to celebrate the Great Jubilee in a spirit of reconciliation which so characterised the mission of Jesus himself.

Keeping in touch with the people

The McCosker Oration, delivered at the Annual Conference of
Catholic Social Services, Australia, Coffs Harbour, NSW,
11 September 2007. Monsignor Frank McCosker was a pioneer
in Catholic social welfare.

Meeting on September 11 2007, we might ask what should be our focus as
Catholic Social Services Australia. This question could be asked of Bishop
Geoffrey Robinson, formerly a member of the Australian Catholic Social
Welfare Commission and currently author of a challenging book calling
for reform in the Catholic Church. We could turn to Monsignor Frank
McCosker who has played such a central role in the development of Catholic social welfare policy and practice in this country. We might reach out
more broadly to Pope John XXIII whose vision led to the convocation of
the Second Vatican Council, the teaching of which gives so much affirmation and direction to our mission.

The visionary pope, the reforming bishop and the imaginative priest
would each answer in his own way but I am sure that at the heart of their
advice to us would be to 'read the signs of the times'. They would recognise
the potential of Catholic Social Services Australia to play a prophetic role in
shaping the future of the Catholic Church in this country and in so doing
to advance the betterment of Australian society as a whole.

Pope John XXIII in his opening speech to the Second Vatican Council
made it clear that the church was moving from defensive mode to a more
open, confident and joyful proclamation of the message of Jesus. He explicitly warned against the 'prophets of gloom' who would seek to undermine
the reforms of the ecumenical council. In his 1963 encyclical, *Pacem in*

terris , the pope used the expression 'signs of the times' in reference to international relations and world peace.

But it was in one of the Council's final and landmark documents, the *Constitution on the Church in the Modern World* that 'signs of the times' really came to the fore. The bishops of Vatican II saw the Church deeply immersed in the heart of humanity. Like Jesus himself, the church must stand in solidarity with the people of this world. The opening words of the Constitution proclaim this boldly.

As the Constitution unfolds, it challenges us to communicate the Gospel message to today's world.

> In every age, the church carries the responsibility of reading the signs of the times and of interpreting them in the light of the Gospel, if it is to carry out its task. In language intelligible to every generation, it should be able to answer the recurring questions people ask about the meaning of this present life and of the life to come, and how one is related to the other. We must be aware of and understand the aspirations, the yearnings and the often dramatic features of the world in which we live ... Ours is a new age of history with profound and rapid changes gradually spreading to all corners of the earth' (#4).

Those familiar with the YCW method of *See, Judge and Act* will recognise the influence of Joseph Cardijn, the founder of the Young Christian Workers. Their method is to seek out the issues facing young workers, reflect on them in the light of the Gospel and set about collaboratively to change things for the better. At the heart of all they do is the promotion of human dignity.

The Second Vatican Council enabled the Catholic Church to engage with contemporary culture, challenged it to seek closer communion with other Christians and to pray and work in collaboration with them. It sought to be in dialogue with other believers and with non-believers. It enabled the liturgy to be celebrated in the language of the people and called on all its members to take an active part in the life of the church. No longer was the role of lay people simply to 'pray, pay and obey'. Human and religious freedom was promoted, as was the primacy of conscience. The notions of collegiality and dialogue were very much part of the aspirations of the Council. John XXIII's successor, Paul VI, wrote a wonderful encyclical *Ecclesiam suam* which spelt out the qualities of respectful listening dialogue. How urgent is that message in today's world.

It saddens me that, in recent times, the 'prophets of gloom' whom Pope John XXIII warned against are exerting more and more influence within the life of the church. There are people who would seek to wind back the reforms of Vatican II. However, I always point out that we should not allow their negativity to obscure the many expressions of the vitality of the church at the grass-roots. I am sure that blessed Pope John XXIII would give a tick of approval to the aspirations and the achievements of the people and agencies who make up Catholic Social Services Australia.

It was the earthiness of Pope John XXIII which appealed to so many people, Catholics and non-Catholics alike. That same quality expressed very differently shone through the person of Frank McCosker. The son of a baker, he grew up in country New South Wales and joined the PMG before entering the seminary and being ordained to the priesthood in 1931. 'Mac', as he was affectionately known in adult life, never lost the common touch. This was beautifully illustrated by Fr John Usher who spoke about his much-loved mentor at his funeral Mass in February 1996. Fr McCosker's first years as a priest, when he was chaplain to Callan Park mental institution, helped to shape his future ministry. Soon after he was very much part of Catholic Action, promoting various forms of lay apostolate in the archdiocese of Sydney. Later, as an army chaplain serving in New Guinea, he saw life at its best and its worst.

Researcher Damian Gleeson's thesis gives many insights into the challenges Fr McCosker faced as he read the signs of the times in relation to social welfare in the archdiocese of Sydney and in wider Australia. Not the least of his problems were financial. That will probably come as no surprise to this audience. He also had the task of convincing his archbishop, Cardinal Gilroy, and Gilroy's auxiliaries of certain strategies in the face of opposing advice being given from other quarters. At a time when the contribution of women to the life of the church was not always acclaimed, McCosker welcomed the talents of such outstanding people as Norma Parker, Mary

Lewis, Pamela Riddle, Dorothy O'Halloran and Margaret McHardy. He also gave assistance to and benefited from the work of the religious orders in the welfare sphere. Gleeson's thesis also notes McCosker's concerns where there was a lack of professionalism and the training programs he introduced to overcome the problem. As well, he highlights Monsignor McCosker's promotion of cooperation between voluntary and professional models of welfare in the Australian church. Monsignor McCosker was a 'big picture' man and the church in Australia will be forever in his debt for the way he positioned it to be a credible voice in the field of social welfare. Yet he never lost sight of the fact that it is people who matter.

Is there a danger in today's climate with so many demands of compliance from government and even church that we become so 'professional' that we lose sight of the human persons involved? Does a whole variety of services guarantee that many people will not fall between the cracks? Do those of us in positions of leadership and authority remain close to people at the grass-roots, ready to listen to their stories of pain, abuse and neglect?

One leader who has listened and remained in touch with his people is Bishop Geoffrey Robinson, the retired auxiliary bishop of Sydney. Having entered the seminary at the tender age of 12, he was later sent to Propaganda Fide College in Rome for the completion of his seminary studies and ordained to the priesthood in 1960. Although he has degrees in Philosophy and Theology and a great love for and knowledge of Scripture, it is his Doctorate in Canon Law which gave direction to much of his priestly life where he made an immense contribution to the life of the Australian church on the matrimonial tribunal. Here he listened to heart-rending stories of people seeking annulments of their marriage; stories that not only related to a broken marriage but very often were life-long sagas of misfortune and deprivation. In his tribunal work he did much to promote the church's ideal of justice tempered with mercy and compassion.

Ordained bishop in 1984, his advice and guidance was sought by his brother bishops on a whole range of issues. He was chosen to represent them at two world-wide synods of bishops and a number of other international forums. But his major contribution came in the late 1980s, when the church first began to be aware of the horror of sexual abuse within its ranks.

By the mid-1990s it was becoming obvious that immense damage had been done to a significant number of people at the hands of church personnel. Often it was Centacare and other church agencies who first received the complaints from victims and their families. Geoffrey Robinson exercised a brave leadership role in helping the bishops and the leaders of religious orders to address the issues. *Towards Healing,* the procedures for responding to complaints of abuse, and *Integrity in Ministry,* a code of conduct for clergy and religious, were the principal documents produced as part of the Catholic Church's response to the terrible chapter in its history. I do not have to tell you how far reaching have been the consequences of abuse within the church and indeed in other parts of society.

Bishop Robinson's book, *Confronting Power and Sex in the Catholic Church,* is a brave exposition of what the author judges to be some of the root causes of abuse. He sees this crisis as an opportunity for the whole church to read the signs of the times in thoroughly re-examining whole areas of its life which are in need of reform. He pleads for open and honest discussion, painful though it might be. Ultimately, he recognises that it is the truth which sets us free. In no area of church life should we back away from the hard questions. At this point in the history of Catholic Social Services Australia we are at a *kairos* moment, a time of challenge and risk but also of great hope and opportunity. Bishop Robinson would be telling his old colleagues to face up to this moment with courage and confidence and in a spirit of dialogue and mutual trust.

It is not without significance that we meet on September 11, the day which saw the terrorist attacks in the United States six years ago, a day which has influenced so many subsequent attitudes and policies and the lives of countless people.

This time last year I was asked by the *Canberra Times* to write an op ed article on peace. Bear with me if I quote from that article because I think some of it has relevance to our aspirations for Catholic Social Services Australia.

> Since the terrible events of September 11, 2001, George W. Bush and his supporters have been outdoing each other in proclaiming a war on terror. I have never understood exactly what such a war

involves, apart from increasing fear in every part of society. It seems to me that it is much more constructive to talk about a war on poverty, rather than a war on terror. With all the rhetoric of the past five years, it obvious that terrorism is now a much greater threat because the divide between 'them and us' has grown much greater. The notion that one side can be beaten into submission by the other is a recipe for conflict rather than peace. It builds up a climate of fear, hate and suspicion alienating rather than bringing people together.

The UN Millennium Development Goals, adopted in 2000, aim at implementation by 2015. They offer a way to peace, security, development, human rights and fundamental freedoms for all peoples. They seek to

— eradicate extreme poverty and hunger;
— achieve universal primary education;
— promote gender equality and empower women;
— reduce child mortality;
— improve mental health;
— combat HIV/AIDS, malaria and other diseases;
— ensure environmental sustainability;
— develop a global partnership for development.

There are no quick fixes for the world's problems, but I take heart in the adage 'Think globally; act locally'. I must say that I very much admired Frank Quinlan's enunciation of Catholic Social Services Australia's response to the government's measures to tackle the problems of child abuse in Aboriginal communities. Such an approach recognises fundamental human rights, the human dignity of every person and community and the need to address the complexities of so many such issues. It is, moreover, a measured voice when so many elements such as the tabloid press are trotting out simplistic remedies.

It is no empty claim when CSSA's discussion paper states: 'Our voice has earned a place in the public discourse of the country on issues affecting the lives of people who are poor and marginalised including domestic violence, taxation, unemployment and work/family balance.'

The same paper 'proposes substantial change to Catholic Social Services Australia. The proposed changes would see its continued growth into an organisation recognised primarily for its success in social policy development and advocacy for those people who are poor and marginalised. Its authenticity and effectiveness in this task will be drawn from the experience of the high quality programs and services offered by its members.'

In our response, Pope John XXIII, Monsignor Frank McCosker and Bishop Geoffrey Robinson would point us to the person of Jesus who not only stood up for the most vulnerable people of his time but became one of them. They would urge us to bring the best of the church's tradition, especially its social teaching to bear on our future direction. They would encourage us to 'read the signs of the times'; to carefully identify our areas of concern and competence; to deliberate wisely in the light of the Gospel and to act decisively and courageously. I am proud, honoured and humbled to part of this noble endeavour. With God's grace may it prosper.

Social policy connections

Paper given at Yarra Theological Union at the request of Rev. Bruce Duncan CSSR, Box Hill, Victoria, 17 April 2013.

Growing up in Queanbeyan, adjacent to Canberra, I never took exception to its nickname, 'Struggletown'. My father politely pointed out that Queanbeyan was the mother of Canberra and it was simply a case of the child outgrowing the parent. In my boyhood in the post-World War II days, Queanbeyan welcomed many refugees from war-torn Europe and my parents were a great example to me of caring for the battlers. Dad was a Justice of the Peace and not only did he witness the signatures of the 'New Australians' on various documents but he helped them to navigate their way through potentially difficult waters. He adopted a similar role as a member of the St Vincent de Paul Society and in community activities. My mother welcomed all comers into our home and showed them unconditional love. To stand up for the poor even as a child was second nature to me and one of the motivations that led me to consider becoming a priest.

From my early days in the priesthood, I had some great role models in promoting justice and respect for the people I was privileged to serve. In many ways, it was the struggling people themselves who gave me some of the best lessons in life. The members of the Young Christian Workers taught me in new ways what it meant to stand up for the rights of vulnerable people. Their apostolate of 'like to like' enabled their members to take control of their lives, empowering themselves and their young colleagues. When I became a bishop, I gravitated towards the movements and bodies that aspired to make our church and world more in tune with the values of Jesus. In my 27 years as an 'active' bishop, I served on bishops' committees and commissions that promoted the dignity of lay people and family life, social justice and social welfare, ecumenism and relationships with the media. Almost a year into retirement, I have had plenty of opportunities to pursue my dreams in those areas without the burden of meetings.

I have been asked to speak on 'What I have learned about the churches and public policy'. I will draw on some of my experiences as a bishop in areas I have just alluded to. I do not in any way suggest that this is an exhaustive list, nor even the most important policy issues. They are simply the ones with which I am most familiar. My ecumenical heart has given me insight into the mission of the other churches living out the Gospel imperative to bring good news to every creature.

The National Council of Churches in Australia, the Anglican Church, the Uniting Church, the Baptist Church, the Salvation Army and indeed all the churches have greatly influenced public policy in the life of Australia. I have not attempted to highlight their achievements, simply because I do not consider myself able to do them justice. But I am keenly aware that the more closely the churches are able to collaborate in the area of social action the more credible will be their voice.

Aboriginal reconciliation

The national apology given by Prime Minister Kevin Rudd on 13 February 2008 to Aboriginal and Torres Islander peoples was one of the most moving experiences in my life. It was even more satisfying in that it followed an era where the previous prime minister could not bring himself to say sorry and it took on further significance when it was endorsed by the whole national parliament across the political spectrum. The emotional scenes of joy among the indigenous people, who had waited so long to hear those words, were embraced right throughout the Australian population.

Credit should be given to those people and organisations who for many years had fought for recognition and justice for Australia's first peoples. I think of Catholic activists such as 'Mum Shirl' (Shirley Smith), Vicki Walker, Elsie Heiss, Pat and Mick Dodson, Graeme Mundine, Jesuit Fr Frank Brennan and Bishops Ted Collins, Christopher Saunders and Eugene Hurley, to name just a few. I recall Mum Shirl giving some straight talk to the Australian bishops and having a strong ally in Fr Ted Kennedy in Redfern. Elsie Heiss and Vicki Walker may have taken a slightly more 'softly softly' approach but they have been extremely effective in their respective states and nationally in raising the level of consciousness within the Catholic Church and beyond of the moral and justice issues involved. I remember listening with pride as Elsie Heiss addressed the Oceania Synod of Bishops in Rome in 1998 in the presence of Pope John Paul II and over one hundred bishops and cardinals. Pat and Mick Dodson, Graeme Mundine and Frank Brennan have called on Catholic social teaching and fundamental principles of justice to articulate very effectively the cause of Aboriginal Australians. The bishops I mentioned and others have helped the members of their flocks to achieve a change of heart. Pope John Paul's Australian visit in 1986, especially his talk in Alice Springs, gave great heart to Indigenous people and a clearer understanding to non-Indigenous Australians. I am told that many Aboriginal people learnt that speech by heart as it so embraced their rich and unique culture.

Popular movements such as the Sea of Hands, launched in Canberra on 12 October 1997, and the Bridge Walks for Reconciliation in May 2000, as well as parish and ecumenical groups across the country, helped break down a lot of prejudice and ignorance and enabled our political leaders to understand the imperative for justice and reform.

Yet we all know that there is a long way to go in 'closing the gap' between Indigenous and non-Indigenous Australians. The Australian Catholic Social Justice statement for 2012-13 puts it graphically:

> It is a source of national shame, that over the past decade, the
> number of Indigenous people incarcerated has increased for women
> by 59 per cent and for men by 35 per cent. Indigenous juveniles
> are detained at 23 times the rate for non-Indigenous juveniles.
> Indigenous parents die younger than non-Indigenous people: on
> average men live 11.5 years less and women ten years less.

It goes on to speak of a much higher proportion of infant deaths and of homelessness. It questions the Northern Territory intervention and suggests other options.

There are much better ways to empower Indigenous families and ensure that they have the support and services most Australians take for granted. Australia has a duty to provide justice for Indigenous Australians by creating jobs, safe environments for children and access to education and health facilities. This must be based on true consultation and partnership, respect for traditional culture and identity and a thorough understanding of the particular needs of each community.

Refugees and asylum seekers

It is a source of national shame to have both the major political parties vying to outdo each other in harsh measures and rhetoric towards 'boat people'. Emotive terms such as 'border protection', 'people smugglers' and 'queue-jumping' all have the effect of creating fear in the community and diminishing the compassion owed to a desperate group of our fellow human beings. People forget the success of the post-World War II and the Vietnamese refugee programs whereby desperate newcomers went on to make outstanding contributions to Australian life, enriching our country as a multicultural nation.

Bodies such as the Australian Catholic Migrant and Refugee Office and the Australian Catholic Social Justice Council (ACSJC) are continually lobbying and making representation on behalf of today's refugees who are among the most vulnerable of people. The ACSJC has publicly restated the concerns of the UN High Commissioner for Refugees concerning conditions on Christmas Island, Nauru and Manus Island. It raises the question as to the humanity of off-shore detention and processing of claims. The Australian Catholic Migrant and Refugee Office accepting the determination of the Australian government to involve other countries has written a paper 'Voluntary and Compelled Migration in the Asia Pacific'. Recognising the complexity of the whole issue, it writes 'For the Catholic Church, regional cooperation on migration is of paramount importance. The Catholic Church aims to provide pastoral care to all people, regardless of their legal status as they move through different nations. Regional cooperation on this issue is therefore fundamental in facilitating the effective assistance of the Catholic Church and other organisations.'

I vividly remember when the refugees began to arrive in the 1970s and 80s how many parishes had wonderful schemes to welcome, accommodate and guide the newly arrived, helping them to settle into their new environment. Am I naive in thinking such initiatives adopted by parishes across Australia today would be more effective and humane than our current harsh strategies?

Catholic welfare/Catholic social services

For almost all of my 27 years as a bishop I was involved in the church's social apostolate at the national level. I came into it through Natural Family Planning but that is another story. I am privileged to be part of a tradition which involved some great pioneering women and people like Monsignor McCosker, Bishop Eric Perkins, John Usher, David Cappo, Toby O'Connor, Frank Quinlan, Joe Caddy and the current National Director, Paul O'Callaghan. Drawing on the first hand experience of people in the field, the Australian Social Welfare Commission and its successor, Catholic Social Services Australia (CSSA), have been able to be credible advocates for some of Australia's most marginalised citizens.

Following my father's example, I had an interest in politics as a youngster. As a bishop based in Canberra, I found myself at times in the delicate and sometimes hazardous interaction between church and government through my part in the Catholic Church's social apostolate. Some of the most effective interventions have been in concert with the agencies of the other Christian churches. I was privileged to represent Catholic Social Services at the July 1992 Youth Unemployment Summit and again in the National Tax Forum in October 2011, both being held in Parliament House in Canberra. The various national directors with whom I worked have had regular access to members of parliament and many of their key staff. The relationships that developed enabled them to represent the needs of their constituents, many of whom were among Australia's most vulnerable people.

In more recent years, Catholic Social Services Australia have held some of their meetings and conferences at Parliament House in Canberra, part of which involved meetings with ministers, members and staff. Breakfasts at the House were an effective way of Catholic Social Services staff from around Australia to make contact with their local members and to showcase some of the important projects at the grass-roots. Over the years, I took part in some rather robust discussions over areas such as the GST and workplace relations legislation. I made the submission to the Human Rights Commission into the Stolen Generations and, I believe, gave the first apology on the part of any of the churches.

Currently, Catholic Social Services Australia is making a 2013-14 pre-budget submission to the Commonwealth government. Its fifteen recommendations cover the following nine areas:

— improved help for jobseekers with multiple and severe barriers;
— income support (especially an increase in the Newstart Allowance);
— a review of working age payments;
— social support services in small rural communities;
— mental health reform;
— support for vulnerable children and families;
— working with the not-for-profit sector;
— creating a social innovation fund (to tackle entrenched disadvantage);
— affordable housing.

Much of CSSA's efforts are directed towards its 67 member agencies which employ around 12,000 people with 4000 voluntary contributors. The network provides community services to over one million Australians each year, with programs valued at around $700 million. CSSA partners with a number of government and non-government organisations to pursue its mission and contributes to social policy development based on the experience and expertise of its member network.

Catholic Health Australia

In May 2009, the Australian Catholic Bishops Conference restructured some of its bishops' commissions, putting Catholic Social Services Australia and Catholic Health Australia (CHA) within the Bishops' Commission for

Health and Community Services. I was elected chairman of that commission. Up to that point I had admired the work of CHA from afar but without any direct involvement. It became very clear to me that CHA, under the leadership of chairman Tony Wheeler and Chief Executive Officer Martin Laverty, is a credible voice on the national scene. I was asked to represent Australia at a meeting of the Pontifical Council for Healthcare Workers in Rome in November 2011. As I reported on Australia and listened to the other reports, I could see that Australia was well placed in the contribution it was making in the health and aged care field. In my report to the Vatican meeting I stated:

> We bishops are very proud of our Catholic hospitals. They are some of the best and most trusted hospitals in Australia. At a time when many Australians are suspicious or cynical about organised religion, they trust the place of Catholic hospitals within the community. The face of Jesus is presented with compassion and expertise to the Australian community through our excellent Catholic hospitals. Governments across Australia have a high regard for Catholic hospitals and aged-care services. Unlike the situation in some other countries, our state governments actively fund 21 Catholic public hospitals to provide services to any person in need. Our 550 aged care services all receive some type of Federal government funding.

CHA focuses very much on the social determinants of health described by the World Health Organisation as 'the conditions in which people are born, grow, live, work and age, including the health system. These circumstances are shaped by the distribution of money, power and resources at global, national and local levels.' CHA sees it as priority to 'reduce the gap in health outcomes between the most and least disadvantaged.' CHA progressed the discussion of the social determinants of health in Australia with the production of its book *Determining the Future: A Fair Go & Health for All*. On 4 December 2012, CEO Martin Laverty made a lengthy submission to a Senate Select Committee Inquiry into the Social Determinants of Health.

CHA also reports

— being the leading voice for providers in the aged care
community's response to the Productivity Commission's report
Caring for Older Australians and in negotiations with the
federal government in its formulation of its response to that
report, culminating in reforms announced in April 2012;
— representing the CHA family on a number of groups advising
the government and the Department of Health and Ageing,
including in the areas of workforce, pathology, hospital pricing
and performance, and aged care reform;
— speaking in conjunction with other national Catholic
organisations on proposed changes to charities and not-for-
profit legislation, working to ensure there are no negative
impacts on the way charities and not-for-profits operate or in
the way they are governed;
— leading the Catholic Church's response to the Senate Inquiry
into past adoption practices;
— continuing efforts to have preventative health measures as a
priority;
— establishing a new website to keep members and the wider
community up to date with CHA's activities, including news
and advocacy efforts; it has expanded its social media presence,
including the establishment of Twitter and Facebook accounts.

The Catholic contribution to health and aged care in Australia is one
of which we can be justifiably proud. The healing mission of the church
reaches out to every section of the Australian community.

Conclusion

I have touched on just four areas of the Catholic Church's engagement with
the wider community as it seeks to bring the good news to every creature,
especially in its interaction with government and the formulation of policy.
Other groups such as the Secretariat of the Australian Catholic Bishops'

Conference under the leadership of General Secretary, Fr Brian Lucas, have made outstanding contributions, building up good relations with those with whom they are in dialogue.

Clearly, the media is a very important player in all such engagement and the strategies and relationships developed there are crucial. While I am too old to understand the intricacies of the newest forms of social media, I recognise their importance in all that I have been speaking about.

The prophet Micah told us that it all comes down to three things, 'to act justly, to love tenderly and to walk humbly with our God'. Two millennia later, Vatican II's *Pastoral Constitution on the Church in the Modern World* would remind us that 'The joys and the hopes, the griefs and anxieties of the people of this age, particularly those who are in any way poor or afflicted, these too are the joys and the hopes, the griefs and anxieties of all the followers of Christ.' I take heart in the way the people and the organisations I have spoken about are responding to these imperatives as part of the pilgrim church.

One hundred and fifty years of grace

Homily given on the occasion of a Mass commemorating 150 years since the establishment of the Diocese of Goulburn, Riversdale, Goulburn, NSW, 17 November 2012.

As the Catholic Church in Australia celebrates a Year of Grace and the Universal Church observes a Year of Faith, we in the Archdiocese of Canberra and Goulburn commemorate our beginnings as the Diocese of Goulburn by the Decree of the Sacred Congregation for the Propagation of the Faith in Rome on 17 November 1862. We do so by celebrating Holy Mass at Riversdale, on the site of the first Mass celebrated in Goulburn by the great pioneering priest, John Joseph Therry, on 3 August 1833.

For that historic first Mass, the faithful congregated in Matt Healy's Inn, while today we are gathered by the parish priest of Goulburn, Fr Dermid McDermott, whose father, Ernie McDermott, was a much-loved publican in this city and for 17 years its mayor. I have in my possession a holy water font presented by Fr Therry to my great great grandfather, Morgan Power, on the occasion of his marriage in 1826.

There is a certain symmetry with these sesquicentenary celebrations beginning while the archdiocese is without a bishop, when we realise that the Diocese of Goulburn did not manage to consecrate a bishop until almost five years after the Roman decree of its foundation. On 10 March 1864, the Bishop of Adelaide, Franciscan Patrick Geoghegan, was named Bishop of the Diocese of Goulburn. At the time, he was seeking medical help for a throat condition in his native Ireland and by 9 May that year he had died following an operation in Dublin. The search for a new bishop rivalled some of the intrigues of modern day politics but eventually concluded with the appointment of Fr William Lanigan, parish priest of Berrima, even though in the latter stages of the selection process the new bishop was unsure whether he was to be Bishop of Goulburn or of Armidale! He was duly consecrated Bishop of Goulburn on Pentecost Sunday, 9 June 1867.

Patrick Geoghegan's influence on the Diocese of Goulburn would continue through the Sisters of St Joseph, whose founder, Mary MacKillop, Australia's first saint, was baptised in Melbourne in 1842 by Fr Geoghegan who had also celebrated the marriage of Mary's parents. It is significant that in these days of historical celebrations, the two streams of the Sisters of St Joseph known as the Black and Brown Josephites have just been united.

Similarly, the Goulburn Sisters of Mercy, who have made such a major contribution to the life of the Archdiocese of Canberra and Goulburn and the Diocese of Wagga Wagga for more than 150 years have now merged into a wider Mercy Congregation covering the whole of Australia.

Any celebration of the Catholic history of this diocese must acknowledge the impact of the Sisters of Mercy and the Sisters of St Joseph in the fields of education, health and aged care, spirituality, pastoral life and social welfare. Records show the 'big picture' achievements of both congregations of sisters, but God alone knows the countless ways in which the sisters touched the lives of so many people, young and old, and not just Catholic. The site of this Mass in proximity to the Goulburn Jail, the old Kenmore Hospital, St Joseph's Orphanage and latterly the House of Prayer is a further reminder of God's grace being mediated to a large variety of people through the ministrations of the whole People of God.

For a time, the Daughters of Charity ministered here in Goulburn while the St John of God Sisters continue to provide a living witness to God's love after many years of outstanding service in their hospital in Bourke Street. The Good Samaritan Sisters, founded in the Benedictine tradition by Australia's first bishop, John Bede Polding, have given dedicated service in Braidwood, Moruya, Queanbeyan and Canberra, while the Presentation Sisters taught at Young and a great variety of religious sisters came to Canberra mainly at the invitation of Archbishop Eris O'Brien to staff the Catholic primary and secondary schools in the growing national capital. The Franciscan Missionaries of Mary founded Marymead Children's Home in Narrabundah, while the Little Company of Mary in Canberra continues to operate Calvary Hospital and Clare Holland House as a hospice for the dying. The Carmelite Sisters have been part of Catholic life in Canberra since the 1970s.

Christian Brothers, Marist Brothers and De La Salle Brothers are all an important part of the Catholic education story, while the Redemptorist, Passionist, Dominican and Jesuit Fathers and the Missionaries of the Sacred Heart have drawn on the particular charisms of their founders to enrich the life of this diocese over much of its 150 year history.

To mark this milestone in our diocesan history, Fr Brian Maher has chronicled the clergy – bishops, priests and deacons – who have played such a central role in its unfolding. Today, Catholic education, in many ways the jewel in the crown of our archdiocese, is almost totally staffed by highly competent and dedicated lay people, very much aware of their vocation within the mission of the church.

The 150 years we reflect on today have seen the growth of Australia as a nation with federation in 1901, and the naming of Canberra as national capital in 1913 and the opening of the original Parliament House in 1927 and the current one in 1988. We have also witnessed two World Wars and other major conflicts involving Australian military personnel, the Great Depression, as well as impressive sporting achievements, including the 1956 and 2000 Olympic Games. The 1967 Referendum and Prime Minister Kevin Rudd's apology to our Aboriginal population have gone some way to recognising the people who have occupied this land for more than 40,000 years but much still needs to be done to redress the injustices suffered by Australia's original inhabitants. I wish to pay tribute to Archbishop Carroll for all that he did to create awareness of such important questions long before it was fashionable to do so. Especially since the end of the Second World War, but even before that, Australia has opened its borders to people seeking a new life in this country for a whole variety of reasons. Many such people and their descendants have made excellent citizens of Australia. Sadly, such a welcoming approach to refugees is singularly missing from Australia's major political parties at the moment.

The Catholic Church has undergone much change in the past 150 years. Bishop Lanigan attended the First Vatican Council from 1869 to 1870 while Archbishops O'Brien, Young and Cahill as well as Bishop Cullinane were Fathers of the Second Vatican Council from 1962 to 1965. Vatican II had a major impact on the life of the church in its self-understanding, its call for greater involvement of the laity, its liturgy, its relations with other churches and other faiths and indeed its place in the modern world. The immediate aftermath of Vatican II was not without its tensions but it was a time of great hope, reflective of the spirit of the pope who began it all, John XXIII.

We celebrate the 150 years of our local church as the Universal Church celebrates the fifty years since the opening of the Second Vatican Council. In each case, it is an opportunity to look forward as well as to look back. The readings so thoughtfully chosen for today's Mass point the way to the future. The gospel calls us to leave aside our fears and hesitations. In the spirit of Vatican II, we are to 'read the signs of the times' and follow Jesus' command to make disciples of all people by proclaiming the Gospel message in a way that is comprehensible and does not shy away from the hard questions confronting us. We must be prepared to listen as Jesus listened and we must engage with people in the way that he did. Six hundred years earlier, the prophet Isaiah had delivered the Lord's message to have a care for justice and to act with integrity. It is by these criteria that Jesus' followers are being rightly judged today. Isaiah challenges us to reach out to foreigners, to be truly catholic and all-embracing, not an inward-looking group lazing in our comfort zones. St Paul calls on us to recognise the great variety of gifts among the whole people of God. We are challenged to find unity within diversity and to honour God's goodness and love even in unexpected places and people. In this way we will be open to the *God of Surprises*.

I would hope, in the years ahead, the Archdiocese of Canberra and Goulburn would be in the forefront of a church which is more missionary, more inclusive and more ecumenical. It is a happy coincidence that at about the same time as our celebrations, the Anglican Diocese of Canberra and Goulburn is celebrating its 150 years. It is my prayer that it will not take another 150 years for our two churches to come together. With determination, more cooperation, mutual trust, a lot of prayer and openness to God's grace we could achieve it in less than 150 months. Or what about 150 weeks! Of course, there is as well the call to openness to unity with the other churches and all the followers of Christ for which Jesus prayed so ardently at the Last Supper as St John records in chapter 17 of his gospel.

Finally, I believe that in the years ahead, if our church is not only to survive but to be true to its calling, we must be open to radically new forms of ministry. Bishops Polding and Lanigan, Caroline Chisholm, Mary MacKillop, Catherine McAuley, Mother Teresa and Pope John XXIII in their different ways and circumstances were prepared to break new ground in living out their vocations. Any new forms of ministry must surely be open to a far wider participation of women and a greater deployment of their gifts. I believe the Catholic Church today would not be facing many of its current woes if women had been more significantly part of its governance. Now is the time for the church to embrace the unique gifts of women in new and creative ways.

Let us look forward in hope as we continue to walk with each other in faith and love on our pilgrim journey as God's holy people.

> *Let all the peoples praise you, O Lord,*
> *Let all the peoples praise you.*
>
> Psalm 67:3

Causeway's influence on my life as a priest

A young priest's introduction to the real world. A talk given to the National Trust ACT members' night, Causeway Hall, Canberra, 21 November 2012

I was just out of college and still 23 when I arrived at St Christopher's Parish, Manuka, in early 1966. Shortly afterwards, the suburb of Causeway, one of Canberra's earliest settlements, became part of my 'beat' and it left an imprint on me which continues to shape my life and values. In those days, there were 122 houses with no street names, there were lots of social issues around poverty and hardship, but also an indomitable spirit which I will never forget.

There were other priests before me who were likewise touched by the unique character of Causeway. The first parish priest of Canberra, Fr Patrick Haydon, had a great affection for Causeway and even though he died in 1949 there were still old-timers who spoke fondly about him.

At a Christmas party at the Causeway Hall, Fr Haydon scandalised a few people by giving each unemployed person at the dinner a bottle of beer and a packet of cigarettes.

Fr Vince Butler was another who endeared himself to the people of Causeway. He was responsible for the building of St Therese's Church at the Causeway. It was blessed by Bishop Young in 1948. Fr Butler had organised the transport of two former air-force barracks from Wagga. They were joined together on site and an expert job was done in plaster by members of the Rumble family. The church boasted two impressive stained glass windows, one of the great Spanish saint, Teresa of Avila, and the other of

Therese of Lisieux, the young French Carmelite nun known as the Little Flower. After his time in Causeway, Fr Butler was to go on to the Snowy Mountains where he ministered to the men working on the Snowy River Scheme. Causeway served as a good apprenticeship for that.

It has to be admitted that the Causeway church did not get a lot of local patronage in my time of visiting there but there were many outsiders who came for Mass. There was a 9.00 am Sunday Mass celebrated by the German priest-scientist, Fr Gregor Hagemann. He gave a short sharp sermon leaving the parishioners free to enjoy the rest of Sunday in other pursuits. Most memories are of how cold the church was in winter. As well as Sunday Masses there was a 7.00 am Mass on weekdays. I can remember my hands aching with cold as I celebrated Mass on some mornings. There are stories of the holy water freezing in the font.

Jill Waterhouse, in her excellent community history of Causeway, speaks of Fr John Hoare, another Catholic priest who endeared himself to the people there. I should add that the Salvation Army, the Church of England and other churches took an interest in Causeway as well.

The priest who handed over the reins of Causeway to me was Fr Kevin Barry-Cotter. Kevin returned from Rome in 1964 with a doctorate in Canon Law and shortly afterwards was assigned to Causeway. Kevin suspects that his superiors may have felt that he needed some grounding after a number of years in the lofty realms of the Vatican. What better place and what better people to do it than the Causeway community! Kevin was quickly embraced by the locals and like me, many years later he looks back on those early years as being formative in his pastoral life. Kevin and I have just spent a few days on retreat together and we had a couple of nostalgic conversations where we were able to jog each other's memories of Causeway in the 1960s.

I should point out that not all the people living in Causeway over the years suffered great deprivation. Many of course did, but for others it was a first stop when they arrived in Canberra. People such as Gerry Kilmartin, Frank and Kath Scott, got a start in the Causeway. They always looked back on those days with pride and affection.

Kevin Barry-Cotter points out that it made good economic sense for many people to have affordable housing (a pound a week rent) while they established themselves and their families.

Causeway was familiar to me when I went there as a young priest in 1966. I had done all my primary schooling at St Christopher's in Manuka in the 1940s and early 1950s and had many school mates from Causeway. Some I remember are the Johnson sisters, Marie Thornton, Judy Hawke, Tom and Colleen Kelly, Michael Harrington and Alan Lamb. Members of their extended families were still part of the Causeway community when I arrived as a newly-ordained priest, still wet behind the ears. Some of the older families, the O'Briens, the Gowings and other names which now escape me were part of this close-knit community.

In the 2010 Canberra Day Oration, I spoke of 'Canberra and its battlers'. Causeway was my starting point:

> If the rest of Canberra ignored Causeway or looked down its nose
> at it, there was a fierce community pride among the residents
> themselves. While there was a great deal of poverty in Causeway
> and many other social problems, the loyal community spirit meant
> that the residents looked out for each other and shared one another's
> burdens in a way which I found to be truly remarkable. Their
> houses were always open to each other and I personally felt humbled
> to be so welcomed into the homes of Catholics and non-Catholics
> alike.

For me the person who best epitomises Causeway is Maureen Wyatt. Some time before I arrived on the Causeway scene, Maureen was deserted by her husband, leaving her to look after their four young children. It was a struggle but Maureen had good support from her mother, Mrs Howard, and, as usual, many of the locals helped out. Maureen herself was always available to others as a mother figure. She called a spade a spade and there were no pretensions about her. She may have been a bit rough around the edges but she had a heart of gold. She was fiercely protective of her children but made them face up to the consequences if they were out of line. Maureen used to tell me that the roof of the church would fall in if she went inside. It always saddened me that someone like Maureen would feel excluded from God's family because of her poverty or sense of unworthiness, when I knew that it was the Maureens of Jesus' day who were closest to his heart. Right up to the time of her death a few years back, Maureen kept in touch with me by phone. 'G'day' would be her opening line, knowing that I would recognise her voice. When the time came, I was pleased to be able to officiate at her funeral and pay tribute to a good and colourful life.

In the seminary, everyone told the truth and somehow or other I thought that was the way it was in life. But I soon learnt otherwise in Causeway. Maureen and her teenage protégé, Lynette Burke, were spinning me a yarn about something or other and I just took it to be true. When I found out otherwise, I confronted them both and they were surprised at my indignation. They pointed out to me that the odd porky was part of life and survival. I no longer remember what the issue was, but I learned that sometimes you have to question what you are being told.

Tom Nichols and his wife were separated and Tom worked hard at being a good father to his three kids even if he drank a bit too much at times. I tried to help out a bit, especially with regard to the youngest lad. He seemed to be responding well to a couple of fatherly talks I had with him. Then one day I was summoned by the head nun at St Christopher's telling me that Graham had been caught pinching a chocolate from J. B. Young's over the road. She told me to read the riot act to him. I was never much good at such tasks, but when I caught up with Graham, I said, 'What's come over you, Graham? You've been doing well and now you do this. What made you do it?' 'It must have been the devil, Father', was Graham's disarming reply. Tom died happily a few years ago, and the three children have been excellent citizens in adult life.

Ernie Corey was a great character who came originally from the Monaro, had a distinguished war record and spent his last years as an elder statesman in the Causeway. Jack Lette was known to me from the days that he and my uncle, Perce Power, drove trucks for Pittmans carting pipes for the Snowy River scheme. Jack and his wife spent many years in Causeway and Jack was seen as the unofficial mayor, often being an articulate spokesman for the community.

The Tallaridas were a prominent Italian family. It is said that their plum tree produced some potent drink. There was another friendly Italian family whose name escapes me, but I often remember with shame my first visit to their home. The husband came in with three glasses of wine, one each for me, his wife and himself. In those days I had taken the pledge and I tried to tell him that I did not drink alcohol. It is very difficult to explain that to an Italian. 'But it is good wine, Father.' These days I do have a drink, but I think now of my immaturity at that time in not accepting such gracious hospitality.

Towards the end of my time in the late 1960s the Railway resumed the land which on which the church and Causeway Mess were built. I don't have memories of many visits to Causeway Mess which housed single men but I do recall doing a sad funeral of one of the residents. It was a graveside service with only four mourners who were tasked with lowering the coffin. Unfortunately one of them was under the influence and was in danger of dropping in the coffin and falling into the grave himself. I quickly put aside my prayer book and filled in for him.

With the closing of St Therese's Church, I gained permission to celebrate Mass in the Causeway Hall. I asked Archbishop Thomas Cahill to say the first Mass in the hall and he readily agreed. I suggested that he might leave aside his more fancy bishop's gear, but he insisted on using it all saying that to do otherwise would be to sell short the people of Causeway. I have to say that, after some initial enthusiasm, numbers fell away and we had to abandon the weekly Mass.

I was transferred to Goulburn at the beginning of 1971, thus ending my association with Causeway as such, but I am always delighted when I catch up with an old friend from those days. At the beginning of my life as a priest, I learnt some important lessons from the people of Causeway: simple goodness, lack of pretence, a wonderful sense of sharing and community, great resilience and a love of life and a love of people. It gives me great joy to be reminded of all that tonight.

Remembrance ceremony

Talk given on 16 October 2006 at the annual ceremony commemorating those who lives have been lost through illicit drug use. It is sponsored by Families and Friends of Drug Law Reform, Weston Park, Yarralumla, ACT.

Last Friday, one of my brother priests presided over the funeral ceremonies for his youngest brother who had died from drowning after an overdose; the man in question had struggled with mental illness and alcoholism for most of his adult life. Before Christmas, many of us here were present at a vigil, organised by Amnesty International, in front of parliament house in support of Van Nguyen who was about to be hanged in Singapore. Each of those people powerfully demonstrate how precious is the gift of human life.

Just now, we have heard the names and circumstances of 170 people who have died as a result of illicit drug use. This is not a mere statistic. These are 170 human beings. Each one is someone's son or daughter, a sister or a brother, an aunt or uncle, a spouse, a partner or a lover. They are surely the dear friends of many, including some of us here today.

We are taking part in a *remembrance ceremony*. We are doing what we do on Anzac Day and other similar occasions. Yesterday, here in Canberra there was a ceremony to remember 353 people who drowned when their boat, known as the SIEV X, sank in shocking circumstances. It can be argued that these 353 died unnecessarily and as a result of government policies.

Today, we are remembering and in doing so we are honouring. We are recognising the dignity, the worth and the achievements of each one who has died so prematurely. We are also acknowledging the struggles of each one and the tragic circumstances that led to their death. We hold up each life as precious and unique.

In remembering, we are also learning. We are learning from people's experiences, good and bad, in the hope that their life and death will not have been in vain.

We gather today with a sense of commitment. All of us here are committed to doing everything we can to see that no more lives are lost. We recognise that there are different roles that we have to play. We are in awe of all that is done by Families and Friends of Drug Law Reform. We see what can be done by legislators, the police, the legal profession, religious and community groups, the media, supportive friends and many others. But most of all, I trust that all of you here recognise the power you have as advocates. Telling the stories, as you do, make you most effective advocates in seeing that community attitudes are changed in a way that will lead to the saving of human lives.

One of the messages read this afternoon came from Great Britain. It told us that where there is life there is hope. I remember once a union leader addressing his constituents. He said to them rather controversially, 'Don't be a hopeless lot.' He went on to explain that we should never give up hope. There is always a future and each of us is empowered in one way or another to shape that future for the better. That surely applies to each of us here.

We should never lose sight of our ability to raise community awareness, and to effect changes that will make ours a more just and compassionate society.

Many of you here today are grieving for family members or friends. Those deaths may have been recent or some time ago, but whenever they took place the memories and the pain are still very vivid. One small piece of advice I offer is to *be gentle with yourself.* It is natural and so easy to go through the 'if onlys'

— If only I had recognised the warning signs.
— If only I had listened.
— If only I had understood what was happening.

— If only I had been more patient.

— If only I had kept the door open.

— If only I had been more loving.

— If only I had been firmer, had taken a tougher stand.

But don't lose sight of the fact that we are all human. The wisdom of hindsight is a luxury we don't have when faced with decisions that may have long-standing consequences. But today we can tell our deceased loved ones that we are sorry for how we failed or how they failed or how society may have failed them. We can tell them how dearly we love them. We can tell them how proud we are to be honouring their memory in this fashion.

Today, we are in a sacred space, sharing precious memories. I ask God to bless each one of us and those we remember with deep affection, confident that all of us and our world will be better for what we have done together.

Real action on climate change

Talk given in front of Parliament House, Canberra, following a walk from Commonwealth Park in support of care for the environment, 5 June 2011.

When I walk up Mount Ainslie, as I do most mornings, I constantly thank God for the unique character of Canberra, the rich natural diversity of Australia and the wonders of the world we inhabit.

When I visit children at school or talk with my grand nephews and nieces, I witness their joy in living, their grateful acceptance of the good things in life: their families and friends, the animal world and the world of nature in general.

Every living person today in appreciating the beauty and integrity of creation surely has a responsibility to preserve and enhance it for future generations. As a person of faith, I believe that care for our environment is one of the great moral challenges of our day. We should not allow short term solutions or the temptation to instant gratification to sabotage the future of our beautiful world.

I hope that even those who do not hold to a religious belief would appreciate the sentiments expressed in the 2002 Social Justice Sunday statement: 'In justice, it is an urgent task for Christians today to be reconciled to all creation, and to undertake faithfully our responsibility of stewardship of God's gifts. To achieve such reconciliation, we must examine our lives and acknowledge the ways we have harmed God's creation through our actions and our failure to act. We need to experience a conversion, a change of heart.' What was true in 2002 has become much more urgent today.

The measures that have been spoken about today will come at a cost, but what is the cost of inaction? If we continue with a 'business as usual' attitude, we will gradually go down a course that will lead to the degradation of so much of our natural environment. It is the poorest and most vulnerable people of our world who are most at risk. Just think of the people of Tuvalu, Kiribati, Bangladesh and other low lying nations who have so much at stake right now with rising sea levels.

If the price of protecting our environment is to be a reduction in the standard of living in countries like Australia, is that an altogether bad thing? 'Live simply, so that others can simply live' makes a lot of sense to me. It is my hope that whatever measures are introduced would carry safeguards to ensure that Australians on lower incomes would not be forced into deeper poverty. The rest of us should be prepared to make the necessary sacrifices to see that future generations are not left lamenting the consequences of our short term greed.

I am proud to have walked across Commonwealth Bridge with you all today as I was proud to join 250,000 others marching over the Sydney Harbour Bridge in May 2000 calling for justice for our Indigenous people. Today we are in solidarity with our fellow Australians in other towns and cities seeking justice in our country's attitude towards the environment and to future generations. As we assemble in this beautiful location in front of our national parliament, we urge our parliamentary representatives of all persuasions to show courageous leadership in offering all Australians a vision of a sustainable future.

Conversation over a meat pie

An article written for *Catholic Voice* in support of those priests no longer in active ministry, 4 October 2000.

Some time ago I estimated that in this archdiocese there were about forty married Catholic priests no longer serving in the active ministry. In late September, while the rest of the nation was focused on the Olympic Games, I met with five of them over a meat pie in my Favier House office.

On Palm Sunday 1996, I had travelled to Brisbane for a meeting of Epiphany, a group of former priests, their families and friends. It was an interesting and at times intense dialogue with about fifty people. I believed it was very worthwhile and productive. In the latter part of 1998, there was a national meeting of Epiphany here in Canberra. Most of the personnel were different to those I had met in Brisbane and I was limited in the time I spent with them, but again my impressions were very positive.

The recent informal meeting in my office grew out of concerns expressed in the diocesan Reconciliation Task Force which has been seeking to take some concrete steps to advance reconciliation in various areas during this Jubilee Year. We were aware of initiatives taken in at least two other dioceses (Ballarat and Toowoomba) to give recognition and thanks to priests no longer in active ministry.

The five men invited are all good friends of mine and are all very committed to the Catholic Church. I thought I knew most of their stories but I was deeply moved by what we shared in a little over an hour. What does reconciliation mean in their situation? What can be done by the official church to address their issues? How can healing be brought about, not just for them but for others in similar situations? We probably came up with more questions than answers.

There were expressions of sadness, regret, guilt and anger, but I did not detect any bitterness. There were also sentiments of relief, satisfaction, peace and the recognition of God's love, the love of wives and families and acceptance by the community.

But in many ways they are people still living in the shadows, sometimes able to contribute to the life of the church but in a way that can never be too obvious. All of them, although they would be too humble to broadcast it, are making an enormous impact in their professional lives and are blessed in being part of a loving family life. They are advancing the reign of God but in a way that the official church seems unable to acknowledge.

My five friends made no claim to speak on behalf of their brothers in similar situations. In fact they were quite adamant that everyone's experience is different, just as there are differing needs, hopes and expectations.

I had hoped that they might be able to make some suggestions as to how some reconciling steps could be made towards people in their situation. My friends did not warm towards the idea of any grand event or gesture, but were enthusiastic about the kind of conversation in which were engaged that day. They recognised that the reconciliation process was severely limited by the current discipline binding the universal church.

It occurred to me that there could be some benefit in having similar informal meetings with other small groups of 'former' priests. Then there is the question of the twenty or more who served as priests of this archdiocese but are now living elsewhere. It would seem beneficial to extend the hand of friendship to them as well. My friends pointed out to me that circumstances often dictated that they left their parishes and friends without the chance to say goodbye. There must be a lot of unfinished business for all involved.

There could be the opportunity to thank them for their years of service, to apologise to them for hurts they may have experienced and to enquire as to what are their current needs and hopes.

God's love for us all is without limit. Sometimes, however, I fear that we place limits on that love. I would hope that during this year of Great Jubilee we might be liberated from some of the fears and limitations which bind us; that we might remember that Jesus came that we 'might have life and have it to the full'.

I would be interested to hear from people with reactions to this story. There are many more conversations to be had. I hope that our conversation over a meat pie might provide food for thought and strength for future action.

Mary, our model

A reflection written for *Catholic Voice*, April 2007.

One of the highlights of a visit to St Peter's Basilica in Rome is to see Michelangelo's *Pietà*, the magnificent sculpture of Mary holding in her arms the dead Christ. The haunting beauty of this great work of art depicts the deep sorrow of a mother mourning her child. Did Mary at that point recall the words of Simeon when Jesus was presented as a baby in the Temple? Simeon had prophesied that Jesus would be a sign of contradiction and that a sword would pierce the heart of Mary as well.

In the gospel accounts, Mary is never far from Jesus and Catholic tradition has always recognised the important role she played in Jesus' work of redemption. She is prominent in so many of the beautiful works of art down through the centuries, a reflection of the veneration in which she has been held for nearly 2000 years.

Leading up to the Jubilee Year 2000, Pope John Paul asked that 1997 focus in a particular way on the person of Jesus Christ. In that context he asked that recognition be given to the role of Our Lady. 'Mary constantly points to her Divine Son and she is proposed to all believers as our model of faith.'

Mary can be a great model of faith for young people. I often remind senior high school students that Mary was their age when she was invited through the Angel Gabriel to be the mother of Jesus. The 'yes' that she was to give to God was to have profound effects not only for herself but for the whole human race. Her decision, made in trepidation and only after questioning, reflection and prayer, is one that will resonate with many young people today. They are so often faced with difficult personal, moral and vocational choices that will at times have significant and even life-long implications for themselves and for others. Like Mary, they will often feel very much alone in making such decisions, but hopefully they will do so with minds and hearts that are open to God who loves us and wants only what is best for us.

Mary is clearly a model for women today. Although she lived in a society and at a time when women were seen in a culturally different light, Mary was by no means a passive wall flower. Stamina and determination, as well as love and devotion, were needed to undertake the hazardous journey to visit her cousin, Elizabeth, when both of them were pregnant. How socially acceptable was it for a woman to travel alone in such circumstances? Her role in Jesus' first miracle, changing water into wine at the wedding feast of Cana showed her assertiveness as well as her concern for the newly married couple and their guests. Her strength of character as she walked with Jesus in his public life and especially to Calvary is inspirational.

Mary is a consoling model for today's parents. How often we meet parents worried and concerned for their children in all sorts of situations. As Mary escaped to Egypt with Joseph and Jesus she must have been fearful for the harm Herod might do to her son.

Any parent who has lost a child even for a short time will identify with Mary's experience when Jesus was 12 years old. Could any mother experience greater heart-break than that of Our Lady as she watched Jesus dying on the cross? While all parents will easily seek the intercession of Mary in their concern for their children, I believe that Mary's unique circumstances make her a special source of hope for single parents.

People who are poor or struggling in all sorts of ways will find a ready companion in Mary of Nazareth. One of Jesus' detractors was to ask, 'Can anything good come out of Nazareth?' Even today, Nazareth is pretty basic in material terms. Yet Mary was able to rise above poverty and shame, finding her strength in God. Her *Magnificat* prayer gives beautiful expression to her faith: 'The Almighty works marvels for me ... He puts forth his arm in strength and scatters the proud hearted. He casts the mighty from their thrones and raises the lowly. He fills the starving with good things and sends the rich away empty.' Mary's *Magnificat* not only places her in solidarity with the poor and victims of injustice but challenges all Christians to have a real heart for justice and fairness.

Finally, Mary is a model for all believers. Undoubtedly, each generation has its own faith challenges to meet. Being a Catholic today is not always easy for a whole variety of reasons. Young people face enormous peer pressure against practising their faith; being a believer today is not part of being politically correct; and the church itself has had to face up to scandals and divisions within its own ranks. Mary was part of the infant Church which endured opposition, persecution and internal struggles as it sought to bear witness to Jesus and the good news he brings. May Mary's serene faith, her openness to God's love and influence, and her trust in the Holy Spirit bring each of us closer to Jesus.

Pope John Paul says it all in summing up his hopes for the Great Jubilee of the Year 2000:

> I entrust this responsibility of the whole church to the maternal
> intercession of Mary, Mother of the Redeemer. She, the Mother of
> fairest love, will be for Christians on the way to the Great Jubilee
> of the third millennium the star which safely guides their steps to
> the Lord. May the unassuming young woman of Nazareth, who
> two thousand years ago offered to the world the Incarnate Word,
> lead the men and women of the new millennium towards the One
> who is 'the true light that enlightens every person'.

Galong Mass

Homily given at the Mass marking, inter alia, the 90th anniversary of the laying of the foundation stone of St Clement's Monastery, Galong, NSW, 14 April 2007.

Readings: 1 Kings 8:22-30; 1 Corinthians 3:5-11;
Matthew 7:24-27

The opening hymn reminds us that we are standing on holy ground. Yet there is every reason why we might not have been here today. They sometimes say that God writes straight with crooked lines.

Father Max Barrett's splendid book *King of Galong Castle,* the story of Ned Ryan, relates the intriguing story of how this property came into the hands of the Redemptorists. John Nagle Ryan inherited the property from his father, but being a bachelor had no descendants to whom he would pass on his inheritance. The arrangement was for his sister, Anastasia Ryan, to have the occupancy of the property but on her death the Catholic Church in some form was to be given its ownership. According to the will, John Nagle Ryan's first choice was the Cistercians and in the event of their refusal the Redemptorists. After a fair period of indecision, the Cistercians resolved not to take up the offer. But, as it transpired, it was not just a matter of the Redemptorists stepping into the breach. Dr John Gallagher, the Bishop of Goulburn, tested the waters in a claim for the diocese. There was some legal argument, but eventually the Redemptorists won the day. To his credit, Bishop Gallagher gracefully welcomed the Redemptorists to Galong and the diocese. It was he who laid the foundation stone ninety years ago on 15 April 1917.

It should be remembered that World War I was still raging at the time, and another Benedict, Benedict XV, was the pope of the day. Like today, it was the Sunday of Easter week. In the Easter spirit, it was the beginning of a story of hope and promise.

Today's gospel reminds us that a building must be constructed on firm foundations. By this time, the Redemptorists were firmly established in Australia for over thirty years and had shown the capacity to preach the word of God effectively in this part of the world. In the second reading, St Paul writing to the Corinthians uses the analogy of planting, watering and growth to highlight the importance of collaboration where we are all expected to do our bit, but ultimately it is God who grants the increase. This has surely been the story of Galong Monastery.

It is a ninety year story lived through the Great Depression, another world war, times of boom and bust, more wars, spectacular growth of the church in this country, the Second Vatican Council, but then a period of decline in religious influence in society generally and a diminution in the number of priests, religious and religious houses. All these phenomena had their influence right here in Galong as well as in every other part of Australia and the world.

Life at Galong has also been able to exemplify the best of what Vatican II made possible in the growth of the role of lay people and the engagement of the church with contemporary society and culture. Right now, when our country is being severely tested by drought and a rural crisis, it is pleasing to see that St Clement's has an environmental and water conservation policy which is part of its present and future planning. Gabrielle Cusack is to be commended for her leadership in this area.

I am proud of the collaboration and partnership with the Archdiocese of Canberra and Goulburn which brings security to the project and adds a further dimension to the life of the archdiocese. In this regard, I particularly commend the leadership of our previous archbishop, Francis Carroll, and the archdiocesan business manager, Herbie O'Flynn. I should point out, as well, that our new archbishop, Mark Coleridge, has expressed his joy in having such a great spiritual asset in our archdiocese. It is only that he has commitments overseas that he is prevented from being with us today.

When I celebrated the 40th anniversary of my ordination to the priesthood, I took the opportunity to write a reflection on my years as a priest. What became very evident to me was that over that time, I had been privileged to have walked with people in many happy moments but sometimes in very difficult and sometimes tragic circumstances. I often stood in awe of such people who not only survived but even grew through such hardship. So often, it could only be explained by two things: the great resilience of human nature and the grace of God. In similar fashion, that is the story of Galong Monastery throughout its ninety year history, often the seemingly impossible being achieved by faith-filled people cooperating with the generous grace of God.

For me, one of the great joys of taking part in the 1998 Oceania Synod of Bishops in Rome was meeting up with the newly-elected Superior General of the Redemptorists, Father Joseph Tobin. As a result of our similar talks, Joe and I found instant rapport and struck up a lovely friendship at the Synod which we were able to renew here at Galong a couple of years ago when he was visiting the community. I spoke at the Synod on 'Marginalised people in society and in the church'. I forget the exact title of Father Joe's talk, but it was similarly addressing God's mercy towards his 'little ones'. After all, that is what *redemption* is all about – God giving us a second chance, and not just a second chance but over and over again granting his forgiveness and merciful love. It is a reminder that God's grace is far more powerful than our human weakness. It is, as the Easter message proclaims, the power of Christ's suffering, death and resurrection.

The story of Galong is the embodiment of all that redemption means for God's children. It is a story of openness to all. I think that the Redemptorists would agree that this dimension has expanded since 1985, with the coming of the Sisters to Galong, first the Dominicans and now the Sisters of St Joseph. Invariably, people's experiences here are stories of acceptance, love and help. As recently as last night, I listened to one such moving story. All those stories illustrate in a very powerful manner the unconditional love of God which is at the heart of all that we live and long for. Both the mission statement and the vision statement give expression to these beautiful ideals.

In the first reading of today's Mass, the majestic language of the Book of Kings not only describes the beauty of restorations and magnificent buildings but the splendour of God reflected in every person involved in this community and these breath-taking restorations. God is truly honoured today. Each person here is clearly touched by God's grace.

For Catholics, the Eucharist is the great prayer of thanksgiving. Today we thank God for Ned Ryan and his family. We thank God for the pioneer Catholics, especially of this district. We thank God for the Redemptorist fathers and brothers. We give thanks for generous lay people, local and from afar, and for the Dominicans and the Sisters of St Joseph. We acknowledge with deep gratitude the Friends of St Clement's, Catholic and non-Catholic alike.

May you all, in the words of the vision statement, 'consistent with the Redemptorist tradition [continue to] spread the Good News of God's merciful compassion and abundant saving love for all people.'

Good Samaritan Sesquicentenary Mass

Homily given in St Christopher's Cathedral, Canberra, 18 March 2007.

In all things may God be glorified.

1 Peter 4:11

It is St Luke's Gospel alone which recounts the parable of the Good Samaritan. Time and again in that gospel we are given moving stories of the hospitality and compassion of God, lived out in the person of Jesus. In many ways, the implications of the parable are shocking: it is not the respectable or religious people who respond to the demands of those in need, but rather someone who would be consistently looked down upon by such people. It is a story about reading the signs of the times, about finding God's love in unexpected places, of crossing all kinds of religious and cultural barriers, of giving without counting the cost, of putting into practice the unconditional love of God. Yet the parable is always in danger of losing its impact, especially when we isolate ourselves from the sometimes grim reality of life around us.

It is precisely because Archbishop John Bede Polding and the founding Sisters of the Good Samaritan were able to read the signs of the times and recognise the struggles of a largely convict population, that they set about finding ways of bringing the healing love of Jesus to people in need.

On 2 February 1857, five women aged between 19 and 56 were formally received as postulants in a new religious institute which was to become the Sisters of the Good Samaritan. Archbishop Polding, himself a Benedictine monk, gave them the Rule of St Benedict as a way of life that called them to seek God in the daily rhythm of prayer and work. He placed them under the care of Mother Scholastica Gibbons of the Sisters of Charity. She is seen as the co-founder of the Good Samaritan Sisters.

It is significant that the beginnings of the Good Samaritans go back to a refuge in Pitt Street in the heart of Sydney in what is now the location of Central Railway Station. Here the plight of destitute women, including those forced into prostitution, was most apparent. Historian Margaret Walsh was quoted in last month's issue of *Catholic Voice*:

> The Sisters walked the streets and back lanes of inner Sydney visiting the sick and poor in homes and hospitals, catechising and comforting. The Good Samaritan tradition of integrating compassion with the educational development of the whole person, of striving to know and respond to the individual's context and circumstances and of reaching out inclusively and preferentially to the poor was begun early and has never been lost.

Archbishop Polding's vision for the Good Samaritans was set out in their Rule: 'The Sisters are ready to teach in schools, to visit and assist the sick in their own homes, to conduct orphanages, to reform the lives of penitent women, and to apply themselves to every other charitable work.' The Sisters are called to a life of prayer, simplicity, humility, obedience, community, hospitality and service of others, of gentleness and compassion.

In 1859, Archbishop Polding sent three of the founding sisters to the Roman Catholic Orphan School, a government institution in Parramatta, where they made a home for children suffering from the disruption caused by the gold rushes in a society still scarred by its convict beginnings. In the following years, the sisters founded houses in Sydney and rural New South Wales as bishops urgently asked for their help to staff Catholic schools when government funding ceased in 1880. A new refuge was opened for women at St Magdalen's Retreat, Arncliffe, in 1887 and, when the government closed the orphan school at Parramatta, a home was provided for the children, first at Manly, then at Mater Dei, Narellan, in 1910.

The twentieth century opened with significant challenges for the sisters. The government resumed the land in Pitt Street for Central Railway Station and the sisters re-established their mother house and college at St Scholastica's, Glebe Point. The number of foundations increased as more Catholic schools were built across the country. During the years of the Depression and World War II, the sisters struggled to help poor families by keeping the schools functioning, frequently surviving through the generosity of parish communities. In 1948, six sisters were sent to Japan in response to an appeal from the Bishop of Nagasaki, made in the aftermath of the destruction of the atom bomb. Today the Sisters of the Good Samaritan are also to be found in the Philippines and in Kiribati.

We owe a great debt of gratitude to the Sisters of the Good Samaritan in this archdiocese. They were here as part of the establishment of the Parish of Canberra in 1928. The first parish priest, Patrick Haydon, is legendary. So too is Mother Dympna whose name can be seen inscribed under the altar here in St Christopher's. Prior to that there were Good Samaritan foundations in Queanbeyan and Braidwood in 1879 and Moruya in 1883.

On the occasion of Mother Dympna's death in 1935, Father Haydon acknowledged the vital contribution made by her and the other sisters in the emerging city and church.

> There have been many prominent personalities in Canberra, many eminent visitors from overseas, and many honoured sons of our native land, but I venture to say there has been none more pleasing to God than the little sister pouring out her heart to God in the school room. The outside world knew little of her because she had withdrawn from it for the sake of the little ones of Christ. We are confident, however, that, although the busy world may not herald her as one of the great builders of Canberra, Mother Dympna's name is inscribed in letters of gold in the Book of Life and her memory is secure with God.

Father Haydon's words were prophetic. The extent of the charitable work done by the Sisters of the Good Samaritan here in Canberra is known to God alone. While Canberra is often seen as an affluent city, the sisters were very much in solidarity with their people in hard times. And even in the best of times there are always many who are less than fortunate and struggle to survive. The Good Samaritans sought out such people often through the school and treated them with dignity, generosity and compassion. I remember in the late 1960s when I was chaplain to what is now St Clare's College, Sister Clare had a great heart for the girls from Causeway, bringing out the best in her pupils. I could tell many stories of Sister Clare's wonderful leadership as founding principal of both Merici and St Clare's Colleges. The charism of the Good Samaritan Sisters was brilliantly lived out in her down-to-earth and faith-filled teaching life.

The educational opportunities offered by the Good Samaritan Sisters to the children of Queanbeyan, Braidwood and Moruya date back to the 1880s. It was no easy life for the sisters in those pioneering days as they shared with their pupils and their families much of the hardship they were enduring. The sisters were an integral part of the life of the parishes and the towns and much loved by Catholics and non-Catholics alike. For the past eighty years, the people of Canberra have similarly benefited from the dedication of the Good Samaritans. Beginning here at St Christopher's in 1928, the sisters were later to be found in St Patrick's, Braddon, St Benedict's, Narrabundah, St Bede's, Red Hill, St Francis of Assisi, Calwell, as well as Sister Clare's founding role at the Braddon and Griffith high schools. Sister Sue Hallams continues the Good Samaritan tradition today at St Francis Xavier's High School in Florey.

I am privileged to be one of the thousands of ex-students who owe so much to the sisters for what they taught us about God, about life and about ourselves. They helped us to appreciate what we had and to make the best of what life had to offer. I might add personally that as a seminarian, priest and bishop I have been a continuing beneficiary of the kindness of the Good Samaritans. So, too, many of you here today will have your own stories of the way that the sisters gave you a great start in life.

The missionary spirit has always been part of the Good Samaritan vocation as the sisters sought to bring the Gospel message to those people and places that might otherwise be deprived of the good news. When in 1948 the call came from the Bishop of Nagasaki for the sisters to go to Japan, there were two from this archdiocese: Sister Marie Eustelle from

St Christopher's and Sister John from Queanbeyan. Later on, Sister Jacinta Shailer, whom I had the good fortune to have teach me in 5th Class at St Christopher's, was to spend many years in Japan. Sister Geraldine Kearney, who made such an impact in Queanbeyan in the 1980s, has not long returned from Kiribati and is great champion of the people there.

Sir William Deane, arguably St Christopher's most famous ex-student, often reminds us that a society is best judged by the way it cares for its most vulnerable members. That care shown by the sisters for their students in school situations has always been a hallmark of their total vocation. But the Good Samaritan outreach has always been further than schools. Around Australia and now overseas, the sisters are to be found in many areas of the welfare apostolate. I think of the work here in Canberra carried out by Sister Mary Gregory, Sister Jeanie Heininger and currently Sister Rita Reilly. The sisters' former convent at Red Hill has been generously given over to Centacare which provides much of the archdiocese's service to those in need. Sister Beverley Caffery is engaged in pastoral care here in Canberra as well as Braidwood and Moruya where the sisters are no longer resident. Sister Joy Edwards in Queanbeyan for a long time has been a great champion of the Aboriginal people. Sister Elizabeth Delaney in her role in the Australian Catholic Bishops' Conference office here in Canberra brings a very Christ-like presence to many arms of the official church which would be less Catholic without her influence.

In today's liturgy, St Paul reminds us that we are to be ambassadors for Christ. We thank God during this Eucharist for the many ways through which the Sisters of the Good Samaritan have modeled for us what it means to be an ambassador for Christ. For 150 years they have reflected the love and compassion of Christ to people of all ages and circumstances, especially those in any way poor or afflicted. Their deep love for God has found expression in countless forms in the lives of God's people. When St Paul exhorts us to be reconciled to God, we readily think of the sisters' reconciling love gathering us into the arms of our loving God.

Last week Pope Benedict XVI gave to the church an apostolic exhortation on the Eucharist as the source and summit of the church's life and mission. He could well have been speaking of the Good Samaritan Sisters when he wrote: 'The church's charitable institutions carry out at various levels the important work of assisting the needy, especially the poorest. Inspired by the Eucharist, the sacrament of charity, they become a concrete expression of that charity; they are to be praised and encouraged for their commitment to solidarity in our world.'

It is the privilege of all of us here today to be in solidarity with the sisters as they continue on the journey begun 150 years ago. May we be inspired and challenged by the words of the Eucharistic Prayer of today's Mass:

> Open our eyes to the needs of all; inspire us with words and deeds to comfort those who labour and are burdened; keep our service of others faithful to the example and command of Christ. Let your church be a living witness to truth and freedom, to justice and peace, that all people may be lifted up by the hope of a world made new.

Goodbye to the Good Samaritans

Homily given in St Raphael's Church, Queanbeyan, NSW, as the Good Samaritan Sisters farewelled the parish after 134 years of service, Feast of St Scholastica, 10 February 2013.

While Canberra celebrates its 100 years in 2013, Queanbeyan boasts a proud history of 175 years. For 134 of those years, the Good Samaritan Sisters have been an integral part of the life of Queanbeyan. It was just 22 years after the foundation of the Good Samaritan Sisters in Sydney in 1857 that the sisters arrived in Queanbeyan.

It was because Archbishop John Bede Polding and the founding Sisters of the Good Samaritan were able to read the signs of the times and recognise the struggles of a largely convict population, that they set about finding ways of bringing the healing love of Jesus to people in need. There would be many opportunities in Queanbeyan in the ensuing 134 years.

Archbishop Polding's vision for the Good Samaritans was set out in their Rule: 'The Sisters are ready to teach in schools, to visit and assist the sick in their own homes, to conduct orphanages, to reform the lives of penitent women, and to apply themselves to every other charitable work.' The sisters are called to a life of prayer, simplicity, humility, obedience, community, hospitality and service of others, of gentleness and compassion.

We owe a great debt of gratitude to the Sisters of the Good Samaritan in this archdiocese. It was here in Queanbeyan and in Braidwood that communities were first established in 1879. On 10 February, the feast of St Scholastica, Mother Lucy Nihill, Sisters Benedict Lawn, Pius Hillier and Magdalen Clancy arrived here. They had been invited by the parish priest,

Father James McAuliffe, and encouraged by the new archbishop of Sydney, Roger Vaughan, remembering that until 1917 Queanbeyan was still part of that archdiocese.

Catholic education had been provided by lay teachers in Queanbeyan since 1852 when St Gregory's Denominational School was opened. That school continued in 1879 while the Good Samaritans conducted a 'Higher School for Ladies'. However at the end of that year, the sisters assumed responsibility for the education of all Catholic children in Queanbeyan and continued in their teaching role for the next one hundred years.

Apart from the parish priest, Father McAuliffe, one of the driving forces responsible for the sisters coming to Queanbeyan was Martin Byrne, ably assisted financially by Thomas Dwyer of Molonglo. The usual round of bazaars and other fund-raising activities helped build St Benedict's Convent in several stages. It was completed early in 1886 and blessed by Cardinal Moran on 16 May of that year. It is said that that Australia's future Prime Minister, Ben Chifley, was named after St Benedict's Convent. Stories are told of the sisters negotiating the river by stepping stones, coming and going to Mass in St Gregory's Church. In reverse, children coming to school were described as the little wet feet coming from Irishtown, as Dodsworth was then known. The opening of the suspension bridge in 1901 overcame those difficulties.

For a number of years, the Good Samaritans also taught at St John Vianney's, behind the Hotel Queanbeyan, and, in 1957, Sister Anne Miles, who is with us today, and Sister Colombière pioneered Sacred Heart School in Crest Road, West Queanbeyan. During the post-World War II years, the sisters both at St Gregory's and Sacred Heart did much to help many of the migrant families settle into life in their new surroundings.

I am sure that the sisters here today are delighted to witness the vibrancy of St Gregory's School. That is a great tribute to Claire Frazer and her staff and all their dedicated predecessors who have carried on the great tradition of the Good Samaritan Sisters by reading the signs of the times and meeting the challenges of today's church and world.

The educational opportunities offered by the Good Samaritan Sisters to the children of Queanbeyan cannot be overstated. It was no easy life for the sisters in those pioneering days as they shared with their pupils and their families much of the hardship they were enduring. The sisters were an integral part of the life of the parish and the wider community of Queanbeyan and much loved by Catholics and non-Catholics alike. I am sure that many people here will have their own stories of how the sisters gave them a great start in life. The missionary spirit has always been part of the Good Samaritan vocation as the sisters sought to bring the Gospel message to those people and places that might otherwise be deprived of the good news. [I have referred to this in detail in the previous piece.]

The Good Samaritan outreach has always been further than schools. Around Australia and overseas, the sisters are to be found in many areas of the welfare apostolate and in the promotion of justice. Queanbeyan's last Good Samaritan, Sister Joy Edwards, has been for a long time a great champion of the Aboriginal people, Sister Mary O'Shannassy formerly of Queanbeyan is now prison chaplain in Melbourne while Sisters Mary Gregory, Jeanie Heininger, Rita Reilly and so many others are to be found in solidarity with some of Australia's most vulnerable people. In recent years, Sisters Evelyn who began the prayer group, Marie Agnese, Michaelene Purcell, Mary O'Shannassy, Helen Avery, Stephanie Hayes, Gwen Bade and Joy Edwards have been a beautiful pastoral presence in Queanbeyan, comforting, nurturing, encouraging, healing and witnessing to the Good News in ways fully known to God alone.

In today's gospel, Jesus comes upon a discouraged group of fishermen, his closest disciples. They had been out all night and had caught nothing. But they responded to Jesus' call not to be afraid. They put out their nets once more and made a great catch. It was in that same spirit of confident faith that for 134 years the Good Samaritan Sisters have served the people of Queanbeyan. If, as members of the Catholic Church today, we are feeling something of a sense of despondency, let us take heart from the Sisters of the Good Samaritan who for all those years have been to us a source of light, hope and Gospel joy.

In the Eucharist, the church's great prayer of thanksgiving, we thank God for all the sisters have been to Queanbeyan. We thank their congregational leader, Sister Clare Condon, Sister Joy Edwards and all the sisters who have served so generously in Queanbeyan. As we are nourished by the Word of God and the Eucharistic presence of Jesus, we pledge to uphold and continue in the years ahead the great spirit of the Good Samaritans in Queanbeyan. For all we remember and celebrate today, we pray unashamedly in the words of the responsorial psalm: 'Before the angels, I will bless you, Lord.'

St Clare's College

Golden Jubilee Mass. Homily given at the Mass marking fifty years of the life of St Clare's College, Griffith, ACT, 31 May 2015.

St Clare's College motto exhorts us to *Seek Wisdom*. For fifty years, students, teachers and the wider school community of St Clare's, as well as parents and families, have been engaged in the search for wisdom. I'm sure that during the jubilee celebrations this year, there will continue to be lots of sharing of memories tapping into that quest for wisdom. The 12-year-olds in Year 7 through to grey-haired people like me will all have stories to tell which will give insight into the life of St Clare's and the growth in wisdom. I hope that there will be lots of story telling during this jubilee year.

A good friend of mine, Father Edmund Campion, published a book called *Australian Catholic Lives*, featuring a whole range of interesting characters. Ed is now in his early 80s but he is still vibrant and remains young at heart. He would be very much at home and appreciated in the student community here at St Clare's. In the introduction to his book, he writes, 'We human beings are story-tellers, we pass on our values through the stories we tell. This is particularly true of Catholics who get their identity through their history, which they see as salvation history linking them to the saving actions of Christ.'

Thousands of people have been associated with this wonderful college over its fifty year history. In the letter inviting me to celebrate today's Mass, Paul Carroll and Vivienne Joice reminded me that 'St Clare's students have gone on to make significant contributions in all walks of life, be it in nurturing future generations, working in the community or pursuing careers in the arts, public service, health and welfare, politics, education and business.' Some may feel that they have not achieved a great deal or that their life has been pretty ordinary. But every person, Catholic and non-Catholic alike, has a story to tell of the grace of God touching their lives in a way which has made the world a better place.

I recall a few years ago seeing a delightful picture in the *Canberra Times* of a group of ex-students of the college. I think the occasion was them turning 50. I remembered most of them from the days that I was their school chaplain. I was touched by the candour with which they described their colourful lives. A few weeks ago, I heard a fascinating interview by Alex Sloan on ABC Radio, in which three generations of St Clare's students, Sue, Emma and Sophie, spoke glowingly of the college's impact on their lives. The differing paths you have travelled enrich the family life of God in which we all share. It is this participation in God's life that we celebrate and seek to embrace as we *Seek Wisdom* on the Feast of the Blessed Trinity.

As we speak of God as Father, we know that it is our mothers and fathers who in a special way have witnessed to us the unconditional love of God. Secure in the love of our parents we are able to reach out in love to others. But our parents would be the first to admit that they don't always get it right. The same can be said of teachers and others who love and care for us. Jesus, the Son of God, has given us the great commandment, 'Love one another as I have loved you.' He has also taught us the need for forgiveness and compassion as we cope with our own frailty and that of others. In today's second reading St Paul speaks of nine beautiful qualities that are sometimes referred to as the fruits of the Spirit: love, joy, peace, patience, kindness, generosity, faithfulness, gentleness and self-control. Over the years, as I celebrated the sacrament of Confirmation, I encouraged the young people to see the living out of these virtues as an achievable way of making a difference in a world desperately in need of decent values. I know that this same emphasis has been part of the ethos of St Clare's throughout its fifty year history.

The impressive symbols on display today remind us of the important role that religious orders of sisters played in the founding of this college. Each group of sisters lived out the special charism of their founder as they witnessed to the joy of the Gospel in being faithful to Jesus' commission to take his message to all people. Remembering that 1965 was the year that this college opened, we should be aware that it was also the final year of the Second Vatican Council. Vatican II was a turning point in the life of the Catholic Church, empowering all its members to have an active role in promoting the church's mission. The dignity of the whole people of God, not just clergy and religious, was highlighted. All people were called to holiness and we heard more of the love of God than of fear. We were encouraged like our Protestant brothers and sisters to have a love and understanding of the Scriptures. And we were able to celebrate Mass in our mother tongue. As church we were called to be engaged with our fellow Christians, with non-Christian religions and with the modern world. As I look back, I recognise the vision of the first teachers of this college: the religious sisters, but also the lay teachers, non-Catholic as well as Catholic. They embraced the leadership of Sister Clare who had always been recognised by her fellow Sisters of the Good Samaritan as a person ahead of her times. As I see St Clare's College today embodying the best of the Second Vatican Council, I wish to acknowledge Sister Clare and the founding staff for their vision for this great college. Over its fifty year history, St Clare's is to be commended for the way it has prepared its students to take their place as competent and confident women in the contemporary world.

The Second Vatican Council also teaches us that we belong to a pilgrim church, always on a journey seeking to 'read the signs of the times', learning from the past, living in the present but looking to the future as we *Seek Wisdom*. The educators among you know this better than I do. But you also know that we need to apply not only our minds, but also to engage our hearts and to do so being open to the wisdom and experience of others. The Benedictine tradition of which Sister Clare was a part reminds us to look to the young ones in our midst in the search for wisdom.

Even though they lived eight centuries ago, St Clare and St Francis are still very relevant models for today's world. They were surrounded by Christian-Muslim conflict but they saw understanding and dialogue, rather than war and killing, as the way forward. In a world of inequality, like Jesus they embraced poverty in sharing what they had with the poorest in their midst. They believed in open doors and open hearts, rather than closed borders. Over the centuries, they have been honoured for their care for the environment so that future generations can share in the blessings which at times we are apt to take for granted. Anyone fortunate enough to visit Assisi cannot but be inspired by these two Christ-like saints. It would be ingenuous of me to suggest that any of us could totally embrace their life-style in our affluent surroundings. But I am continually uplifted when I hear stories coming out of St Clare's and similar schools of the idealism of the students and the whole school community reaching out to those less fortunate in their midst and in the wider world. When the challenges seem to be overwhelming, I take heart in the advice of development agencies when they encourage us to 'think globally and act locally'.

No wonder Pope Francis, under the patronage of the great saint of Assisi, has won the hearts of so many people well beyond the confines of the Catholic Church. Like St Francis and St Clare, his simple, down-to-earth goodness, his shunning of opulence and power and his embracing of the poorest of people gives us someone with whom we can identify while at the same time being challenged by his example. In proclaiming a Jubilee Year of Mercy to begin on 8 December 2015, Pope Francis invites us to take up the example of Jesus: 'Let us open our eyes and see the misery of the world, the wounds of our brothers and sisters who are denied their dignity, and let us recognise that we are compelled to hear their cry for help! May we reach out to them and support them so they can feel the warmth of our presence, our friendship and our fraternity.' I am confident that St Clare's College in the days and years ahead will *seek wisdom* in searching for innovative ways of responding to Pope Francis' invitation to reach out to those people most in need.

Today we give thanks for the proud history of St Clare's College over fifty memorable years. We do so in the context of the church's great prayer of thanksgiving, the Eucharist, on the Feast of the Blessed Trinity. Let us embrace the challenge of our recessional hymn in honour of St Clare:

> Then let us seek, seek wisdom. It is found in Jesus Christ with the Father and the Holy Spirit. He is God, he is Lord of all. Seek Christ, seek wisdom. He is our way, our truth, our life. He is the light, joy and courage we need to live each day to the full.

May God bless us all on our continuing journey of life and of faith.

The value of a life

A opinion piece on the unique value of every human life,
Canberra Times, 9 November 2004.

I listened recently to a challenging talk by Rev. Tim Costello who pointed
out that the world was rightly devastated by the horrible deaths of 3000
people in the United States on September 11, 2001. He pointed out, however, that on the same day 5000 children around the world had died of
preventable diseases. The same thing happened the next day and the following day and still continues. Is life of any less value when it belongs to
a poor person in an obscure country without the focus of the media on its
misery?

During the lead-up to the invasion of Iraq, I repeatedly asked the question: Is an Iraqi life of any less value than an American, a British or an
Australian life? It seems so, if we are able to be given exact figures of the
unfortunate loss of life among foreigners in Iraq but no accurate statistics
for the loss of life among Iraqi citizens.

Somehow or other, we have conveniently adopted a 'them and us'
mentality with regard to the importance of human life. If you belong to a
group which is strong, rich, influential, vocal and powerful, there is a good
chance your rights and your life will be safeguarded. But if you are poor,
defenceless and without a voice, it is a different matter.

Once a society decides that it can pick and choose and say that one life
is of more value than another, that not every person is of inestimable value,
that out of sight is out of mind, then that society becomes diminished.

The current abortion debate focuses on unborn human life which
must be seen in the context of a whole-of-life understanding. Is an unborn
child of less value because it hasn't yet seen the light of day, because it can-

not speak for itself or because many people are unwilling to speak up for it for fear of offending various groups of other people?

Every Australian should be alarmed at the fact there are 100,000 abortions annually in this country. We pride ourselves in being a civilised nation. Yet every day we allow countless innocent, defenceless lives to be snuffed out before birth. History will surely judge Australia and the world harshly for our neglect of such basic human rights.

Invariably, protagonists of abortion defend their position by pointing to the 'hard cases' such as pregnancy following rape and the danger to the life of the mother. But how many of the 100,000 annual Australian abortions arise out of such circumstances?

I understand that pre-natal screening is becoming more commonplace, leading to the aborting of babies who are possibly less than perfect. No doubt, a great deal is asked of parents whose children suffer severe defects, but how often their heroism greatly enhances such a family. Jean Vanier and members of L'Arche communities remind us of how much we have to learn from people suffering disabilities. Our recent history has shown the world how pernicious it is to eliminate people judged to be defective or different.

How many abortions come about for social or economic reasons? How many unwanted pregnancies are caused by failed contraception or through casual sexual liaisons that take little or no account of the consequences of their actions?

It saddens me to see how promotion of abortion has become a 'badge' of feminism. Over the years, women (and many men!) have advocated strongly and justifiably for the rights of women. It is ironic that one such right is to deny the right to life to some children at the sole discretion of their mothers.

Of course, it is not enough to condemn abortion. It is the responsibility of governments, communities, the medical profession, church and welfare groups, families and individuals to give support to women experiencing difficult pregnancies. Is it too much to strive for a world where no one would feel forced to seek an abortion? Surely, even the strongest 'pro-choice' advocate would desire a climate in which there would be no need for abortion.

I appeal to the women of Australia to speak out for the protection of unborn human life. So often I hear from women, some of whom have had abortions themselves, who express distress over the path Australia has gone down in the 'abortion explosion'. In the current debate, it is being said that this is just another example of men seeking to dominate women, often putting them on a guilt trip as well. Women who hold strong pro-life views should not be intimidated from defending the rights of the unborn against those pretending that no such rights exist.

Defending the right to life means doing everything possible to counteract suicide, especially among the young, reducing Australia's road toll and giving much more attention to deaths (and other injustices) in custody.

Equally, our respect for life should cause us to grieve for those people who have died through illicit drug use. Each year many of them are remembered and named by their families and friends at a moving ceremony at Weston Park in the ACT. [See 'Remembrance ceremony', pp. 97-99.] Nobody can be happy until these tragic and senseless deaths are eliminated. Again there are responsibilities right across our society to prevent such deaths.

The fact that Aboriginal people have a life-span of twenty years less than the rest of Australians is a national shame and disgrace. Better health care, educational and employment opportunities and positive discrimination towards Aboriginal people will go some way towards restoring the value and dignity of the lives of our indigenous people and righting many of the injustices they have experienced over 200 years and more.

Australia's attitude to refugees, to poverty at a national and global level and to people at the edge of society hardly rated a mention during the recent federal election campaign. As a nation we need to lift our game, to demonstrate at every level that we value every life – in Australia and beyond – and that we have a special heart for those lives most at risk.

Further reflections on abortion

Written for *Catholic Voice*, 17 November 2004.

In many ways the current controversy around abortion is the debate we need to have. If there is an assumption that the status quo is satisfactory, it is a stinging indictment of Australian society in accepting without question the death of 100,000 unborn children each year.

However, I would like to think that Australians might become involved in a conversation on this issue, rather than a slanging match where there can be no meeting of minds and hearts.

As Catholics we believe that every human life is precious and that we have a special duty to protect lives most at risk. We see that even before birth a child has rights and especially because of its vulnerability needs a special measure of protection.

Supporters of abortion concentrate on the rights of the mother, often to the exclusion of the rights of the child. Most would also say that in ideal circumstances, there would be no need for abortion. Is there some common ground here which might lead to a productive way forward in countering abortion?

I recently took part in a conversation on abortion on the *Insight* program on SBS TV. Several people spoke of the need for more support for women experiencing difficult pregnancies. One said that she would not have had an abortion if there had been more financial help available at the time. Others spoke of feeling alone in their predicament. Some asked for more government assistance at such a time.

Clearly, families, friends, counsellors, doctors, Centacare, parish and community groups can all play an important part in giving such support.

I think of groups like Pregnancy Support and Karinya House for mothers doing wonderful work in this area.

It is not enough for us as a church to be condemning abortion if we are not doing everything possible to relieve the pressures leading to it.

Help, too, needs to be given to young people in enabling them to see the meaning and consequences of a sexual relationship. We should not be afraid to teach chastity as a viable and healthy choice.

It is not inconsistent to be strongly opposed to abortion while still showing every understanding and the forgiveness and compassion of Jesus towards those women who have had abortions. It was clear from the *Insight* program that many women who have had abortions carry hurt and guilt for a long time afterwards. Groups such as Project Rachel are to be commended for the help they offer for post-abortion healing.

It is my hope that the current debate will enable all Australians to review their attitudes towards abortion and to do everything possible to reduce dramatically the number of abortions taking place in our country.

The Royal Commission

Reflection written 14 November 2012 at the request of *Eureka Street* following Prime Minister Julia Gillard's announcement of a Royal Commission into institutional child abuse in Australia.

Clearly, the Prime Minister took the only course open to her in agreeing to a Royal Commission into child sexual abuse in our country. There has been more than enough media coverage to convince any fair-minded person of the terrible damage done through the abuse of children.

Over the past twenty years I have listened to people who have suffered such abuse, sometimes many years ago, and every time I hear a heart-rending story I see another facet of the horror of this criminal behaviour. The loss of childhood innocence, the secrecy that means little ones carry a burden that they can share with no one, the misguided sense of guilt they often carry for many years into adult life, blaming themselves for what someone else has done to them, their shame before God, and the times when they do try to unburden their troubled souls not being believed or understood.

Speaking to such people who have experienced failed marriages, it becomes clear that sexuality, which is meant to be God's joyous gift to us, has been a source of confusion and great hurt because of destructive experiences in childhood. Every person's experience will be different, but I believe that the present publicity, painful though it be, will give more people the opportunity to unburden themselves and thus take the first steps towards finding healing and peace.

Whatever form the Royal Commission takes, opportunity will be given to those who have suffered abuse to be heard and taken seriously in a way that not only their own case is dealt with but that systems can be put in place to afford children greater protection in the future.

I welcome the fact that the Royal Commission's scope will be wider than the confines of the Catholic Church because the abuse of children is surely a much wider issue. But at the same time, I believe it important that as a church we Catholics need to face up to the particular factors that have contributed to the occurrence of sexual abuse among the ranks of clergy and religious. Having said that, I think that what has already been done in Australia to address the problem should be acknowledged. Since 1996, *Towards Healing* which has sought to accept and investigate claims of abuse, and *Integrity in Ministry*, which provides guidelines of behaviour, and other measures have attempted to provide justice and healing for all involved. People such as Sister Angela Ryan and Bishops Geoffrey Robinson, William Morris, Peter Connors and Philip Wilson have been in the forefront of such reform.

Most people would accept that as a church we have been overly negative in our teaching on sexuality. Many of the pronouncements of the church at the highest level have caused me to question how an all-male celibate voice can realistically enunciate such teaching in a manner which is able to be understood by the whole human family. Unless women and married people are made part of the governance of the church, there will continue to be a lack of balance and reality in all our teaching, especially around sexuality. I would include homosexuality in that critique.

These are painful times to be a Catholic, but they can also be an occasion for us all to look to Jesus and to know that 'the truth will set us free'. If we are humble enough to admit that at times we have got it wrong, sometimes horribly wrong, then there is the opportunity to make reparation and to do all that we can to see that the same mistakes are not repeated.

Opening the Second Vatican Council fifty years ago, Pope John XXIII called on us to 'read the signs of the times' so as to bring the light of the Gospel on to every aspect of the life of our church. My hope is that the Royal Commission can become for the Catholic Church a true instrument of grace and healing.

The Royal Commission revisited

A further comment on the calling of the Royal Commission, written for *The Good Oil*, the online publication of the Good Samaritan Sisters, 11 December 2012.

Not long after the announcement of the Royal Commission, I led the annual retreat for the clergy of the Archdiocese of Canberra and Goulburn. My brother priests and deacons were battling to know how to best respond to the awful issues that are constantly before us at this moment of our history. But they were unambiguous in acknowledging that the damage and hurt to victims and their families should be our first concern. They shared their experiences of raising the issue of abuse in their homilies and other forums and in one-to-one conversations with their parishioners and the positive response that they were given for doing so. I encouraged them in their openness and asked them not to withdraw but to continue to preach and live the Good News, doing so in a spirit of humility which acknowledges the human frailty we all carry.

Most people would accept that as a church we have been overly negative in our teaching on sexuality. I think much of the current negative reaction to the Catholic Church is a result of Catholic moral teaching disproportionately concentrating on details of sexual morality. Many of the pronouncements of the church at the highest level have caused me to question how an all-male celibate voice can realistically enunciate such teaching in a manner which is able to be understood by the whole human family. Unless women and married people are made part of the governance of the church, there will continue to be a lack of balance and reality in all our teaching, especially around sexuality. I would include homosexuality in that critique.

Listening is crucial in every facet of the church's response. I well remember in the 1990s, Bishop Geoff Robinson repeatedly appealing to his brother bishops to listen personally to the victims of abuse and to engage with them. He said that it was only having had such experience that we could even begin to understand the impact of abuse on a person's life. I remember too a touching moment not so long ago, when the apostolic nuncio, Archbishop Lazzarotto, shared the impact on him of listening to a family whose child had suffered from abuse within the church. It was refreshing to hear in the last week of Bishop Bill Wright of Newcastle listening to a mother at the launch of a book describing the abuse of her son at the hands of a (now-deceased) priest. That the book launch took place in the cathedral was also powerfully significant.

These are painful times to be a Catholic, but they can also be an occasion for us all to look to Jesus and to know that 'the truth will set us free'. If we are humble enough to admit that at times we have got it wrong, sometimes horribly wrong, then there is the opportunity to make reparation and to do all that we can to see that the same mistakes are not repeated. The whole church is in need of the good healing oil which the Good Samaritan offered the wounded man on the road to Jericho.

Caught in the cross-fire

An article written for *The Swag*, highlighting the pain of good priests in the face of the scandal of sexual abuse within the church, January 2014.

Recently I had the privilege of leading the priests of the Diocese of Ballarat in their annual retreat. As I prepared for the retreat, I was very conscious of the burden the priests of that diocese were carrying in relation to clerical sexual abuse. Yet I knew that, as an outsider, I had no words of wisdom to impart to a group of men who had clearly agonised over the issue for some time. So, early in the retreat, I asked those who wished to share with each other their thoughts, feelings and experiences around this painful and shameful time in their lives as priests.

That session was arguably the most productive time of the whole retreat. Each priest who spoke was heard respectfully by his brothers without any critique from following speakers. They were all painfully aware of the terrible harm done to victims of abuse, their families, the wider community and the church as a whole. They spoke of the dreadful damage done and the need for healing, forgiveness, reconciliation and the continuing examination of ways to ensure that the climate in which such abuse was perpetrated would not continue. Many of them spoke of their own experience of trying to help people affected, as well as how they themselves were coping with the fallout in these times when almost daily they are confronted with revelations of abuse.

Most of all, they acknowledged that there are no simple solutions to what is a highly complex question touching people at the very core.

Later in the retreat, I had a heart-rending conversation with one of the priests who stated very passionately, 'I am not a paedophile, and I am not a bishop, but a priest who feels he is carrying the can for all the sins committed and mistakes made by others.' My friend gave me permission to write about that conversation which, I believe, represents what many priests today are experiencing.

Most priests believe that the Royal Commission or something similar was very much needed to face up to a terrible episode in our church's history. They also believe that sexual abuse took place in an environment of clericalism which was imposed by the highest authority in the church and which they felt powerless to confront. 'Father is always right' operated from the pope down and any questioning of it was seen as disloyal or even heretical.

One of the most blatant expressions of such clericalism is propagated in an Instruction of the Congregation for the Clergy, 'On certain questions regarding the collaboration of the non-ordained faithful in the sacred ministry of the priest'. This was issued on 15 August 1997 after being approved by Pope John Paul II two days earlier. It can still be found on the Vatican website. In many ways it became the basis for the Statement of Conclusions presented to the Australian bishops following the 1998 Oceania Synod of Bishops.

Generations of Australian priests have shared the lives and aspirations of their people, listening to their stories and responding to their needs. Yet the Statement of Conclusions criticised such attitudes for being too egalitarian. Good priests across Australia were and still are appalled at such expressions of clericalism. Many, myself included, believe that unbridled and unquestioning acceptance of authority in so many aspects of church life is one of the key factors contributing to a climate which gave rise to clerical sexual abuse.

It is precisely that which angers my friend quoted above. He and so many dedicated pastoral priests believe that they had absolutely no say in the direction church authorities were dictating and now they are bearing the brunt of its consequences. Today, they witness individuals and groups who call for reform being ignored and treated as trouble-makers while their hearts are breaking for the church they love. My friend suggested that we bishops should collectively submit ourselves to the Third Rite of Reconciliation for our part in this whole sorry episode in the life of God's people, acknowledging the pain caused in so many lives. He points out that such a penitential act would demonstrate the collective and social nature of the sin involved. Clearly the victims of abuse are those from whom we should ask forgiveness first and foremost, but let us be very much aware of the countless good and faithful priests who are caught in the cross-fire and must daily give an account of themselves.

'Blessed are you when people abuse you and persecute you and speak all kinds of calumny against you on my account' are Jesus' reassuring words to all his followers. Every Australian bishop should say 'Amen' to that. Is the humiliation currently experienced by the whole People of God a way forward for the church in identifying more closely with Jesus the Suffering Servant?

Pope Francis has so often been described as a breath of fresh air in his gentle, down-to-earth pastoral love and care. His denunciation of all forms of clericalism is unequivocal. Throughout the retreat with the Ballarat clergy, I quoted consistently from the pope's recent apostolic exhortation, *The Joy of the Gospel,* which I have earlier described as the most enriching and life-giving papal document I have read since Vatican II. May Pope Francis' inspiring words and example give hope and direction in these troubled times.

Saint Patrick
Champion of the oppressed

Address at the annual ecumenical service held in honour of St Patrick at the Australian Centre for Christianity and Culture, Canberra, 17 March 2010.

Around this time two years ago I spent ten days in Ireland walking in the footsteps of my great-great-great grandparents, Morgan Power and Bridgette Byrne. They were transported to this country as convicts, arriving on our shores in 1797 and 1803.

My cousin, William Power, has written a detailed family history, but sadly has been unable to make contact with any known relatives in Ireland. But I was able to visit Morgan's home town of Roundwood in County Wicklow and Bridgette's in Trim in County Meath. I was also able to visit the beautiful harbour of Cobh, near Cork. It was from there that, six years apart, Morgan and Bridgette were taken forcibly off to Sydney. William Power's history reveals some of the shocking details of the five and half month journey via Brazil.

The day I visited Cobh harbour in 2008 was a beautiful spring day. At the time, a huge American cruise ship was docked and tourists were coming and going, seemingly without a care in the world. I couldn't help but think what a contrast that was to what my ancestors must have experienced in the same place over two hundred years earlier. Morgan and Bridgette faced a cruel and sickening sea journey to a distant country with an unknown future. As I walked around the harbourside, I saw a plaque to the great Irish pioneer missionary priest to Australia, Father John Joseph Therry, who would minister in Australia to my ancestors and countless others who embarked from Cobh harbour in similar circumstances. As I further reflect, I think of Patrick, the future apostle of Ireland, being taken against his will from his native British shores and led into slavery in Ireland. But I will return to that later.

In Bridgette's town of Trim I went on a tour of Trim Castle and looked over the River Boyne and wondered what role they played in Bridgette's life prior to her arrest. I took a photograph of the magistrate's court and asked what kind of justice Bridgette had received in her sentencing. My earlier visit to Wicklow Prison gave me some idea of how Morgan spent his time before being shipped off to Sydney.

Those of you who know Ireland better than I do will know that it isn't far from Trim to Tara. I arrived about 9.00 am to be told by the locals they didn't expect to see anyone so early! I reflected on the vigilance which was so much part of St Patrick's character. As I walked across the grassy mounds of the Hill of Tara I recalled Patrick's fierce clashes with the Druids all those years ago. I thought of the next 1600 years and the cost of the wars and disputes around the world which were seen as a contest between good and evil. How many of those differences may have been resolved with the spirit of humility displayed by Patrick in his *Confessions*? How many lives would have been saved as result? At Tara I drank from the Holy Well hoping to imbibe something of my patron saint's faith, tenacity and missionary zeal.

On a lighter note, in Ireland I was also on a quest to find the relatives of my Irish Wolfhound, Bridey. I had heard the story of the great grey dog that had led St Patrick through the mists of Ireland when he had returned to evangelise. Maybe he was a ghost of one of the hounds mentioned in the *Confessions*, escaping on the boat with the young Patrick. We could also speculate on Patrick's Dialogues with Oisin and how the legendary figure had sought the company of his faithful companion dog when he entered eternal life. Although I was told in Trim and in Tara that there were a couple of Wolfhounds in the districts, I failed to sight any in the land of Bridey's ancestors.

I stayed in Dublin as a guest of Fr Mark Noonan and the staff of All Hallows College. Walking along the corridors of this great missionary college, I looked up at the 'rogue's gallery' to see the photographs of many familiar faces and of so many priests who have made an indelible mark on the life of the Australian church and wider society. With their companions scattered around the world they would proclaim the Gospel with the ingenuity and zeal of St Patrick.

The gospel reading we have just heard depicts Jesus with the power of the Spirit upon him returning to his home town of Nazareth. He goes into the synagogue, familiar to him from his childhood days. He applies to himself the words of the prophet Isaiah (61:1-2):

> *The spirit of the Lord has been given to me,*
> *for he has anointed me.*
> *He has sent me to bring good news to the poor,*
> *to proclaim liberty to captives*
> *and to the blind new sight,*
> *to set the downtrodden free,*
> *to proclaim the Lord's year of favour.*

It was with that same grand vision that Patrick returned to Ireland. As a 16-year-old he had been kidnapped from his British homeland and forced into slavery in Ireland. After eventually escaping, he returned to his home country, only to be called by God to go back to Ireland. The response to any vocation taken seriously is a daunting one. Patrick knew that his would come at an enormous cost. Yet he knew he would not be alone or unaided.

He would write heroically in his *Confessions*:

Who am I, Lord, and what is my calling that you should cooperate with me with such divine power? Today, among heathen peoples, I praise and proclaim your name in all places, not only when things go well but also in times of stress. Whether I receive good or ill, I return thanks equally to God, who taught me always to trust him unreservedly. His answer to my prayer inspired me in these latter days to undertake this holy and wonderful work in spite of my ignorance, and to imitate in some way those who, as the Lord foretold, would preach his Good News as a witness to all nations before the end of the world.

I remember a number of years ago being enthralled by Archbishop

Francis Carroll's homily at this ecumenical service. He compared St Patrick with the great missionary apostle, Paul. How much of Patrick's writing resonates with the teaching of Paul: each was painfully aware of his own weakness and limitations and totally reliant on God's grace. Each was inspired to preach the Good News with great zeal and enthusiasm, sharing with everyone who would listen the details of their own graced life. One of the most powerful experiences in my 44 years as a priest has been the witness of the people I have been privileged to serve. On many occasions I have seen good people plunged into unimaginable tragedy and I wondered how they would ever survive. Yet time and again I have seen such people not only come through those awful events but somehow almost miraculously grow through them. I can attribute that to three things: the great resilience of human nature, the support of good people around us and the grace of God. St Patrick is the embodiment of all that. How much his character and spirit must have given heart and hope to my ancestors and the multitude of Irish people landing in what is now Australia in humanly impossible conditions.

Not only the Irish priests and religious coming to Australia but lay people including and especially convicts could identify with this passage from Patrick's *Confessions*:

> I came to the Irish heathens to preach the Good News and to put up with insults from unbelievers. I heard my mission abused, I endured many persecutions even to the extent of chains; I gave up my free-born status for the good of others. Should I be worthy, I am ready to give even my life, promptly and gladly, for his name; and it is there that I wish to spend it until I die, if the Lord should graciously allow me.

The *Confessions* vividly describe the harsh conditions endured by the youthful Patrick in his life as a shepherd: living roughly in the woods and experiencing snow, frost and rain. But rather than crush him, it led the future Apostle of Ireland even closer to God through a life of continuous and faithful prayer. Undoubtedly that experience of solitude and deepening relationship with God would impel and sustain him in his future ministry

Patrick's own experience of being sold into slavery as a teenager en-sured that when he returned to Ireland as a pastor he would speak out strongly against an abuse which was still seen as acceptable in Christian quarters. His *Letter to the soldiers of Coroticus* is a strongly worded protest against the slaughter and kidnapping of Irish Christians by a small-time British 'king', Coroticus. Patrick is particularly concerned for the fate of the women he rightly sees as being most vulnerable. He appeals to the soldiers of Coroticus to listen to him even if their master fails to do so. He expresses his hopes in these terms:

> If only God may inspire them to come to their senses eventually and return to God, so that, however late, they repent of acting so sacrilegiously (murderers that they are of the Lord's brethren!) and free the baptised women whom they previously took captive, so that they may be free to live for God and be made whole here and forever.

Some of you will be familiar with Thomas Cahill's 1995 book *How the Irish Saved Civilisation*. The chapter on St Patrick powerfully illustrates the part the Apostle of Ireland played not only in his adopted country but in subsequent world history. Cahill makes some brave claims:

> Patrick's emotional grasp of Christian truth may have been greater than Augustine's. Augustine looked into his own heart and found there the inexpressible anguish of each individual, which enabled him to articulate a theory of sin that has no equal – the dark side of Christianity. Patrick prayed, made peace with God, then looked not only into his own heart but into the heart of others. What he saw convinced him of the bright side – that even slave traders can turn into liberators, even murderers can act as peacemakers, even barbarians can take their places among the nobility of heaven.

Watching *Songs of Praise* on ABC television, I was moved to hear Rev. Ian Paisley speak with such admiration about St Patrick and openly declare that he personally and all Irish people owed their freedom to Patrick. To hear him speak of St Patrick as an agent of reconciliation not only gives hope for the unity of Ireland but for peace in our wider world. World leaders such as Nelson Mandela, Mary Robinson and Barack Obama bring a spirit of hope and reconciliation to a world so much in need of unity and harmony.

I am painfully aware of the trauma currently being experienced by the Catholic Church in Ireland in the wake of revelations of widespread abuse by people in positions of trust and the failure of church leaders to adequately respond to complaints of such abuse. I say that without any sense of superiority, aware of similar experiences here in Australia in our recent history. I agonised over whether even to bring up the horrible business today. But I looked to Patrick who railed against injustice and abuse of every kind especially against the weak and the innocent; Patrick who stood up so courageously for freedom; Patrick whose own innate humility led him to a life of penance to which Croagh Patrick is a permanent monument and Patrick who was so aware of the advice of the scriptures that 'the truth will set us free'.

Today we invoke the intercession of St Patrick, praying that victims will be listened to and taken seriously and that they will find healing and peace; that those responsible for abuse will recognise the enormity of their actions; that church leaders will seek the wisdom and help of others, Catholics and non-Catholics alike, in seeking to reform the structures and practices of a church that allowed such abuse to take place; and that the love of God and the example of Jesus may be enabled to shine through the gloom giving hope to a church which has been the instrument of so much good and so many blessings since the time of St Patrick.

My theme for this address has been 'St Patrick: Champion of the Oppressed'. That was very much part of Patrick's contemporary role. Down through the centuries not only has he been a source of inspiration and hope to the people of Ireland, in good times and bad, but in the direst of circumstances men, women and children everywhere have been given strength, wisdom and hope as they looked to him as a model of Christian living and the best of human values. At the same time the great Apostle of Ireland continually challenges us to live out his spirit by following the dictate of the Prophet Micah 'to act justly, love tenderly and walk humbly with our God'.

The Missionary Sisters of Service

Homily at the Mass commemorating the 70th anniversary of the founding of Missionary Sisters of Service, St John the Evangelist Church, Mitcham, Victoria, 6 July 2014.

How often since his election have we heard Pope Francis described as a breath of fresh air? I celebrated Mass in my home parish of Queanbeyan last weekend and made that observation. One of the parishioners after Mass said, 'That should not be a surprise since he was the archbishop of Buenos Aires, which means "good air".'

In the fewer than 18 months since becoming pope, or Bishop of Rome as he likes to call himself, Francis has offered so many powerful gestures, words and symbols which have consistently brought us back to the person and teaching of Jesus. He has revived so much of the joy and the hope of Pope John XXIII and the Second Vatican Council.

Sadly, in my opinion, up to the election of Pope Francis the institutional church went through a period where that spirit of hope and light seemed to have faded. But grace prevailed where individuals and groups such as the Missionary Sisters of Service never lost heart, never lost hope and were a constant source of encouragement and inspiration to Christ's little flock. I will come back to that later.

One of Pope Francis' great gifts to the church is his apostolic exhortation, *The Joy of the Gospel,* published at the end of 2012. As I quote from this inspiring document, I am sure you will see much of its message lived out by the Missionary Sisters of Service for the past 70 years.

> The joy of the Gospel fills the hearts and lives of all who encounter
> Jesus. Those who accept his offer of salvation are set free from
> sin, sorrow, inner emptiness and loneliness. With Christ, joy

is constantly born anew ... The Gospel joy which enlivens the community of disciples is a missionary joy ... This joy is a sign that the Gospel has been proclaimed and is bearing fruit. Yet the drive to go forth and give, to go out from ourselves, to keep pressing forward in our sowing the good seed, remains ever present ... The joy of the Gospel is for all people: no one can be excluded (*EG* 1, 21, 23).

In many ways, Fr John Wallis was a priest in the mould of Pope John XXIII and Pope Francis. John Wallis was a beautiful, well-grounded human being. He was able to 'read the signs of the times', he identified with the needs of his people and he used his faith-filled imagination to bring the good news to the People of God in the down-to-earth circumstances of their lives. That is very explicitly stated in the sisters' constitution quoted in today's Mass booklet: 'In the spirit of the Good Shepherd we go to people wherever they are. We walk with them in the joys and hopes, griefs and anxieties of their lives.'

I am disappointed when occasionally I see priests trying to do everything themselves. The best apostles and leaders empower others, enabling their God-given talents to be shared with all God's children.

For seventy years, the Missionary Sisters of Service have accepted the challenge of today's gospel to take themselves *into the highways and by-ways*, as well as the streets and alleys, the open roads and hedgerows. It is there that they have lovingly encountered and ministered to the poor, the crippled, the blind and the lame and many other modern day equivalents. They have done so by living out their own deep relationship with Jesus and sharing it with their sisters and brothers. They have embraced the counsel of St Paul writing to the Christians of Philippi when he urges them to be united in their convictions and love with a common purpose and a common mind. They have learnt from the humility of Christ who emptied himself to assume the condition of a slave and finally gave his very life out of love for us.

When I recall Pope Francis celebrating Mass on Holy Thursday this year for the disabled people and washing their feet and last year doing the same for the young people in prison, I think of the many ways the sisters have ministered the love of Jesus to people very much in need in a wide variety of conditions and places. Like Pope Francis, they have reached out to people in a way that enhances the dignity of those they are serving and enables them to feel good about themselves and glimpse something of the face of Jesus and the love of God.

Going back to Pope Francis' apostolic exhortation, I think you will recognise in its words how the Missionary Sisters of Service have lived out their vocation for the past seventy years. The pope has this to say:

> We have to state, without mincing words, that there is an inseparable bond between our faith and the poor. May we never abandon them ... Let us go forth then to offer everyone the life of Jesus Christ. Here I repeat for the entire church what I have often said to the priests and laity of Buenos Aires: I prefer a church which is bruised, hurting and dirty because it has been out on the streets, rather than a church which is unhealthy from being confined and from clinging to its own security. I do not want a church concerned with being at the centre and which then ends being caught up in a web of obsessions and procedures. If something should rightly disturb us and trouble our consciences, it is the fact that so many of our brothers and sisters are living without the strength, light and consolation born of friendship with Jesus Christ, without a community of faith to support them, without meaning and a goal in life. More than by fear of going astray, my hope is that we will be moved by the fear of remaining shut up in structures which give us a false sense of security, within rules which make us harsh judges, within habits which make us feel safe, while at our door people are starving and Jesus does not tire of saying to us 'Give them something to eat.'

Today's thoughtfully prepared liturgy gives expression to the way that the sisters have lived for seventy years confronting the challenges Pope Francis is laying out for the entire church. For the sisters, it has been an ongoing journey as they learnt from the people they have served, reflected on God's love and God's call in relation to each other and the people they are serving.

I was surprised and humbled a few years ago when I was approached to be a patron of the John Wallis Foundation. I have admired the wonderful vocation of the Missionary Sisters of Service and I am in great admiration of the way the foundation seeks to widen their apostolate by sharing it with a great variety of people. It is a beautiful expression of Pope Francis' wish that our joy be a truly missionary joy.

My first encounter with the Missionary Sisters of Service was when I met Jenny Lauritsen who was helping to relaunch the YCW, the Young Christian Workers, in the Archdiocese of Canberra and Goulburn. Some time after that I was invited to participate in an MSS assembly which included people like me who were part of the sisters' outreach. It was an eye opener for me to see so many people with a clear sense of purpose and vocation being formed for leadership and feeling a real sense of ownership. I think it was at the assembly that I first met Fr John Wallis and was touched by his warmth and charisma. John represented much of what I aspired to as a priest. In 1996 I travelled back to Canberra with him by car. We had both been attending the National Council of Priests Convention in Albury. As we travelled along the Hume Highway, we were able to reflect on what had been discussed and experienced during the previous few days. John was taking the opportunity to catch up with Sr Julianne Dunn who was serving the Bishops' Conference secretariat in Canberra, no doubt drawing on her experience working with Archbishop Guilford Young in Hobart. Recently, at a priest's funeral in Hobart, it again came home to me how supportive the sisters have been to priests over the years as together they tended to the flock of Jesus.

It is to the sisters' credit that they are to be found in so many places where otherwise the message of Jesus would not be heard. It is in that spirit that the John Wallis foundation seeks to continue the spread of the Gospel.

Today's Old Testament reading invites us to reflect on our being part of God's plan for all eternity. We are invited to celebrate the wonderful gifts with which God has blessed us. 'Come and eat my bread and drink the wine I have prepared.' I thank Sr Stancea and the other people who have gathered us together in prayer and love today, mindful of similar celebrations in other parts of Australia around this time. May the 31 sisters named in our Mass booklet, and all who have gone before them, remind us of God's eternal love for each one of us.

As we prepare to be nourished at the table of the Eucharist, we thank

God for all the blessings that have come to Australia through the loving and dedicated ministry of the Missionary Sisters of Service. May they continue to inspire us and give us life.

With Pope Francis, let us pray to Mary:

Star of the new evangelisation, help us to bear radiant witness to communion, service, ardent and generous faith, justice and love for the poor, that the joy of the Gospel may reach to the ends of the earth, illuminating even the fringes of our world.

Being a Catholic today

Written for *The Good Oil*, September 2014.

Hardly a day goes by without some form of adverse media criticism being levelled at the Catholic Church or some of its members. Sometimes the criticism is vitriolic, unfair and replete with half-truths. At other times, I must admit, it is totally justified.

It hurts me deeply to see the family of God which is meant to be a source of goodness and grace portrayed as a repository of evil. Much of the current negative publicity flows from the Royal Commission and other inquiries into institutional sexual abuse. Can such public discussion be an opportunity for the church to endorse reforms needed for it to become its best self?

For nearly twenty years I have spoken and written of my hopes for our church which I have seen to be much in need of reform at many levels. Among those hopes are that we will be a more human church, a humbler church and a church that is more intent on reflecting the person and the teaching of Jesus.

Since his election, Pope Francis has demonstrated simply and force-fully those Christ-like qualities the whole church needs to embrace. He has walked away from the pomp and ceremony and triumphalism which has previously distracted from what should have been the true mission of the church. He tells pastors that they need to be at home with 'the smell of the sheep'.

The Holy Thursday ceremony of the washing of the feet has been for Pope Francis more than symbolic as he has included women, who were previously excluded, as well as embracing Muslims, prisoners and disabled people. He has spoken out unambiguously of the horror and criminality of sexual abuse in every form, especially within the ranks of the church. He has called on us to be a 'poor church for the poor'.

Much of the criticism of the church these days is sharpened by the fact that in the past its teaching on sexuality was so negative and unbalanced. This was exacerbated by the fact that it was articulated exclusively by men who were removed from the realities of intimacy and family life.

The 2014 Synod on the family offers an opportunity for the beginning of a healthier approach which will need to admit past mistakes and embrace the wisdom and experience of women and of married people generally.

In a society which seems to take promiscuity for granted, the church has a clear role in promoting values such as fidelity, integrity and healthy sexual relationships. Homosexual people need to be engaged in a conversation which hopefully will result in a better formulation of Church teaching on all forms of sexuality.

In his apostolic exhortation, *The Joy of the Gospel,* Pope Francis writes about the indispensible role of women in the church and of the need to listen to young people and poor people. He makes it clear that the church at every level must be engaged in dialogue and conversation. Ecumenical and inter-faith dialogue is an intrinsic part of being Catholic today as is a healthy interaction with the secular world.

The Good Samaritan Sisters' origins in the middle of the 19th century focused primarily on vulnerable women in Sydney. Today, we see Sister Anna Warlow and her community supporting Indigenous, rural and mining communities in remote Western Australia, Sister Rita Hayes assisting Timorese people in their recovery as a nation, and Good Samaritan sisters in Australia, along with other religious women, campaigning against the exploitation of women through people-trafficking. Although their numbers are diminishing, religious sisters in Australia bring great credit to our church and stand for what is best in the Catholic tradition. This came out very clearly in the tributes paid to Sacred Heart Sister, Philomene Tiernan, who perished in the Malaysian Airlines' plane shot down over the Ukraine.

Pope Francis humbly and realistically recognises that he does not have all the answers, but looks to local communities to search out, reflect and take action on the issues that are impinging on their people.

As I watch the evening news or read the newspaper, I am confronted with stories of the plight of refugees and asylum-seekers, unemployment, homelessness, poverty in a multitude of forms, domestic violence, alcohol-induced violence, suicide especially among the young, mental illness, Aboriginal disadvantage, rural crises and drug addiction, as just some of the ills plaguing Australian society.

At the heart of these tragic stories is the diminishing of the value of human life. Of course, there are many good news stories as well but unfortunately they do not always attract the same publicity. Sometimes we can be overwhelmed by the vastness and the complexity of the problems. But I am heartened by the slogan often used by development agencies which encourage us to think globally and act locally. Personal friendships, neighbourly concern and simple acts of kindness can be powerful antidotes to many of our contemporary evils.

I find the image of the pilgrim church an attractive one for today's Catholics. We are not standing still but are constantly called to move forward, often re-adjusting to changing circumstances, sometimes falling over or getting lost. Always we need Jesus and our fellow Christians as companions on the journey.

Pope Francis gives expression to the deepest sentiments of my heart:

We have a treasure of life and love that cannot deceive, and a message that cannot mislead or disappoint. It penetrates the depths of our hearts, sustaining and ennobling us. It is a truth that is never out of date because it reaches that part of us that nothing else can reach. Our infinite sadness can only be cured by infinite love.

Welcome to Archbishop Christopher Prowse

After-dinner speech welcoming Canberra's new Archbishop, Christopher Prowse, on the evening of his installation, Canberra Southern Cross Club, 19 November 2013.

It is a great joy and privilege for me to be speaking tonight at the end of a wonderful day of celebrations for the seventh Archbishop of Canberra and Goulburn, Christopher Prowse. History and geography were not my strong points at school but I have picked up a bit in the meantime, some of which I wish to share with you all on this happy occasion. Any glaring mistakes or omissions on my part will be noted by our historical experts, Fathers Bill Kennedy, Paul Bateman and Brian Maher.

Our new archbishop could be excused for finding his appointment to this see quite daunting. The Diocese of Goulburn was established by the Sacred Congregation of the Propagation of the Faith on 17 November 1862 and we have just concluded a year of rather low-key sesquicentenary celebrations. However, it wasn't until 10 March 1864 that the ishop of Adelaide, Franciscan Patrick Bonaventure Geoghegan, was named Bishop of Goulburn. At the time, he was seeking medical help for a throat condition in his native Ireland and on 9 May that year he died following an operation in Dublin. The search for a new bishop rivalled some of the intrigues of modern day politics but eventually concluded with the appointment of Fr William Lanigan, parish priest of Berrima, even though in the latter stages of the selection process the new bishop was unsure whether he was to be Bishop of Goulburn or Armidale! He was duly consecrated Bishop of Goulburn on Pentecost Sunday, 9 June 1867, nearly five years after the establishment of the diocese. So our 18 month wait for you, Christopher, has not been too bad in comparison. And Monsignor John Woods did a brilliant job as archdiocesan administrator as we waited patiently for your appointment.

But having arrived here safely and in seemingly good health, you can take heart in the knowledge that of your six predecessors as Archbishop of Canberra and Goulburn only one, Thomas Vincent Cahill, died in office. What might be more worrying to you is that your three immediate predecessors, Edward Bede Clancy, Francis Patrick Carroll and Mark Benedict Coleridge are still living. I cannot recall a stage in Australia's Catholic history where four occupants of a see were all alive at the one time. But I can assure you, Chris, that your three predecessors are all perfect gentlemen and will cause you no interference whatsoever.

While the Diocese of Goulburn was established in 1862, where we are sitting now remained part of the Archdiocese of Sydney until 1918. That was the year in which a large segment of the western part of the Diocese of Goulburn was ceded to form the Diocese of Wagga Wagga with the parish priest of Temora, Joseph Dwyer, named as its first bishop. It was then that Queanbeyan, the Monaro and the coastal part of the diocese became part of the Diocese of Goulburn.

Since 12 March this year, Canberra has been basking in some wonderful centenary celebrations. Not to be outdone, my home town of Queanbeyan is celebrating its 175 years. My father used to say that Queanbeyan was the mother of Canberra, but it was a case of the child outgrowing the parent. Certainly, in ecclesiastical terms, the Parish of Queanbeyan gave birth to Catholic Canberra. Established as a parish in 1842, remembering that it was part of the Archdiocese of Sydney, Queanbeyan welcomed in 1912 a 22-year-old newly ordained Sydney priest, Patrick Haydon, as assistant to Father Matthew Hogan. When the diocesan changes took place in 1918, Fr Hogan decided to return to Sydney and Fr Haydon was made parish priest of Queanbeyan. Canberra, still not a parish, was very much part of Father Haydon's beat. When St Christopher's Canberra was established as a parish in 1928, the much loved Father Haydon was appointed as the first (and it turned out to be the only) parish priest. He had the good fortune to have the ministrations of the Sisters of the Good Samaritan who had been part of the Queanbeyan scene since 1879. Just a few weeks ago, Fr Brian Maher escorted a small group of us to Springbank Island, just across the lake from the National Museum. It was on the Springbank property that the Sullivan family and others offered hospitality to the Queanbeyan priests who travelled there to celebrate Sunday Mass.

The erection of St Patrick's Parish in Braddon in 1955 was the beginning of a burgeoning of parishes in the national capital as the church has battled to keep pace with the rapid growth of Canberra. Although there are still more parishes in the country part of the archdiocese, Canberra boasts the larger part of the Catholic population.

It is wonderful to witness the continuing renovation of St Peter and Paul's Old Cathedral in Goulburn, the seat of the original diocese and the first inland city in Australia. In the meantime, St Christopher's, where Archbishop Christopher's installation took place this morning, has progressively graduated from church in 1939 to pro-cathedral, to co-cathedral and to cathedral with its extension under Archbishop Cahill in 1973.

I am probably showing my personal bias when I say what a splendid area our archdiocese covers. Yass the producer of some of Australia's finest wool, is our oldest parish with its beginnings in 1839 and the claim that Melbourne was at one stage part of its territory. Cooma is the gateway to the Snowy Mountains and the snowfields, Cootamundra is the birthplace of Don Bradman, Paleface Adios hails from Temora and Grenfell has its claims on Henry Lawson but also on Edward Bede Clancy whose father taught at Holy Camp, a settlement out of Grenfell that still remains dear to the cardinal's heart.

Archbishop Christopher, if you wish to savour some delicious stone fruit in the next few weeks get over to Young to taste the cherries and down to Araluen, the Valley of Peace, to bring home a box of peaches. Make sure before too long you get out to your furthest outpost, Lake Cargelligo. While you are there try to get across to Rankin Springs. I put in a plug for them because to my shame I have never made it there in my 48 years as a priest of the archdiocese.

Of course, nothing will hold you back from the enchanting strip of coastline from Batemans Bay to Eden where a little further on at the border you will touch on your former diocese of Sale. It was off the coast of Eden where the *Lyee Moon* was shipwrecked in 1886, taking the life of Mary MacKillop's mother, Flora, and sixty others. The future saint was always grateful to the people of Eden for caring for her mother's body. I am told that a Mrs Power was the principal carer, but I cannot claim any relationship to the good woman. What is factual is that the future bishop, Fr Patrick Geoghegan baptised Mary MacKillop in Melbourne in 1842, having celebrated her parents' marriage a couple of years earlier. Our archdiocese has been particularly blessed with the presence of both streams of the Sisters of St Joseph who officially came together on the feast of St Joseph this year.

The archdiocese also owes a great debt of gratitude to the Sisters of Mercy who have lived up to their name in all sorts of challenging situations and still continue to be found among the poor and struggling in our midst. They too have merged nationally with other streams of their congregation. I have already mentioned Australia's home-grown order, the Good Samaritans. Over the years, the Brigidines, the Presentations, the St John of God Sisters, the Little Company of Mary, the Franciscan Missionaries of Mary, the Carmelites and Mother Teresa's Missionaries of Charity have all witnessed powerfully to the Gospel in our midst.

We honour those orders who staffed secondary and primary schools in Canberra, providing solid foundations for a Catholic education system of which our Archdiocese is justifiably proud. Jenny Jeffery has just launched as a Canberra Centenary project, *Ringing in the Years*, a comprehensive and colourful account of Catholic schooling in Canberra. Preaching at the sesquicentenary Mass in Goulburn just over a year ago, I spoke of Catholic education as the 'jewel in the crown' of our archdiocese, now almost totally staffed by highly dedicated and competent lay people, very much aware of their vocation within the life of the church. I pay tribute also to the Signadou campus of the Australian Catholic University which is going from strength to strength. An historical overview such as this needs to acknowledge Bishop John Cullinane's leadership in the famous 1962 Goulburn schools strike which was to play a significant part in achieving justice for Catholic school funding across our nation.

Our archdiocese has been similarly blessed with the male religious who have served the church and the wider community so well: the Christian Brothers, De La Salle and Marist Brothers, the Passionist Fathers, Missionaries of the Sacred Heart, Dominicans, Jesuits, members of the Society of Christ and most latterly the Missionaries of God's Love about to become a Congregation of Diocesan Right.

The death last Friday of Redemptorist, Fr Joe Carroll, just as the clergy of the archdiocese were concluding our annual retreat was a poignant reminder of the spiritual oasis Galong monastery has been to our own and surrounding dioceses.

On 15 October last year, we mourned the death of Fr Joe Staunton. It was the first time in our diocesan history we had been without the ministrations of the Irish clergy. In fact, it was some time in the early 1950s, some say with the ordination of Fr Neville Drinkwater in 1954, that for the first time in our diocese the number of Australian-born priests outnumbered the Irish-born. It was fitting that when Fr Brian Maher wrote his authoritative history of our archdiocese that he gave it the title *Planting the Celtic Cross*, thereby acknowledging the great debt of gratitude we owe to the Irish church. Though bereft of this Irish presence, the archdiocese now counts among its ranks priests born in Vietnam, India, Singapore, the United Kingdom, New Zealand, Indonesia, Samoa, Lebanon, Croatia and Korea, not to mention the chaplains to the ethnic communities.

Archbishop Christopher, you are inheriting a loyal and dedicated group of priests and deacons even if they are diminishing in number. You will find in them brotherly collaborators willing to give their all in the service of God and God's people. The priests are faithful pastors to their people and the biblically seven permanent deacons bring much needed flexibility to the life of the Archdiocese. But I have to say that they are being stretched to the very limit as is the case in most countries in the western world.

A few weeks ago, I sat in on a meeting at the Australian National University of about fifty people from different parts of Australia looking towards renewal in the church. They examined a statement that looked at the call to be disciples. They pleaded for a Catholic Church that reflects Jesus' message of love, justice, equality, peace and forgiveness

— a Catholic Church in which all people are directed by their conscience and assume their responsibility for the mission of the church;

— a Catholic Church that inspires its people to recapture an experience of the mystical and the spiritual;

— a Catholic Church where God-given authority is used widely and justly to propagate the teachings of Christ, and respects the role of the People of God;

— a Catholic Church where all people, men and women, single and married minister in a spirit of co-responsibility for the church;

— a Catholic Church that influences Australian society to be ever more just, compassionate and egalitarian.

Archbishop Christopher, on 11 October last year, I was part of the congregation in St Peter's Square while you and the other members of the Synod concelebrated with Pope Benedict the Mass marking the 50th anniversary of the opening of the Second Vatican Council. I derived great hope from the Mass that the gifts of that great Council would be freshly received. The election of Pope Francis reinforced those hopes. I see your appointment as our archbishop as further reason for hope. I always remember the speech you gave at the bishops' meeting in 2005 when you were honoured for your 25 years of priestly service. It was clear that your priestly heart was still very much to the fore in your ministry as bishop. Your demonstrated commitment to ecumenical and inter-faith relations, your yearning for greater closeness to our Indigenous people and your enthusiasm to take up Pope Francis' call for us to be a poor church for the poor bring us all closer to the heart of Jesus.

Our archdiocesan synods of 1989 and 2004, with their themes of *Coming Home in Christ* and *One in Christ Jesus*, were based on wide consultation similar to what Pope Francis seems to be asking for in regard to the international synod on the family. However, our archdiocesan experience would indicate that much more time will be needed if the consultation is to be effective. There is no doubt that the gifts of all the People of God need to be drawn upon.

Your recognition of being 'Christopher', Christ-bearer, in St Christopher's Cathedral and all that it represents is a worthy challenge not just for you personally but for all the People of God in our local church. Just a week ago today, members of the newly-elected federal parliament gathered in prayer in St Christopher's asking God's blessings on their leadership of our nation. The Archbishop of Canberra and Goulburn has unique opportunities to be a significant part of the national discourse. You will be a humble yet articulate partner in that important conversation. You will have similar opportunities in the local community as well. Canberra for many reasons has been comparatively free of the sectarianism which has at times bedevilled other parts of Australia. Much of our thanks for that goes to our friend Monsignor Haydon who was held in such high esteem by the whole community, to some outstanding Catholic lay people and politicians, as well as to a fine body of clergy and religious who have engaged with respect and friendship members of the wider community.

Archbishop Christopher, we welcome you to the Archdiocese of Canberra and Goulburn as our chief pastor. We wish you well and we promise you our loyalty, our love and our prayers. *Ad multos annos.*

Jerusalem

Opinion piece written for the *Canberra Times*, reporting on
a conference in Doha, Qatar, in support of the rights of the
Palestinian people, February 2012.

Hardly a day passes without me being appalled by the plight of the Palestinian people and the apparent indifference of much of the western world to the injustices suffered by these beleaguered people. I have to admit that before visits to the Holy Land in 1973 and 1988 my sympathies were with Israel whom I saw as a fledgling nation surrounded by hostile Arab neighbours. The scales fell from my eyes on those visits where I saw a heavy military presence in Jerusalem and other towns, armoured vehicles rumbling up and down the streets, threatening war planes flying overhead and on one occasion just escaping from a tear-gas assault in a busy alley-way in Jerusalem.

In the years since then, successive Israeli governments, with the seeming complicity of the United States, have become more and more emboldened in their violence towards the Palestinian people. The destruction of Palestinian homes, tearing down beautiful olive groves, building a dreadful wall that isolates Palestinians from one another and makes already difficult movement almost impossible, not to mention the barbarism committed against the people of Gaza in recent years, are examples of a major aggressor scorning any effort to find peace based on justice. Why else would Israel be so consistently in breach of United Nations' resolutions?

At the end of February, I accompanied Ali Kazak, former Palestinian Representative to Australia, to an international conference on Jerusalem, held in Doha, Qatar. The conference was convened by the United Arab

League, hosted by the Emir of Qatar and attended by over 350 people from all over the world. I was surprised to find among the participants a number of Jewish rabbis who belong to a group called Jews United Against Zionism. I was able to tell them of the number of Jewish people here in Canberra who have spoken out against atrocities perpetrated against the Palestinian people. I was proud to stand beside Bishop Michael Sabbah, the former Latin Patriarch of Jerusalem and the first Palestinian to be appointed to that role. He unsurprisingly spoke strongly in defence of the rights of his people and of the violence to which they are being subjected.

The Doha Declaration at the end of the two day conference made a wide-ranging appeal for the protection of Palestinian people in Jerusalem and the upholding of their rights.

> We reiterate that the forced eviction of the Jerusalem population by means of the Judaisation plans, denying the rights, obliterating the history and heritage, usurping land, and confiscating properties are violations of International Law. Therefore we are calling on the international powers that are silent about Israeli violations to assume their responsibilities and oblige Israel to implement all international resolutions relevant to Jerusalem. Additionally, we are calling on all relevant agencies of the UN to assume their responsibility towards Jerusalem and its population, ensuring their enjoyment of their city, complete civic, economic and social rights, preserving its sanctities, historical landmarks and human heritage.

Australia's foreign minister, Senator Bob Carr, in his maiden speech, gave some moving historical examples of religious tolerance. It is my hope that he will raise the awareness of our Federal parliamentarians of the need for greater understanding of the injustices being suffered by the Palestinian people. Dialogue, so urgently needed at the political, racial and religious level, will never succeed while there is denial of the facts on the ground. I tire of seeing our parliamentarians of all political persuasions unquestioningly supporting Israel's usurping of fundamental Palestinian rights. Much of the tension with Iran would be lessened if that country were to see the Palestinian people being treated justly by Israel and the rest of the international community.

In a paper submitted to the conference, I concluded,

The 64 years of pain and suffering the Palestinians have endured are enough. The Catholic Church and other Christians have consistently cried out for peace and justice in the Holy Land. The Arab League has rightly demanded that Israel end the occupation and withdraw to the 1967 borders. Jerusalem needs to be secured as a city for all faiths with Muslims and Christians from outside Jerusalem being given the opportunity to pray in the Holy City. Provision needs to be made for the millions of Palestinian refugees by providing right of return and just compensation in accordance with UN Resolution 194.

I plead for patience and restraint on the part of the Palestinian people, for good will, a sense of justice and practical peace-making actions on the part of Israel and a firm resolve on the part of the international community to broker a peace which is based on justice and respects the dignity and rights of all the people involved. I pray for the climate of trust called for by Pope Benedict and I pray that the God of Abraham will bless these steps towards a peaceful solution in the Holy Land.

SIEV X

Address at an inter-faith prayer service on the shore of Lake Burley Griffin, Canberra, commemorating the deaths of 353 people on the SIEV X, 18 October 2003.

I think back to the year 2001 with a great deal of pain and bitterness. I think how hopefully the year began. We had hosted the 2000 Olympics in Sydney and welcomed people from all over the world. Volunteers, ordinary Australians, had played a significant part in the success of the Games. And it wasn't just about winning. Every athlete was applauded for participating. There was everywhere a spirit of welcome.

At the beginning of 2001, Australia celebrated its centenary of federation. Right around the country, with parades, dance and song, there were moving tributes expressing pride and joy in Australia being a multi-cultural and multi-racial society.

But as the year went on, we began to lose our nerve. We became threatened by the fact that people were risking their lives and arriving on our shores in leaky boats. Politicians began talking about border protection. The tabloid press and talkback radio whipped up fear in the Australian community.

It is little wonder that in August, when the Norwegian freighter the *Tampa* came to the aid of a distressed boat carrying asylum seekers, the Australian government drew its line in the sand and refused to accept the hapless people into our country.

After the September 11 terrorist attacks in the United States, Australia joined its American ally in declaring war on terrorism. To this day, I still don't understand what is meant by a war on terrorism. It is a vague enough notion to generate fear in all sorts of ways, hardening our hearts against those we should be reaching out to and embracing.

When SIEV X came to grief on 19 October 2001, with the loss of 353 innocent lives, it should have been recognised as a day of national disaster and mourning. It was truly a day of shame. Yet I don't recall any great outpouring of grief in our national parliament. I don't recall any prayer service in the Great Hall of Parliament House for those innocent lives lost. I don't recall any official intensive investigative process aimed at determining the causes of such a loss of life on a grand scale. (The senate inquiry seemed more like a cover-up, rather than a genuine effort to uncover the facts.) It has been left to individuals of great integrity such as Tony Kevin to try to bring those responsible to account.

The only official reaction I recall has been one of relief that a signal had gone out to people smugglers and others that there is little chance of piercing the net surrounding the Australian coastline.

As a nation, we have closed our borders and our hearts to desperate people in need of a home and security. How can the same government that justified going to war in Iraq to liberate its people continue to justify its position of refusing Iraqi and other asylum seekers entry into Australia?

Those of us gathered here join with fellow Australians around our country to say that we stand for something different. We grieve for the loss of 353 innocent lives on SIEV X. We express our shame that so little has been done on an official level to find out the causes of those deaths and to make some reparation. We uphold the value of every human life; we recognise that we belong to one human family; we say that the strong should protect the vulnerable; that the more affluent should share their resources with the needy; that every person is our sister or brother.

We come together to pray – as Christians, Muslims, members of other great world religions or maybe people struggling with faith or unable to see God's goodness reflected in the people or world around them. We come together as people of good will wanting the best for every human being.

Can I finish on a personal note? Today causes me great sadness because 18 October is my late parents' wedding anniversary. My father's ancestors were convicts from Ireland; my mother's parents came to Australia from Lebanon to find a better life. My parents not only gave a home to their five children, but living in Queanbeyan in the 1940s, 50s and 60s they welcomed into their home and their lives many of the refugees who found a home in Queanbeyan in the wake of the Second World War. I would hope that as Australians we can get back to our roots and re-discover and reclaim our best values. We should then send that strong message to our political leaders.

An appeal to President Bush

A peace message sent to President George W. Bush on the occasion of his visit to Canberra on 23 October 2003.

Last Tuesday morning I was preparing to say a Mission Mass for school students from our archdiocese. The theme of the Mass was 'Peace for Life'. As the students were about to enter the cathedral, a helicopter gunship flew over, seemingly in preparation for your visit to Canberra. The students saw the irony of the clash of the two events and prayed even more fervently for peace in our world.

That is surely the deep desire of every person of good will – that there be global peace, peace based on justice that recognises we are all part of the one human family.

Gathered with the young people last Tuesday, I thought of young-sters of similar age in Afghanistan, Palestine, Iran, Iraq, North Korea and other countries often viewed by you as 'the enemy'. Those children, along with their parents and grand-parents, easily become the innocent victims of threats and hostile actions played out between you, the President of the United States, and their own political leaders.

I appeal to you today to demonstrate to the Australian people and to the world that you are a man of peace. Up to now you have shown yourself to be more intent on issuing threats, on wreaking revenge and on waging war.

Can't you see how your so-called war on terrorism has only succeeded in increasing the threat of terrorists attacks? Can't you see that our world has become far more volatile and fragile since you embarked on this sense-less campaign? Can't you see that there must be a better way of bringing stability into international relations?

I suggest that there is another way. Instead of talking of waging war on terrorism, let us begin to talk about a war on poverty. This means recognising the great imbalance in the distribution of the world's wealth and resources. Can countries like the United States and Australia continue to flaunt their extravagant lifestyles in the face of the dire poverty of Third World countries?

During the Jubilee Year 2000, a campaign was conducted to remit or at least reduce the international debt of those Third World countries whose whole economy was locked into trying to pay off impossible interest debts. A fraction of the price of the war on terrorism would have gone a long way towards lessening those crippling debts.

Surely it is in everyone's interest for the United States and its allies to be viewed as friends to the rest of the world, rather than trying to beat them into submission by threats and brute force. Isn't it time for a bit of humility from you, Mr Blair and Mr Howard, admitting that you got it wrong over the invasion of Iraq, time to act in the interests of the people most affected by the war, rather than what is best for the United States?

It should be clear to you that there will never be peace in the Middle East until there is a resolution of the conflict between the Israelis and the Palestinians. Clearly, the violence and terrorism on both sides needs to be condemned in the strongest terms. But the United States needs to take a more even-handed role in the resolution of the conflict, condemning not only the desperate acts of Palestinian suicide bombers, but also the illegal occupation by the Israelis of Palestinian land, the unjust restriction of movement of the Palestinian people, the building of a wall that makes Palestinians prisoners in their own land and the heavy-handed use of sophisticated American-made weaponry against people barely able to defend themselves on such a scale. A Jewish leader recently wrote that 'peace can only come through deeds of peace'.*

The United States should use its influence (and its financial clout) with Israel to bring about negotiations with the Palestinian people. Only then will the state of Israel be safeguarded and a truly free and independent Palestinian state come into being.

---

*David Knoll, Vice-President, NSW Jewish Board of Deputies, Sydney, writing to *The Tablet* (London), 4 October 2003.

Pope John Paul frequently reminds us that there can be no true or lasting peace unless it is underlined by genuine justice.

It would be wonderful if you and the Australian prime minister this afternoon would declare yourselves men of peace in those terms — leaders prepared to offer a hand of friendship to your former enemies, leaders committed to a fairer distribution of the goods of this world, leaders who acknowledge the dignity of every human person, leaders brave enough to take the risk of loving, leaders renouncing hatred and fear, leaders who will boldly tell the world that every person is our sister or brother.

Breaking the silence

Speech given at a Palm Sunday Rally in support of refugees and asylum seekers, Garema Place, Canberra, 20 April 2014.

In the lead-up to the invasion of Iraq in 2003, I asked the question, 'Is an Iraqi life of any less value than an Australian life, a British life or an American life?' Today I further ask: What value do we Australians place on the lives of some of the most vulnerable people in our world today? How do we view the 45 million people world-wide who are displaced? Do we understand what it is like to be living in fear for our lives, to be persecuted, or to be deprived of the basic necessities of life? Can we put ourselves in the shoes of parents trembling in fear for the safety of their children? Do we see such desperate people simply as a threat to our comfortable way of life? Do we join in the mantra of 'stopping the boats', of trying to have 'problem people' out of sight and out of mind? Are we at one with our government in treating refugees and asylum seekers worse than criminals in hell-hole conditions in Nauru and on Manus Island?

People from all around Australia are gathering today because we wish to break the silence, to say loud and clear to our political leaders that we do not espouse the harsh policies that both major political parties are pushing in relation to refugees and asylum seekers. During the last Federal election campaign, we witnessed an obscene contest where Labor and Coalition parties were seemingly trying to outdo each other with tough and cynical rhetoric aimed at frightening the electorate away from a compassionate, fair and humane approach to the plight of some of the world's most needy people. To the credit of the Greens they attempted to put forward policies more in line with decent Australian values.

But, in deciding who would form government, voters had Hobson's choice in trying to separate ALP and Coalition policies in this whole question. In such a scenario, I dispute the fact that the Abbott government has a mandate to continue enacting its current harsh and inhumane policies. My heart almost freezes every time the prime minister or his minister for Iimmigration appear on television with more of their heartless language in relation to desperate people searching for hope and for a future.

Emeritus Professor Gillian Triggs is president of the Australian Human Rights Commission. She can hardly be dismissed as someone of the radical left. Yet she states that

> For over a decade the Commission has repeatedly recommended that mandatory and indefinite detention be abolished as it breaches Australia's international obligations. There is no evidence that mandatory detention effectively deters irregular arrivals. Moreover, the human and financial costs of mandatory detention have been enormous.

I am told that a United Nations Commission has found Australia to be guilty of 150 breaches of human rights in its arbitrary detention regime. No wonder our government is so anxious to deny independent observers access to the Nauru and Manus Island detention centres.

The Refugee Council of Australia puts it starkly:

> For asylum seekers already traumatised by the persecution or torture they have suffered, and the dangerous journey to find safety and protection, long-term, indefinite detention in a harsh, remote facility creates a highly toxic environment.' I am sure that many of us here today support the Refugee Council's call to the Australian government 'to abandon offshore processing and reintroduce alternatives to detention that provide prompt processing while asylum seekers are supported in the community in Australia.

I reflect on the treatment of the Vietnamese boat people in the 1980s and 90s and the way that many parishes and other community groups sponsored and supported them in the beginning of their journey towards becoming excellent Australian citizens. I think back a generation or two earlier when I was growing up in Queanbeyan seeing my parents and many other open-hearted people welcoming New Australians from war-torn Europe. Those people and succeeding generations have gone on to enhance Australia in countless ways. Today, Mustafa Jawardi from Afghanistan reminds us that he and so many others from similar backgrounds have the qualities needed to make Australia an even better country and one where we are able to celebrate unity in diversity.

After his election as pope, the first journey out of Rome made by Francis was to Lampedusa in the south of Italy in the wake of the tragic loss of so many lives of African refugees. Pope Francis stated unequivocally, 'Refugees are not pawns on the chessboard of humanity.' Isn't this precisely how they are being treated by Tony Abbott's government? Pope Francis went on to condemn a 'globalisation of indifference' and to say that we need to move away from attitudes of defensiveness and fear. I believe that all of us here today are heartily sick of the fear campaigns that have demeaned Australia for far too long in relation to people who need our love and acceptance, not the bitterness of hate and rejection.

Let us applaud those politicians who want more humane attitudes in relation to refugees and asylum seekers: the Greens who have consistently promoted more enlightened and just policies and the many individuals in both the Coalition and the ALP who are deeply troubled by their parties' policies but are caught up in the constraints of party discipline. Today we are breaking the silence to say to all those who exercise some sort of power that we acknowledge the sisterhood and the brotherhood of all humanity, that we believe in the dignity of every person and that as members of one human family, we Australians do really believe in a 'fair go' and want what is best especially for those who most need it. I think of our former governor-general, Sir William Deane, who used to say that a community is best judged by the way it treats its most vulnerable members.

Australia can do better – a whole lot better. Let us see that it happens.

A hundred years of warfare

Speech at a gathering marking 100 years since the beginning of the First World War, Australian Centre for Christianity and Culture, Canberra, 4 November 2014.

On 30 November 2002, I was proud to march beside Sue Wareham and thousands of others from the Sydney Town Hall to the Domain in a Walk against War. Both of us spoke alongside some very passionate speakers warning against the dire consequences of invading Iraq. That day, I asked a question which I have subsequently often repeated: 'Is an Iraqi life of any less value than an American life, a British life or an Australian life?'

A couple of months later, right here at the Australian Centre for Christianity and Culture, on 4 February 2003, I incurred the public wrath of Prime Minister John Howard following an ecumenical service for the opening of parliament that year. I had planned later in the day to take part outside parliament house in a silent protest against the war. It had been organised by the ACT Churches Council and I felt I should be man enough to say to the prime minister face-to-face what I would be saying by my actions later in the day. I simply said, 'Prime Minister, I share the concerns of many Australians about the prospect of us going to war in Iraq.' To my surprise and that of the TV cameramen around us, John Howard launched into a tirade telling me that I did not have a monopoly on an abhorrence of war; that he too had a hatred of war. He repeated it over and over, making me think that he was not totally convinced of the path he was about to embark upon.

We now know that there was no huge build-up of weapons of mass destruction in Iraq, that a terrible dictator in Saddam Hussein was eliminated, that thousands of people including innocent civilians were killed and that the whole political system was destabilised and all kinds of unholy alliances formed. Many sections of the population, especially among minority groups, including Christians, are now far worse off than they were before the 2003 invasion. Afghanistan is another story and I wonder what positives have been achieved there or what lessons have been learnt from that terrible conflict.

In the aftermath of the Second World War, Pope Pius XII stated, 'The calamity of a world war with the economic and social ruin and the moral and social excesses and dissolution which accompany it must not on any account be allowed to engulf the human race for a third time.' He went on to say 'Nothing can be lost by peace; everything may be lost by war.'

As we mark the one hundred years since the beginning of the First World War, are we to look forward to something better in terms of international relations and a recognition of the fact that we all belong to one human family? Can we be happy to be part of a world where every life is not precious, where so many people lack the basic necessities in terms of education, food, clean water, clothing, shelter, health care, social services, protection, freedom of movement and freedom of choice to pursue life's goals and aspirations? It is often stated that there can never be true or lasting peace which is not based on justice for all the people involved. I am acutely aware that many of our own indigenous Australian people are experiencing all kinds of deprivation and lack of justice. But I also know that many of us are living comfortably with scant regard to those less fortunate both in Australia and overseas. Who is my sister? Who is my brother?

The answer to those questions will determine how the current world conflicts are played out. Will it be by might and force, rape and killing, or by a genuine effort to understand that the so-called enemy is made up of real people, mothers, fathers and children who also long for the good things which life has to offer?

The ravages of war are being especially felt in the Middle East right now. Daily there are reports of killing, violence and the displacement of whole communities. I do not claim to even begin to understand the complexities of all the fighting. But I do believe that the continuing harassment of the Palestinian people by the Israeli authorities is a major cause of hostility towards western countries on the part of many Arab nations. The recent slaughter in Gaza, the continuing confiscation of Palestinian land and homes, the denial of freedom of movement and so many other violations of human rights are examples of rank injustice towards the Palestinian people. They are viewed by neighbouring Arab states in terms of the role of the United States in not exerting sufficient pressure on Israel to desist, but rather actively supporting the undermining of the rights of the Palestinian people. I believe that if the question of Palestinian and Israeli co-existence could be justly and peaceably resolved, it would go a long way towards lowering the political temperature in the Middle East generally and help to secure a greater world peace.

Clearly there needs to be much more dialogue and use of diplomatic means in resolving conflict. Two important qualities for genuine dialogue are listening and humility. Bringing warring parties together is no easy matter on any level but somehow or other a spirit of trust needs to be built up. The United Nations clearly has a key role to play and every effort must be made to enable it to function effectively.

I hesitate to say this, but I sometimes think the United States can best help by adopting a lower profile. I believe that many countries see the US as a superpower imposing its will on countries who are no match for it in terms of finance, influence or armaments. Whether it is in regard to oil, other commodities or trade, they see the US as acting in terms of its own selfish interests rather than for the good of all humanity. I recall that at a time when there had been some apparent softening of the stance of North Korea towards South Korea, and some hope for peace there, out of the blue came George W. Bush in his January 2002 State of the Union address naming North Korea along with Iran and Iraq as part of an 'axis of evil'. The immediate effect on the Korean peninsula was a return to the Cold War position. I wonder how much of the current posturing by President Putin is not a reaction to his fears that the Ukraine is coming too much under the influence of the United States and the western world generally.

Given that much of the tension is in predominantly Muslim countries, dialogue with Islam and inter-faith dialogue generally is of the utmost importance. It is my hope that much of the good will here in Canberra, as shown by the recent Mosque Open Day, will spread further afield and be a model for other places as well. It is by knowing each other better that we will better understand each other and learn to love and forgive one another.

Finally, let me say in this forum what I have been saying for the whole of my life as a bishop in the Catholic Church. While the gifts of women are being excluded or restricted, whether it be in leadership, decision-making, or in terms of equality or basic human rights, we will continue to be directed by a male-dominated framework which does not do justice to the best of the human spirit. May that best spirit prevail.

Three days in Dubrovnik

A reflection written in the wake of a moving visit to the historic city of Dubrovnik, threatened by the Balkans War, 20 May 1993.

In 1975, Zelimir Puljic and I were young priests studying together in Propaganda Fide College in Rome. I was delighted when he invited me to celebrate Easter with him in his family's parish in Slavonska Pozega in Croatia. Even under the shadow of communism, the faith of the parish community shone forth as people celebrated the Lord's death and resurrection.

After experiencing the hospitality of the parish priest and the parishioners for almost a week, I was taken by my host to visit Sarajevo, Mostar and Dubrovnik. We spent the night in the seminary of Dubrovnik, neither of us imagining that 15 years later my friend would become its bishop. A few months later, having completed my studies in Rome, I returned to Australia. It was Zelimir Puljic who arranged the little *festa* to farewell me.

We kept in touch over the years, and I was overjoyed when I learned at the beginning of 1990 that Zelimir Puljic had been appointed Bishop of Dubrovnik. I rejoiced with him and his people in the ensuing months when it became clear that they were about to escape the yoke of communism.

But that joy turned to sadness and frustration when after Croatia's declaration of independence, the beautiful walled city of Dubrovnik and its region (almost the total area of the Diocese of Dubrovnik) were brutalised by the forces of occupation.

Dubrovnik could well lay claim to have been one of the most beautiful cities in the world. Because of its beauty and rich cultural heritage, it was placed on the UNESCO register of world cultural heritage in 1979. While Dubrovnik at times has suffered from earthquakes, never in its history, which dates back to the seventh century AD, had it been damaged by war.

But all that changed in the autumn of 1991 when the Yugoslav army, reinforced by reservists from Serbia, Montenegro and Eastern Herzegovina, occupied a large part of the Dubrovnik region. Dubrovnik itself was not occupied but was surrounded by the enemy forces.

It was attacked three times, in October, November and December 1991. The attacks lasted several days and it was during the third attack that extensive damage was caused to precious buildings and monuments in the old city.

I remember the sense of helplessness I felt in Australia when I heard the news reports of Dubrovnik's terrible fate. Many times I tried unsuccessfully to telephone my brother bishop. However, I was able to ascertain that he was alive and that he was remaining in his diocese, protecting and sustaining his flock. Some time later, I received a letter from him appealing for Dubrovnik's plight to be made known to the world outside. I did my best, but with a sense of frustration, to give some publicity to the suffering of the people of Dubrovnik.

In the second week of May 1993, I attended a meeting in Rome at the Pontifical Council for Promoting Christian Unity. Before leaving Australia, I determined to visit Dubrovnik, not at this time as a tourist but in solidarity with its bishop and his people. If I enjoyed my previous visit, this time I really fell in love with Dubrovnik.

I write these words on the feast of the Ascension after three unforgettable days in the Diocese of Dubrovnik. The pain of division, that we talked about in Rome, materialised before my eyes during this visit.

Driving south from Dubrovnik almost to the border with Montenegro, I saw the airport buildings destroyed, whole villages and towns, from which the inhabitants had been forced to flee, senselessly burnt and gutted, crops destroyed, and homes left in ruins. We visited the parish priests who had now returned to what was left of their parishes. I was told of the work of Caritas, which, with special help from Germany, has a plan to put a roof over everyone's head. Maybe one or two rooms will be repaired enabling the family to return to its home and begin re-building for the future.

Walking around the top of the walls of the old city, I was heartened to see what had been done to restore it to its pristine beauty. Although there is scarcely a tourist to be seen, life is getting back to normal among the locals. Walking about the old city, I enjoyed talking to those I could in their halting English or in my broken Italian. Ivo Grbic, an artist and musician, proudly showed me over his exhibition in his burnt-out studio. As I admired the work of a young female artist, she apologetically explained to me that her gallery was called *Inferno* after Dante, not out of any disrespect for religion! I watched another artist diligently painting a street scene. The markets, the shops and the churches were open, all attracting a steady stream of people.

It happened that during my visit the priests of the diocese were meeting for their bi-monthly conference. They were greatly encouraged by my presence at the side of their bishop and my few words expressing my solidarity with them.

On my last evening, I went with Bishop Zelimir to celebrations in two parishes: in the Parish of Slano which was commemorating the anniversary of the town's liberation on the Feast of the Ascension last year, and the Parish of Mokosica, celebrating its patronal feast. In each case, I had the opportunity of expressing the great admiration I had gained for the people of Dubrovnik Diocese for their faith, their determination to persevere and for the seeming lack of any trace of bitterness. I was almost moved to tears as different ones asked me to pray for a brother, a son or a husband killed in the fighting.

On my first day in Dubrovnik after having visited the most devastated parts of the Diocese, Zelimir drove me to the fortress that stands high over the city of Dubrovnik. We were welcomed by the brigadier in charge of the soldiers occupying the strategic fortress. As he was explaining to me the crucial role the fortress had played in the eventual liberation of Dubrovnik in October 1992, he picked up a tiny piece of an exploded grenade telling us of the attack which had killed about fifty of his men.

He allowed me to take with me that piece of otherwise worthless metal which will be for me a sacred relic, a precious reminder of the suffering of a people and of a city but also of their resolute faith and hope which is enabling them to seek new life and the peace which Christ promised.

I pray and ask that all who read this to pray for peace – for Dubrovnik, for Croatia, for Bosnia Herzegovina, indeed for all the Balkans – and that it will be a peace based on justice and a peace that respects the dignity of every person.

A short stay in Medjugorje

An account of a visit to a place of pilgrimage which is not officially approved as such by the Vatican but which attracts thousands of pilgrims each year, May 1993.

By most standards, the three days I spent in Medjugorje between 21 and 24 May 1993 would be considered a short time. But that was all that was available to me after a week's meeting in Rome at the Pontifical Council for Christian Unity and the three unforgettable days spent with my friend, Bishop Zelimir Puljic, in Dubrovnik.

Hardly had I arrived in Medjugorje when I was greeted by two American women pilgrims. One was on her third pilgrimage. I had to admit that I was something of a sceptic. They said they would pray for me.

I have been blessed by God in being deeply convinced of his love (I took as my motto as bishop 'God is love') and devotion to Our Lady has always been important to me. My concerns were more about the extraordinary and sometimes bizarre experiences reported by people who had visited Medjugorje. These experiences rather than a deeper relationship with God in many cases seemed to have been what mattered. On the other hand, I had been deeply impressed by one of the visionaries, Ivan, who visited Canberra in February this year. He came across as a very normal, down-to-earth young man. He spoke about six things central to Our Lady's messages to him over the years: peace, conversion, prayer, fasting and penance, a deeper faith and love. It struck me that they were very much Gospel values.

Why did I go to Medjugorje anyway? Probably as a representative of my family, many of whom were very enthusiastic about Medjugorje. I had read Wayne Wieble's *The Last Apparition*, Jan Connell's *Queen of the Cosmos*, as well as numerous articles about Medjugorje. In January 1992, I had attempted to make a visit with my 15-year-old niece, Louise, but at Venice we had to make a decision (on good advice) not to proceed any further because of the war. This time the dangers were still there but after some deliberation and prayer, I decided to go to Dubrovnik and Medjugorje.

The three days I spent in Dubrovnik were deeply moving. I've written elsewhere about my stay there. Suffice to say that the people and their beautiful city have suffered a great deal, but there is also great faith and determination, with God's help, to rebuild their lives and the many destroyed homes and buildings.

In the three days in Medjugorje, I managed to climb the mountain of the cross on two days, making the Stations, and on the third day to recite the 15 decades of the Rosary while walking up and around the hill of the apparitions. I also took the opportunity to concelebrate Mass each day in English and to attend the Croatian Mass each evening. There were also lots of rosaries, a talk by Father Philip and plenty of time for personal prayer and reflection.

The fighting in surrounding Bosnia Herzegovina has taken its toll on Medjugorje. There were comparatively few pilgrims, many shops were closed, accommodation houses virtually empty, and once-crowded outdoor cafes seating just one or two people. Gun fire could be heard from time to time (Mostar is just 30 km away). Yet, despite all that, there was an atmosphere of prayer and hope and a lovely spirit of friendliness and openness between the locals and visitors.

Many United Nations vehicles could be seen in Medjugorje, and I had the opportunity of meeting with a British group who had brought a great deal of material aid to the many refugees who had come there. I was privileged to meet some of the refugees who were grateful for my interest and the few words of greeting I was able to give them in Croatian. Part of the relief group was a likeable Scotsman, Simon, with whom I struck up a rapport we were able to build up over a beer, some prayer and an exchange of experiences. Simon was a seasoned visitor to Medjugorje who was drawn to give practical help when the war began to take its toll on the people of the old Yugoslavia.

Later in the visit, I again met the American ladies. They wanted to know if I was still a sceptic. They assured me they were still praying for me.

I left Medjugorje on the Feast of Our Lady Help of Christians after celebrating Mass with Fr Wally from Jindabyne and a little group of Australians. I left without experiencing any miracles (although during my time in Medjugorje I got rid of a cold that had been nagging at me for a week and a back and leg problem that had been troubling me for about three months).

During my time in Medjugorje, I kept a low profile as a simple pilgrim rather than presenting myself as a bishop. I was pleased I did. The graces I experienced were largely through the people I met: Veronika and Ivan who took me into their home (as their sole paying guest) and shared with me some of their faith and the joys of their family life; Simon and the American ladies I've referred to; Joanne and Tom who were overjoyed to be able to be married in Medjugorje and have one of the visionaries, Vicka, as their bridesmaid; Vicka herself, smiling throughout as if she were the bride and cheerfully meeting people afterwards; Fr Wally, Ken and Walter from Jindabyne with whom I was always welcome; the refugees and the people who were trying to help them.

But most of all, I was moved by something very sad. Barbara, an Australian pilgrim suffering from cancer became really sick and had to be taken home. Pauline, a trained nurse, was part of Barbara's group but the pair had never previously met. Pauline obtained and administered what medication she could, cut short her time in Medjugorje and gave up an extra week in Rome and London and cheerfully assisted Barbara on the long trip back to Australia. She was ably assisted by her fine 19-year-old son, Sam, who escorted them to Rome before going on to London. I won't describe the shabby treatment the two ladies encountered at Rome airport where I spent two hours (unsuccessfully) trying to sort out their travel arrangements. In the end, both women had to fork out $1800 for another fare home. During all this, Barbara was in considerable pain, while Pauline was so selfless in looking after her new friend. Such heroism touched me profoundly.

I needed no greater miracle than that: the example of good people, under the inspiration of Our Lady, living out the great commandment of Jesus: 'Love one another as I have loved you.' I think that was the answer to the prayers of the American ladies on my behalf.

Pilgrimage to Santiago de Compostela

An account of a pilgrim journey to the supposed burial site of the Apostle James. This increasingly popular pilgrimage attracts a large number of people with many different motivations. The pilgrimage began on 26 March 2003 and the reflection was written in August 2003.

It has been ceaselessly repeated that the Way (*Camino*) is an excellent metaphor of life. And, sure enough, it is, and in every way, not just as a goal but also for the joy of the journey in all its fascination and fullness. The Way of St James, a wayfarer's way offers not only the meaning of the pilgrimage, or of the journey, but also the wealth that, over the centuries, grew up at its sides and under its shelter: art, scenery and diversity, legends and communication between different people, the underlying idea forming the background to a way of living and feeling that arose along this route.

It is said that at the beginning of the 9th century a supernatural light signalled to a hermit the burial place of the Apostle (James the Greater, brother of John). In the early years of Christianity, he had been sent to evangelise Spain. Things did not go well for him and he had to return to Jerusalem, where he had the dubious honour of being the first of the twelve apostles to be martyred – by Herod in 42 AD. Herod refused to allow the decapitated body to be buried, but a dedicated group of Christians were able to rescue it, place it in an unmanned boat and from there it was taken by the angels across the rivers and seas to the capital of Roman Galicia to a place which would become known as Compostela.

The Road to Santiago: Edilesa Guides

Legends abound and not all of them are politically correct today, especially the image of James the Moor-slayer. Apparently in the first millennium, when the Christians were getting a hard time of it from the Moors and about to drop their bundle, a vision appeared in the sky of James slaying the dreaded Moors. This gave heart to the crestfallen Christians who took up the fight with renewed enthusiasm. Along the way and in Santiago itself there are lots of depictions of James on his horse, sword in hand and the heads of hapless Moors lying on the ground.

Around the turn of the first millennium, Santiago de Compostela became a place of pilgrimage and in fact is the oldest pilgrim destination after Jerusalem and Rome. These days about 100,000 pilgrims a year traverse the many pilgrim routes, mainly on foot, but also on bicycles and horses.

Geraldine and I joined the 'French Way' at León, 311 km back from Santiago. We had picked up our pilgrim passports at Burgos further down the route but took the bus to León. Many of our fellow pilgrims began 500 km further back at St Jean Pied de Port on the French side of the border or at Roncesvalles in Spain. In 1998, Mary Wilkie from Armidale NSW, then aged 59, walked 1800 km from Paris to Santiago and has recorded her journey in the interesting book *Walking to Santiago*.

Our *camino* began on 26 March 2003, just as war was breaking out in Iraq. We shared with many of our fellow pilgrims (and 91 per cent of the Spanish population) an abhorrence of the war, so in many ways it was a walk for peace. Every person's motive for undertaking the pilgrimage would be unique, just as everyone's experience. But there is a real bond shared by the 'companions on the journey' and great encouragement given by the locals along the way.

The refuges at the end of the day and the bars along the way give respite to weary travellers while the yellow arrows marking the route are an indispensable guide. Often it is a walk in faith and a real relief when a yellow arrow appears to confirm that you are still on track. It isn't long before the pain of sore limbs becomes part of the story and blisters and possible cures are much discussed by sufferers. The weight of the backpack is an ever-present reality, happily put aside on reaching the refuge.

Rain and mud were not unexpected. The internet had warned that the region would expect 14 days of rain in April. As it turned out, it rained for the first five days of our walk (but never too heavily) but was fine for the next 11 days, just beginning again as we arrived in Santiago.

Coming from drought-stricken Australia, we were delighted by the clear flowing rivers and streams, often with little trout swimming around. (They tasted nice when served up in the restaurants.) If I were to do it all again I would photograph the splendid bridges we crossed: the most spectacular (which we did capture on camera and postcard) was at Hospital de Obrigo, over 200 metres long and with more than twenty arches. (There is a story around that at this bridge men had to prove their gallantry to female admirers.) I remember out in the middle of nowhere, not too far from Melide, a wonderful single-arch pedestrian stone bridge with a steep rise and fall. Its architect must have been a genius.

The beauty of spring awaited us as we descended after some steep climbing between Astorga and Rabanal. Somewhere there we came upon Foncebaden where we appreciated the bar on a wet cold morning. Inside there was a glorious mural of ten splendid bishops. It must be a recent work of art because I've seen no reference to it in the guide books. Out of devilment, I had my photo taken in front of them, they in their finery with me in my wet clothes holding up my bottle of beer. I'm not usually a beer drinker but I enjoyed a small one on the way while Geraldine usually settled for a cup of tea which isn't exactly a forte for the Spaniards. However, they make great coffee.

We were a bit ahead of the season which meant that we had no trouble getting a place in the pilgrim refuges once we produced our pilgrim passport. We had our own sleeping bags but the refuges provided us not only with a roof over our head, but a bed (usually in a dormitory), a hot shower, usually a place to eat and sometimes to cook and an atmosphere to share something of the experience with fellow pilgrims. The snoring at night could be a trial. We had a terrible night in the over 50s dormitory at Villafranca and a couple of others were not far behind. But I must say I never felt deprived of sleep and was rested and ready for the trek each day.

Being out of the peak season also meant that we weren't always able to see inside the churches and the pilgrims' Masses at the end of the day hadn't yet begun. Most days we managed a quiet Mass together. Some of the bigger places such as León, Astorga and Burgos had magnificent cathedrals and the Benedictine monastery at Samos was spectacular and special to Australia because from there came Bishop Salvado, a great pioneer bishop for WA. Along the way, and especially in Santiago, we were touched by the earthy Madonnas with plain but beautiful faces, quite different from anything I was used to. We were fascinated by the storks nesting high up in the bell towers of the churches and liked the pair cheekily at home in the spire of the bishop's palace in Astorga.

The biggest group of pilgrims were the Spaniards, followed by the Germans. We came to make some good friends among the Germans and I saw a softer side of them than I had previously experienced. Our favourite was Alfred, a doctor from Berlin. He was completing the second half of the pilgrimage, not being able to take too much time away from family and his practice to do it all in one hit. Our great friend, Irma, from Holland, was doing her eighth *camino* and proved to be a mine of information and an invaluable help and guide for us. We met her at Triacastela, about half way through. Not speaking Spanish was a real drawback for us. I had mistakenly imagined that if I spoke Italian and they spoke Spanish we would understand each other. We found very few people spoke English, except dear Irma, whose Spanish was very good as well.

Geraldine especially enjoyed the spring wildflowers coming into bloom and later as we got within a 100 km of Santiago, we might have been in Australia with all the gum trees. She was taken too by the great variety of dogs greeting us as we went by. I was pleased that some of the bigger ones were behind fences. Two little mutts gave serious chase on one occasion but finally gave up, sparing me torn trousers and a dose of Spanish rabies. The local people were always encouraging, wishing us *Buen camino* as we trudged along.

We had the best paella on a cold Sunday night in El Acebo. And an interesting interlude with Tomás at Manjarin in the middle of nowhere. He served bad coffee, played Gregorian music and got a bit jealous of his dog giving attention to Geraldine: for all that, I liked him, but I was pleased that unlike three brave lads we were not staying the night. The guide book promised us an English speaking pharmacist at Molinaseca; she was very helpful and chuffed to see the reference to herself in the book. Ponferrada proved to be quite a meeting place for pilgrims and we met up with Jim, an Irishman we had met at the beginning at León. He turned out to be a UN soldier who had served in Lebanon and Kosovo and needed to get away from it all occasionally. He organised a communal meal that night.

Villafranca, already mentioned, had a character called Jesús running the refuge which was described as atmospheric. We didn't see much of Jesús, but Mrs Jesús wasn't overly helpful. That was really exceptional, because overall we were overcome by people's kindness and patience. At O Cebreiro up in the cold high country we appreciated the warmth of the inn and the home cooking of the lady of the house. (We decided that we would occasionally take a break from the refuges.) It was leaving there that we met a lively group of teenagers from Seville. They and their teachers came to our aid on a couple of occasions when we were the walking wounded. We appreciated, too, the kindness of the policeman at Cacabelos. He not only opened up the refuge for us but gave us a much needed lift in the police car. We enjoyed our feed of *pulpo* (octopus) at Melide. We were told that this was not to be missed as it was a specialty of the Galician region.

Sixty-seven km from Santiago, I planted an Australian one dollar coin and wrote a note to Neil Harrigan directing him how to find it. Six weeks later, Neil struck the jackpot and has photos to prove it. He selflessly replanted the coin in case another more needy Australian pilgrim comes by.

Arriving in Santiago on 10 April, after 16 days on the track, we were greeted with light rain reminding us of our beginnings. Receiving the *compostela* after an inspection of the stamps on our pilgrim passport, we were a bit overcome when we went into the cathedral for the first time. We were first greeted by the homely face of Salome, James' mother, on one side of the sanctuary and Zebedee, his dad, on the other side. The rest of it was a bit overwhelming until Irma gave us a guided tour the next day.

The pilgrims' Mass at noon the next day was memorable for us both. Pilgrims are not mentioned by name, but we were honoured to be the two Australians recorded as beginning the *camino* at León. We met for the last time some of our dear fellow pilgrims and it was a time to bring to prayer some very special people who were sick or recently deceased. It was the first anniversary of the death of my dear friend, Lex Johnson, and just a week or so after we had got word of Kris' death. The Gregorian chant, a moving Taizé chant for the responsorial psalm, led by a vibrant nun, and a special feeling of belonging to the people of God were all part of a wonderful liturgy. When they lit and swung the *botafumeiro* at the end, we felt 'our cup had runneth over'. The giant censer is more than a metre high and six trusty handlers had it swinging almost to the roof over the transepts. (We were pleased we were in the main aisle.) The priest told us to view it as a prayer, rather than a spectacle, but we had to admit to finding it quite spectacular. Apparently it was employed in earlier times to clear the air polluted by smelly pilgrims!

Two more days interspersed with rain gave us a chance to see a few of the sights, including the pilgrims' museum and some other parts of the city. The Mass on Palm Sunday was celebrated by the archbishop and we were moved by the fact that the solemn procession of palms at the beginning included an impromptu appearance of a Down Syndrome lad who very nonchalantly joined the archbishop and his entourage as they set out on their ten minute tour around the large cathedral. We had a couple of free feeds at the Parador, a plush hotel across the square from the cathedral. They undertake to feed ten pilgrims a day, but it is the staff's food, served in the basement of the hotel. I enjoyed the experience more than Geraldine. We also tasted and bought a Santiago tart which was to sustain us for a day or so after we left the city. We departed Santiago rather unceremoniously on Palm Sunday on a crowded overnight train to Madrid.

Nearly four months later, the *camino* is still very much in my being. I've enjoyed sharing the experience with others, especially those who have embarked on it themselves. I've recalled the documentaries that first got me interested and the helpful advice from people like John Stephens and Pat Kenna. Geraldine prepared a lovely paella meal with them shortly after we got back and subsequently it was good to catch up with the Harrigans and John Armstrong to hear of their later exploits.

People naturally ask why did you do it and what did you get out of it? In fact, they ask you something like that when you are claiming the *compostela* in Santiago. There is clearly a sense of achievement, the thrill of being part of something that is based on one thousand or, more broadly, two thousand years of tradition, the joy of communing with God in nature and in the special people we met, a welcome respite from work pressures, a time to get some balance and perspective back into life and an opportunity to enjoy so many new aspects of living.

I've always been drawn to the notion of life as a pilgrimage and the image of the pilgrim church. Many of the blessings of the *camino*, as well as some of the hardships, were a mirror for me of what it means to be a Christian today. I hope I returned to Australia a better person and a wiser pastor.

After leaving Santiago, we still had a couple more weeks in Spain, visiting Madrid, Avila, Cordoba, Granada and Oreto. The last mentioned won't be found on a map, but it is the site of my titular see,* about 150 km south of Madrid. Its modem name is Granatula and it has a population of about a thousand people, a very large church (at the time of our visit, closed for renovations), no resident priest and no accommodation for visitors. We had hoped to be there for the Easter ceremonies but were forced to stay at Almagro, 12 km away, and make a couple of day visits. It was a bit disappointing not to be able to make contact with the priest or parishioners, again finding my lack of Spanish a decided handicap. However, we witnessed one of the *Semana Santa* (Holy Week) community processions and had a meal at the Oreto bar. Granatula is in the middle of olive growing country and I found out for the first time to my great pleasure that it is in the heart of the La Mancha province, with all the stories of Don Quixote. It made me wonder if the legendary figure tilting at windmills and fighting lost causes has not had some influence on my ministry as bishop!

---

*Auxiliary bishops, not having their own diocese, are given a titular see, a now defunct diocese.

Lebanon
A personal encounter

**During some long-service leave in 2008, the author, son of
Ken and Olga Power (nee Bookallil), spent a week in Lebanon
discovering his Lebanese ancestral roots. This reflection, from
September 2008, uncovers some of them.**

I often say that it has only been in the second half of my life that I have
appreciated my origins, Lebanese on my mother's side and Irish on my
father's.

Morgan Power was transported to Australia in 1796-97 and his future wife, Bridgette Byrne, in 1802-03. My mother's parents, Nicholas and
Margaret, and many other extended family members arrived in Australia
from Lebanon in the 1890s. Nicholas Bookallil was quite a bit older than
his cousin Margaret and they were married here in Australia. They settled
in Cooma NSW and four children were born to them, Fred, John, Olga
(my mother) and Alec. I never knew my grandparents who died well before my parents married, but I remember my great-grandmother, Rose, who
lived to her nineties and died in 1950. My mother was able to understand
Arabic but they always spoke English in the home because Nicholas and
Margaret did not wish their children to be discriminated against because of
their race. When I once asked Mum why they came out to Australia from
Lebanon, she said simply, 'For a better life.' At the same time, some other
family members went to the United States and Mum used to speak of a (female) cousin over there who was a doctor. Australia was home and I never
heard Mum express any desire to visit Lebanon, remembering of course that
overseas travel was not very accessible in her younger days.

At the end of some study in Rome, I planned to visit Beirut in May 1975, but had to change my plans at the very last minute when war broke out. Since then I have watched with sadness so much loss of life and destruction in what is such a beautiful country. I have witnessed the Lebanese people so often being the meat in the sandwich in the conflicts of neighbouring countries. In good times in Lebanon, Christians and Muslims have got along harmoniously and the constitution provides for power-sharing between the various religious groups. The neighbouring Israeli-Palestinian fighting has impacted directly on Lebanon and its people, and over recent years I have been involved in a number of campaigns in Australia calling for justice and peace for all concerned. In 1988, on a pilgrimage to the Holy Land, there was a poignant moment when our little group stopped and looked across the border to Lebanon but we were unable to cross into the land of my ancestors. I was invited to lead the group in a prayer for peace.

In 1998, mainly through the initiative of David Bookallil and Denise Baraki Mack, a Bookallil reunion took place at the Kensington Sacred Heart Monastery grounds in Sydney. Many of the early family had settled in that area. 'Everyone's your cousin' was the theme of the reunion which saw many distant cousins meeting, sometimes for the first time. After a Mass which I celebrated, there were many exchanges of stories, additions made to the family tree and even some healing among estranged family members.

Part of my plans for some 2008 long-service leave was to spend a week in Lebanon. I was put in touch with Pascal Abukhalil and we communicated by email. It transpired that Pascal's father, Khalil, and I are second cousins, our grandfathers Nicholas and Boutros (Peter) being brothers. They came to Australia together in the 1890s but Boutros returned to Lebanon while Nicholas remained in Australia.

My sister, Pauline, gave me Catherine Taylor's book, *Once upon a Time in Beirut*, to read in preparation for my visit. I spoke with Jamil Skaff who had established contact with Khalil and met up with him in Beirut. Last Christmas, I visited the graves of my grandparents and great-grandparents in Cooma, asking them to watch out for me on my visit to the land of their birth. I anxiously watched the news as the time for my visit approached, hoping that yet another conflict would not break out in the meantime. One time I emailed Pascal telling him that I would rely on him to advise me on how safe it would be to visit. He replied, 'You'll have to make your own decisions; we live here [under that sort of cloud] day by day.'

As it was, I planned to be in Lebanon for the last week of February. My mother would have turned 100 on 29 February and I felt it was fitting to celebrate in the country of her forebears. Thanks to Khalil, accommodation was arranged for me at the Melkite Patriarchate at Rabweh which is high up in the hills overlooking the harbour in Beirut. I was given a grand welcome at the airport by Khalil, Pascal, several other cousins, Bishop Salim el Ghazal and Maroun Bourjeily, President of the Greek Catholic League. (The Melkites refer to themselves as Greek Catholics. Their patriarch normally lives in Damascus, but I had the good fortune to meet him on a brief visit while I was in Beirut.) Khalil generously gave up a week of his life to care for me while I was in his country and his wife, Marcelle, and sons, Pascal and Alain, made me at home in all kinds of ways.

The two things I had hoped to achieve were to meet my relatives and to visit Mashghara, their home town. Everything else would be a bonus. Mashghara is about two hours from Beirut, in the southern part of the Bekaa Valley, and we made our way there the day after my arrival. We were accompanied by Bishop Salim who is also a native of Mashghara. Two weeks earlier we would not have got through because of snow which was still very much in evidence. We stopped at Zahle where we met the archbishop, Andre Haddad, a very kind and down-to-earth person. We travelled through a series of towns and I should add that we passed through many army checkpoints, but without drama. Just before we reached Mashghara we stopped for a coffee at a resort overlooking a large artificial lake and were served by a young man called Baraki, a native of Mashghara, and, I was told, quite possibly related to the Macks in Australia (their Arabic name was Baraki). Along the way we had great views of snow-covered Mount Hermon of biblical fame. The last time I had viewed it was from Israel in 1988.

My heart leapt as I saw the sign telling us we had arrived in Mashghara. Bishop Salim had arranged for the church to be opened for us and it was so special to bless myself from the font in which my ancestors had been baptised. Outside, I picked a small sprig from a cedar in the grounds. It remains a treasured souvenir. I was shown the bell tower which was financed from Australia in 1921 by Amin Bookallil, another brother of Nicholas and Boutros. Khalil showed us four of the family homes, all quite near the church. Although he was born in Senegal (in 1940), Khalil and his brother, Sammy, lived in Mashghara during the time of their primary schooling. Apparently, Mashghara means 'lots of water' and I enjoyed drinking from the abundant fountain just outside the church. It used to be a thriving town with about 5000 Christians, but there are now only 300, the remainder being Muslim. Most of the former Christian population are to be found today in Ottawa. There is a regular Mass celebrated in Mashghara by a priest who cares for a number of neighbouring towns. Bishop Salim celebrates a Mass on 15 August each year and this is a time of reunion for many of the former townspeople. Khalil told me that at the time of World War II an Australian Bookallil had visited Mashghara. I told him the only person I could think of was Gordon Bookallil and David Bookallil has since confirmed that to be correct.

During 2006, when I said a Mass for peace in Lebanon for the people of Canberra, I based my homily on the premise that hospitality was the outstanding quality that I had observed in Lebanese people. I was treated to an abundance of it during my short stay. Relatives and many others, all previously unknown to me were the soul of kindness. After a delightful day at Harissa, a shrine to Our Lady high up overlooking Beirut, I was treated to a sumptuous meal by Magdalen, wife of cousin Tony, before being taken to a meeting of the Greek Catholic League of which Khalil is a member. They are similar to the Knights of the Southern Cross in Australia. They asked me to encourage Lebanese people in Australia to take a greater interest in what is happening in their country of origin, and to take out dual citizenship to enable them to vote in Lebanese elections.

They expressed concern at the exodus of Christians from their country. They also told me of what they were doing to promote Muslim-Christian dialogue, showing me replies of gratitude they had received for good will messages sent by them on the occasion of a Muslim feast. They came from the President of Iran, the King of Saudi Arabia, the President of Egypt, the King of Jordan, the President of Kuwait and the President of Yemin. In 2007, Bishop Salim el Ghazal received in New York an international peace award for his promotion of dialogue among Christians and Muslims. I witnessed him giving a lecture to Muslims and his own people during my visit. I was reminded of what Bishop Issam Darwish, the Melkite bishop in Australia, is doing to give a lead in inter-faith dialogue. The members of the Greek Catholic League presented me with an inscribed plaque as a memento of my visit.

As well as the ever-present army checkpoints, I saw scars of war all through Beirut, including the shell of the destroyed Holiday Inn. One evening, after a meal at Khalil and Marcelle's home, I heard nearby gunfire which caused me not a little concern. Apparently it was a show of support for a Muslim politician who was talking on TV at the time. During my stay, Lebanon had been without a president for a number of months, causing considerable concern. The day before I left Beirut I was taken to meet the Maronite cardinal patriarch. Given that the president has to be Maronite, this gentle old man has a great deal of influence on the political life of the country. Khalil told me he is a reluctant power-broker. Something like the pope in Rome, he conducts daily audiences with all kinds of people. I was briefly on TV that night meeting him, while other more important people were giving interviews. I might add that the whole compound was heavily guarded. One evening, as I was travelling in the car, the radio was broadcasting the news. While I could not understand what was being said, I was fascinated to hear the word 'Hezbollah' in just about every sentence. There was no fighting during my week in Lebanon, but it seemed to be a fragile peace.

On 29 February, after going to the chapel of the patriarchate to pray for my mother who would have turned 100 that day, I was taken down the coast to the south in the direction of the biblical town of Sidon. Just before Sidon we travelled inland to St Saviour's Monastery. It was here that Khalil and his brother, Sammy, did their secondary education. Today it educates Muslim as well as Christian children. The monastery was founded in 1711 and the church in 1720. The church houses a chandelier which was a gift of

Napoleon III. The monastery produces for sale, wine, olive oil, soap, jams, preserved fruit, arak, rose and other syrups. During World War II, it had a thriving bakery which provided for the needs of the local community as well as the monastery.

From there we proceeded to the town of Mantara, with its shrine commemorating the place where Our Lady is supposed to have waited for Jesus while he preached in nearby Sidon (Mark 7:24). The tradition has it that because Sidon was a pagan town, Mary could not go there so she waited in Mantara through which Jesus would have to pass as he was returning to Galilee. The image of Mary waiting patiently was beautifully depicted. On my mother's birthday, I recalled her great patience and prayed that I could possess something of the patience of the mother of Jesus and my own mother.

Leaving Mantara, we passed by a Palestinian refugee camp before reaching Sidon as the sun was setting over the historic port city. I would have liked to have visited a Palestinian refugee camp while I was in Lebanon, but I was acutely aware of the sensitivity of the camps and the opportunity simply did not present itself. After leaving Sidon, I read of a project which has resulted in the building of an ancient Phoenician rowing boat which is planned to be rowed around the Mediterranean Sea in quest of peace with 17 crew members of differing religions.

Among other blessings of a productive week, I had about an hour with the Melkite patriarch, Gregory III, with whom I identified in many ways. The next day, many of the extended Abukhalil family gathered at the patriarchate to be present at a Mass celebrated with him before adjourning to the Royal Hotel for a splendid family dinner. I am told that there are up to 75,000 Abukhalils in Lebanon. Khalil tells me that about 5000 of them are Shiite Muslim. Apparently some time back one of the Christian men fell in love with a Muslim girl and the only way they could marry was for him to become a Muslim. Khalil would say that there is something different, something special about Abukhalil Shiites, as if their Christian roots are still bearing fruit.

Before leaving Beirut, Khalil took me to the north to the ancient port town of Jbeil which served as a fortress. From there we went almost vertically up the mountain to where St Charbel's body is venerated. He lived a saintly life as a hermit, but what attracted me to him is that he is venerated not only by Christians but by Sunnis, Shiites and Druze as well. After we descended the mountain, Khalil picked up some photos taken with the Maronite patriarch earlier in my stay and gave me an excellent selection.

I wrote at the end of my diary: 'He then drove me to the airport. We have developed a lovely bond this week and I'll never forget his goodness to me in making this last week one of the most memorable of my life.'

When I left my motherland, it was not only with nostalgia but with a real sense of hope that this peace-loving people would finally achieve their dream. Some time later there was a major conflict but one that was quickly resolved and, in the aftermath, there was an 'outbreak of peace' with the appointment of a president who seems to be a good leader. Yet I know that it is very much an ongoing saga, just as I experienced in the rest of my journey which took in Lourdes, the *camino* to Santiago de Compostela and Ireland, the land of my father. We plan as best we can, but then take one step at a time and trust in God to walk at our side.

East Timor

An account of a momentous first visit to this country which has been part of the author's psyche since he witnessed the brave people's struggles for justice and independence in the 1990s, written in January 2013.

Although in the 1990s I campaigned vigorously for the rights of the East Timorese people, I had not had the opportunity to visit Timor-Leste till Christmas 2012. Thanks to Nat McGahey and Domingos Oki and his family, and having retired in the middle of the year, I was able to spend two fascinating weeks among one of Australia's nearer neighbours. It is only an hour's flying time between Darwin and Dili and it is hard to understand how the atrocities that took place in East Timor since 1975 were largely ignored by Australia.

Domingos Oki is the first Timorese graduate from RMC Duntroon and I was honoured to be present at his and Sally's wedding in Canberra and later to attend the baptism of their son, John. Oki has since gained his Masters from Macquarie University and now holds an important position in the Defence Department. His former boss, Taur Matan Ruak, one of the freedom fighters of the Resistance, is now the President of Timor Leste, having defeated Jose Ramos Horta for the position. While I was in Timor, Jose Ramos Horta was appointed to a key role in the United Nations.

For the past 12 years, Nat McGahey has supported Timorese students here in Canberra, Oki being one of them. Many have stayed in his home and all have been helped in a great variety of ways to take advantage of educational opportunities that will enhance theirs and their country's futures. Sally and Oki and their extended family offered the most generous hospitality to Nat, his son Tim and me during those two weeks.

We didn't travel too far from Dili, but we ventured up into the hills to Dare where we saw the tributes to the Timorese people protecting Australian troops from the Japanese in 1942; those same hills where the Timorese resistance fighters campaigned against the Indonesian army. We visited the War Heroes' Cemetery in Metinaro where Sally's father is honoured and later met Sally's mother in nearby Hera. Sally's mother also had been a freedom fighter and I had seen a picture of her holding an AK46 rifle. I had expected to meet an old lady but I met a vivacious woman who could have passed as Sally's sister. I was asked to bless the house when we arrived. This was a small ritual which was observed in just about every family we visited. They would set up a little shrine with holy pictures, statues, etc., and provide me with some water to bless. I brought with me a stole and fortunately Nat had a missal which offered some suitable prayers and readings.

While we were in Dili, the University of Peace had its graduation and I was taken to two families where there were celebrations during which I was asked to bless the graduates and the houses as well as the families and guests.

On the two Sundays we were there we went to Mass at St Anthony's Church at Motael and on Christmas Day we went to the cathedral. I met the priest after the Christmas Mass and he invited us all to call on the bishop on Christmas afternoon. I thought the bishop might be too tired to be entertaining us but the priest insisted and Bishop Ricardo was very hospitable to us all and not at all upset when little John knocked over the dish of nuts! The two Sunday Masses at Motael were animated with lots of participation and wonderful singing by the largely youthful congregation. The same priest celebrated the Mass on both Sundays and had a great gift of engaging the congregation. He had them in fits of laughter for much of the time, but Oki assured me that he had a serious message in each case.

It was in that church that an 18-year-old student, Sebastian Gomes, was shot dead by the Indonesian army in October 1991. On 12 November there was a commemoration of his death which included a procession from the church to the Santa Cruz cemetery. Members of the Indonesian Army surrounded the cemetery opening fire and killing over 200 people. This has become known as the Santa Cruz massacre. Much of it was filmed by Max Stahl who secretly sent the film to England where it was shown on BBC

TV. The brutality exposed there alerted the world to what had been happening in various ways since 1975 when the Indonesians took over from the Portuguese. Thousands of East Timorese were killed in that time. I had a chance meeting with Max Stahl at a coffee bar while I was in Dili.

At the Dili airport on the way home, I bought *Circles of Silence,* Shirley Shackleton's book which outlines the events surrounding the murder of her husband, Greg, and four other journalists at Balibo in 1975. It is not just a probe into their tragic deaths but a powerful history of the recent struggle of the Timorese people to determine their own future. Shirley is not a Catholic but recognises the important role the Catholic Church has played in the Timorese quest for independence. Early in my visit, I was taken to the huge field where Pope John Paul celebrated Mass in 1996. Shirley believes that the Indonesians manipulated much of that, but were unsuccessful in having the Mass in Indonesian. Instead the Pope celebrated the Mass in English with Bishop Belo translating into Tetun. She also points out that the Nobel Peace Prize awarded to Bishop Belo and Jose Ramos Horta brought much-needed world attention to the struggle for independence. Much of all that was dramatically depicted at the Resistance Museum which we visited in Dili not long before we left.

On another day trip we visited Liquica, the scene of another church massacre in which hundreds were killed, including a priest and three nuns. At the church we met a diminutive old lady, a catechist, who was a survivor of that terrible day.

The time of our visit to Timor was the wet season and although we avoided the worst of it, we were prevented from reaching our destination to Railaco one day when we were hit by a deluge up in the hills. I had hoped to visit the mission of Good Samaritan Sister Rita Hayes, even though I knew she was back in Australia for Christmas. Similarly, I missed seeing Josephite Sister Julianne who had returned to New Zealand for Christmas. However, Nat was able to pass on some material at the Mary MacKillop Centre in Dili which he had brought from Australia.

Sisters of St Joseph, Susan Connelly and Josephine Mitchell, have been stalwarts in Australia in solidarity with the people of East Timor. I will never forget those dark days in September 1999 immediately after the East

Timorese people had voted overwhelmingly in favour of independence. All hell broke loose as the militia went on a killing spree with the support of the Indonesian army. Things were so bad that I feared that the whole population of East Timor would be slaughtered. The United Nations withdrew and all foreigners were forced to leave. I will never forget an interview given by Sister Susan Connelly on ABC radio. The interviewer asked Susan what was on my heart: 'Is this the end of the East Timorese people?' Susan replied with hope and conviction, 'Nothing will crush the spirit of the Timorese people.'

While I was in Dili I met an impressive couple from California who have lived on and off in Timor Leste for a long time. Gabriel teaches high school science (in Tetun), but it was his wife, Pam, that I managed to speak with. When she told me that they had been in East Timor since the 1990s, I asked her whether she was there for the referendum and its terrible after-math. She told me of the huge dilemma faced in a particular way by herself and three other women. They feared that if they left Dili they would be leaving the local population to a cruel fate. As it turned out, the decision was taken out of their hands and they were flown out of Dili to Darwin. As soon as they landed they were met by a host of journalists who were able to take their heart-rending stories to the outside world. Pam described her own personal experience as she became very emotional describing the hor-rible events she had left behind. Finally, the United States under President Bill Clinton and Australia under PM John Howard could see that enough was enough and a United Nations force returned to provide the stability and protection needed for the people of East Timor. I spent two weeks in hospital in December 1999 after a serious car accident. I clearly remember the exuberant TV images of the Australian soldiers under General Peter Cosgrove celebrating the lead-up to Christmas with the Dili population, especially the children. From memory, I think they got rained upon, but it didn't ruin their parade. My nephew, Geoffrey de Jongh, then a captain and an engineer in the Australian army would spend four months in Dili in 2006 as part of the reconstruction process.

Because of the mass killings after 1975, there is almost a whole genera-tion missing, with very few people of my age. But there are lots and lots of kids, many of whom are poor but all that I saw were delightful. They are soccer-mad and many wore T-shirts with names such as Ronaldo, Rooney and Messi on their backs. As I was on a walk one day, I passed a dusty field where there was a muck-up game of kids' soccer in progress. A goal was scored and the defending goalie was the smallest lad on the field. He was really cranky with himself for having conceded the goal. In the ensuing play shortly afterwards there was another raid on his goal and this time the little bloke saved it. I will never forget the verve with which he then kicked the ball up the other end of the field. In some ways that little scene said so much about the people of Timor Leste and their unwillingness to accept defeat.

There is seemingly no bitterness among the people towards the Indonesian people and in fact there is some intermarriage. They recognise that it is not the Indonesian people who did such terrible things but a harsh regime who often perpetrated the same cruelty on their own people. Shirley Shackleton makes that point many times in her book.

Canberra and Dili have a friendship city relationship and I took with me a couple of letters from our Chief Minister, Katy Gallagher, telling among other things of the Dollars for Dili project which is part of Canberra's centenary celebrations.

On the final night in Dili, we were taken to dinner by a dozen of the former students whom Nat has supported in their university studies. All have graduated, some with a number of degrees. It was touching to see them honouring Nat and also to know that Timor Leste has such great talent among its future leaders. Many of them are in key positions already. At the airport, as we were leaving Dili, I met a group of impressive Carmelite seminarians with their Australian superior, Fr Keith Clark. They were farewelling an Australian lad preparing to join the order. In another sphere they too were symbols of hope and strength for their country and their church.

The two weeks in Dili gave me only a glimpse of a limited part of life in a nation just over ten years old. I saw a lot of material poverty and many health and educational challenges, but also a great spirit and resourcefulness among beautiful people. I hope that foreign aid and the royalties from the gas and oil resources will provide the much needed finances to help this emerging nation to realise its full potential. Timor Leste deserves a great future.

Funeral Mass for Pope John Paul II

Homily given at St Christopher's Cathedral at the Canberra Funeral Mass for the recently deceased Pope, 8 April 2005.

On 24 November 1986, Pope John Paul's plane touched down at Fairbairn Air Base on the first stop of a wonderful Australian papal visit.

The pope recalled his 1973 visit as a cardinal to Canberra and Queanbeyan – a visit which is still especially remembered vividly and fondly by the Polish community in this area.

He told us that in his 1986 visit he was coming as a *pilgrim*, as a *pastor* to the Catholic community, as a *fellow Christian* to all who believed in Jesus and as a *friend* to every person of good will.

All those hopes materialised when, in one short week,

— he met with Australia's political leaders, the governor-general (Sir Ninian Stephen), the prime minister (Bob Hawke) and the leader of the opposition (John Howard) here in Canberra;

— he uplifted the handicapped and disabled people in Brisbane;

— he danced with young people at the Sydney Cricket Ground;

— he donned a hard hat and met workers on the factory floor in the western suburbs of Sydney;

— he affirmed a skill-share program for unemployed people in Hobart;

— he sat in a classroom with primary school children in Melbourne;

— in what was probably the highlight of his Australian visit, at Alice Springs he acknowledged the Aboriginal people as

Australia's first inhabitants, gave support for their land rights, affirmed their spirituality and culture as precious and not incompatible with Christianity, and stressed the need for reconciliation among all Australians;
— he upheld the dignity of old people in Perth on the final leg of his visit.

Throughout his Australian visit, John Paul II showed his deep commitment to ecumenism by meetings and prayers with other Christian leaders.

His 1986 Australian visit proved to be a microcosm of his twenty-six and a half years of papal ministry.

Many of us recall the Canberra Mass at the National Exhibition Centre for nearly 100,000 people. The Mass celebrated by the pope was for Justice and Peace, themes so consistently part of John Paul's teaching. It was earlier that year that the Pope had called together in Assisi the world's religious leaders – Christian and non-Christian to pray for peace. At the Canberra Mass he reminded us that there could be no true and lasting peace without an underlying commitment to justice.

Last Sunday morning, we awoke to the news of Pope John Paul II's death. At Mass that day the gospel gave us the first words of the Risen Lord to his disciples: 'Peace be with you.'

Each year, in his New Year Message, John Paul has given to the world his message of peace. He has reminded the people of the world as he did in Canberra that there can be no true peace without justice, that we need to find inner peace with ourselves, that we must seek peace with God and peace with one another.

Many times in his pontificate he made direct appeals to world leaders, especially in times of war or the threat of war. I think especially of his consistent opposition to the invasion of Iraq where right up to the last he appealed for diplomatic and peaceful remedies to be found for the problems besetting Iraq.

He made many personal visits to trouble spots, sometimes putting his own life on the line. I think of his visits to Lebanon, to Sarajevo in Bosnia during the Balkans war and his Jubilee 2000 visit to the Holy Land which offered every possibility for peace in that troubled part of our world.

The pope saw forgiveness as a vital ingredient for peace and what more powerful example could be given than the image of him visiting his would-be assassin, Mehmet Ali Ağca, in his prison cell and embracing him in forgiveness.

In the Jubilee Year 2000, the pope offered his apologies for the hurts the Catholic Church had inflicted in the course of its history. This evening I would like to update and extend that apology to any people here who have found themselves hurt by the church or by any member or members of the church.

As a champion of peace, Pope John Paul was a vigorous defender of human life in every form. Not only did he defend vulnerable unborn children in condemning abortion, and the frail, elderly and dying in speaking out against euthanasia, but he pointed out the deadly aspects of war and advanced the church's teaching in his opposition to the death penalty. At times he specifically pleaded for the lives of people on death row.

Tonight, almost simultaneously with Pope John Paul's funeral liturgy in Rome, we celebrate his life and death in the context of the Eucharist. Tonight's gospel gives us Jesus' words: 'Those who eat my flesh and drink my blood will have eternal life and I shall raise them up on the last day.'

The celebration of the Eucharist permeated the whole of John Paul's priestly ministry. He continually taught that the Eucharist is at the heart of our Christian life. He proclaimed a Year of the Eucharist which we are now celebrating from October 2004 to October 2005.

In the apostolic Letter for this Year of the Eucharist, he writes: 'The Christian who takes part in the Eucharist learns to become a promoter of communion, peace and solidarity.'

He then takes up the theme of his homily here in Canberra in 1986. He pleads for the Year of the Eucharist to be a special opportunity to respond with fraternal solicitude to the many forms of poverty in today's world. 'I think for example of the tragedy of hunger which plagues hundreds of millions of human beings, the diseases which afflict developing countries, the loneliness of the elderly, the hardships faced by the unemployed, the struggles of immigrants ... By our concern for those in need we will be recognised as true followers of Christ. This will be the criterion by which the authenticity of our Eucharistic celebrations will be judged.'

May I add one more challenge – an ecumenical one. Tonight and on many similar occasions we are constrained to deny the Eucharist to our non-Catholic sisters and brothers even though many of their churches feel free to offer Eucharistic hospitality to fellow Christians. This is a very painful reality to all concerned. As Catholics, we see Eucharistic communion flowing out of full ecclesial communion. Surely this must be a heart-felt goal for all of us. Pope John Paul promoted it strongly in many of his writings, especially his 1995 encyclical *Ut unum sint.* A prominent part of his ministry as pope was his meetings with the world's religious leaders, and his visits to other countries invariably included prayer services and meetings with non-Catholic Christians. May we all make a special prayerful effort during this year's Week of Prayer for Christian Unity which culminates at Pentecost on 15 May.

This last week has been a momentous and moving time for us all. I wish to pay special tribute to the media for the way in which you have enabled Australians and the world – Catholic and non-Catholic alike – to focus on the outstanding life, achievements and holiness of a wonderful leader and an extraordinary human being. The depth and breadth of the coverage of Pope John Paul's life and ministry has encapsulated a great legacy to human history.

We will all have our deeply personal memories and emotions of this past week. But for all of us it has been a time of grace when we have thanked God for the second longest serving successor of St Peter, when we have reflected on Pope John Paul II as a peace-maker and a bridge-builder, as a holy man of God and as a shepherd of his flock who has revealed to us more clearly the face of Jesus and the unconditional love of God.

Pope John Paul II has departed this life, but we continue to walk as a pilgrim people praying on our journey with hope and confidence: 'The Lord is my shepherd, there is nothing I shall want.'

Graham Greene

An article written for the *St Vincent de Paul Profile* , June 1991, and further reflections.

Just after Easter I was on holidays at Narooma where I met a young woman trying to make sense of her life. She had been through a broken marriage, was struggling with alcoholism and drugs – and she was in the middle of reading *Monsignor Quixote.*

We both spoke of Graham Greene as if he were an old friend. In a way he was; and we both found in him and in his characters much with which we could identify. A day or so later news came of his death and I returned to my friend to drink (a cup of coffee!) in his honour and to mourn his passing.

A week further on, there was a brief news report stating that the great man had been buried in Geneva after a Requiem Mass attended by sixty people including his estranged wife. The celebrant of the Mass was a Spanish priest friend who had earlier ministered to him the last rites of the church. A person whose writings had reached millions of people was buried in near obscurity. Yet I suspect that Greene chuckled at such irony.

I think I was still at school when I first read *The Power and the Glory.* Coming back to it when I was older, I developed a real fondness for Greene and his characters. It is now quite a while since I read *Brighton Rock, The End of the Affair* and *The Heart of the Matter,* but I remember being engrossed by them at the time.

Monsignor Quixote especially, on film with Sir Alec Guinness and Leo McKern, was delightful. Written just a few years ago, *Monsignor Quixote* contains the paradoxes and struggles of Greene's earlier writings, but it is all in a much lighter vein.

Graham Greene, the great Catholic novelist, often questioned his own Catholicity. I always felt sad when Greene referred to himself as something of a half-baked Catholic. He became a Catholic on the occasion of his marriage but he was far from being a nominal Catholic. His Catholicism runs through so many of his writings from *The Power and the Glory* to *Monsignor Quixote*.

The brilliant novelist had a real understanding of the struggles of human life, of the reality of original sin and of the weaknesses of human nature. But he also recognised the reality of Jesus' redeeming love and God's forgiveness, mercy and compassion.

In one way, the whisky priest in *The Power and the Glory* got it all wrong, but ultimately through God's grace he got it all right. Monsignor Quixote was able to have a deep and genuine friendship with Sancho, the communist mayor, without in any way compromising his own principles. That the bishop and the civil authorities did not understand was their problem.

Many of Greene's characters were sinners, but they were also searchers. Undoubtedly, they reflected much of the tension in the author himself. He felt that made him less of a Catholic. I personally found those characters attractive because there is much about them with which we can all identify, if we are honest enough to admit it. I suppose I must acknowledge, too, that I have an admiration for the 'little people' who are brave enough to poke fun at the establishment occasionally.

Most of all, Graham Greene recognised the triumph of God's grace over sin and human failure. He never lost sight of God's love (which sustained him through some dark times) and he never gave up on the Catholic Church. In fact, he was at the time of his death a trustee of *The Tablet*, the international Catholic weekly published in London.

Pope John Paul II in his latest encyclical writes: 'The poor ask for the right to share in enjoying material goods and to make good use of their capacity for work, thus creating a world that is more just and prosperous for us all.' Graham Greene would undoubtedly say 'Amen' to that. Like good members of the St Vincent de Paul Society, our friend was at home with the poor and the oppressed; he upheld their dignity and called for justice and fairness for everyone.

I leave the last word to Tom Burns, writing in *The Tablet*.

Some serenity came to us both in our eighties. I recall a weekend in Antibes with him, when there was some feasting and a Mass shared in the local church while like two publicans from the gospel we stood at the back; my 80th birthday party at home when Graham came, to be devoured by my family and friends. It is not for me to make judgement of anyone, but in Graham's case I shall always value his life-long resistance to world fame. Blessed are the poor in spirit.

Afterword

Just before beginning eight months long-service leave in 2008, I was delighted to come upon a treasure in a secondhand bookshop: *Graham Greene, Friend and Brother*, by Leopoldo Duran, the priest earlier referred to as presiding over the great man's funeral. I eagerly looked forward to reading it, but had to put it aside until I returned from travelling overseas, part of which would include trekking part of the pilgrimage to Santiago de Compostela in Spain.

Part of my daily ritual on the pilgrim walk was to stop each morning after a couple of hours on the track go into a bar and enjoy a cup of coffee and a pastry, say my morning prayer from my little breviary and have a glance at the newspaper which was usually available. In April, just a day or two before I was due to arrive in Santiago after almost a month's walking, I came across this report:

Deceased in Vigo, Leopoldo Duran, intimate friend of Graham Greene. The most knowledgeable authority of the personality , the thinking, the sentiments and the work of the British writer, Graham Greene, the priest Leopoldo Duran died on Thursday aged 90. He was buried yesterday in his birthplace, Penedo de Avion, surrounded by his family. How he became the loyal friend and trusted guardian of the personal keys of Graham Greene in the last part of the life of the great English novelist can be traced in the novel, *Monsignor Quixote,* which came out of their travels together in Spain and Portugal.

The newspaper report went on to detail some of Father Duran's writing on his dear friend:

'The crisis in the priesthood in Graham Greene'
'A study on *The Power and the Glory*'
'Graham Greene, friend and brother'
'The doctors and Graham Greene'

Needless to say, I could not wait to get back to Australia to read Fr Duran's moving biography of his very dear friend. The book is a chronicle of the rich friendship shared by two men coming from very different backgrounds but united in their shared humanity, sense of humour and belief in God's love for us all.

The book's back cover invites would-be readers to an exciting adventure:

In the later years of his life, Graham Greene's closest male friend was Leopoldo Duran, a Spanish Catholic priest. Over more than twenty years the two men would meet at least once a year and each summer set off by car, journeying through North-West Spain and Portugal. These holidays were tremendously important to Greene, inspiring his last great novel, *Monsignor Quixote*. Duran's book gives the first informed account of the older Greene's Roman Catholic faith. Contrary to much opinion, Greene never divorced himself completely from the church. His attitude is succinctly summarised in his words to Duran. 'The trouble is I don't believe my unbelief.'

Bishop Geoffrey Robinson

A defence of a brave bishop in the face of criticism by his brother bishops, written for *Catholica Australia*, **May 2008.**

The lot of a prophet is rarely a comfortable one. Geoffrey Robinson, with his great knowledge and love of the Scriptures, would understand that better than most. Yet he chose such a path when he wrote *Confronting Power and Sex in the Catholic Church: Reclaiming the Spirit of Jesus.*

In many ways, he had no other option but to write such a book. Since the late 1980s when revelations of sexual abuse within the Catholic Church began to surface, Bishop Robinson was at the forefront in addressing the issue. He began by listening to victims, hearing first hand the stories and witnessing the pain and damage of those most affected. He saw too the effects on families, parish and school communities and other people involved. He began to understand something of the complexity of factors which led to abuse. He saw it as necessary as well to get inside the skin of those responsible for the abuse.

It was largely his leadership among the Australian bishops which led to the publication of *Towards Healing* which gives protocols for receiving complaints of abuse by church personnel and, also, *Integrity in Ministry* which sets standards of conduct for those involved in the ministerial life of the Catholic Church.

At the same time, he urged his brother bishops to listen to victims and to deal decisively with complaints of abuse. But he saw the need to go deeper. It is imperative to look not just at the causes of individual instances of abuse, but to try to understand the systemic weaknesses and failures which underlie such a betrayal of trust and power.

The Australian bishops in their recent statement on Bishop Robinson's book acknowledge their indebtedness to him for his huge contribution in this area. But it goes much deeper than that. When I became a bishop in 1986, Geoffrey Robinson had been a member of the Bishops' Conference for two years and even at that early stage he was consistently called upon for advice by his brother bishops. I remember the late Archbishop Guilford Young enthusiastically nominating him to represent Australia at a Synod of Bishops in Rome, extolling his distinguished qualities. I regard him as possessing the finest mind among my fellow bishops in the 22 years I have been part of the Conference.

Those aware of Geoffrey Robinson's contribution to the Marriage Tribunal, to Catholic education at all levels, and to the pastoral life of the church generally, have seen him as a truly Christ-like person. Through retreats, lectures and seminars he has enabled laity, religious and clergy to develop their potential among the People of God. He has sought to promote conversation within and beyond the Catholic Church through Catalyst for Renewal and Spirituality in the Pub, thereby connecting with many people who otherwise would be left on the outer.

When I read Bishop Robinson's book, I recognised anew the author's great love for God and his people, his deepest desires for the church to be true to its mission in bringing Christ to the world and his great honesty and courage in naming the challenges facing the Church today. Here was a faithful son of the church wanting it to be its best self, while knowing it was *ecclesia semper reformanda*, a church continually in need of reform.

The bishop has drawn on his expertise in the Scriptures to tackle some of the thorny questions surrounding the nature of Christ and the church which have occupied the attention of saints and scholars for most of the church's 2000 year history. So many of these heroic members of the church have been dismissed or condemned in their own day only to be fully understood and appreciated later on. I think of Blessed Mary MacKillop and Catherine McAuley, as well as many distinguished theologians under a cloud prior to the Second Vatican Council. History has shown that immediate judgements very often are subsequently proved to be wrong.

In calling the Second Vatican Council, Pope John XXIII sought to 'open the windows' to allow the winds of the Holy Spirit to renew the life of the church. It saddens me that much of the openness which Vatican II stood for is now being shut down.

In response to Geoffrey Robinson's book, I detected a renewed sense of hope among those who read it. I am told that it has sold like no other religious book in Australia in recent years. That is surely a message from the grass-roots where people's deepest sense of faith is finding its expression.

Pope Benedict's recent visit to the United States has been acclaimed a success, largely through the Pope's honesty in facing up to the issues around sexual abuse in the life of the church. I dare to say that is precisely what Bishop Robinson has been doing for twenty years and what he has courageously set out in his book *Confronting Power and Sex in the Catholic Church: Reclaiming the Spirit of Jesus*.

I recently saw a quote from Pope John XXIII which could aptly be applied to Geoffrey Robinson:

All believers must be a spark of light, a centre of love, a vivifying leaven amidst their fellow human beings: and they will be this all the more perfectly they live in communion with God. In fact there can be no peace between people unless there is peace within each one of them.

Bishop Bill Morris

A response to the Toowoomba Leadership Group who had written to all Australian bishops in the aftermath of the sacking of their much-admired bishop, 10 August 2011.

Rev. Peter Schultz JCL, Associate Judicial Vicar
John Elich, Chair, Toowoomba Diocesan Leadership Group

Dear Peter and John,

I am responding to your 3 August letter with the accompanying petition containing 2722 signatures expressing concern around a number of aspects of the forced retirement of Bishop William Morris. I note from your letter that a further 411 signatures have since been added.

At the outset, I wish to express my deep disappointment at the treatment Bishop Morris has received. Like you, I see him and the whole diocese as being victims of a great miscarriage of justice.

When I gave the priests' retreat in Toowoomba in 2003, when I spent time in the diocese during the National Council of Priests Convention in 2006 and in many other instances when I have observed with admiration so many positive features of the diocese, I have consistently been given the impression not only that the Diocese of Toowoomba was in good shape but that it was responding positively to the Second Vatican Council's vision for the church today. I saw Bishop Morris' inspiring leadership as being an integral part of such a healthy local church. I noted too the strong bonds of communion existing between bishop, clergy and the faithful.

My observations showed a far-flung diocese doing everything possible to see that individual and community needs were being met in Christ-like fashion with healthy ecumenical and community relations and with a real care for issues of justice, peace and development.

In an age when so many people both within and outside the Catholic fold are asking legitimate questions about the life of the church today, Bishop Morris courageously gave voice to such issues. Among Bishop Bill's strengths are that he is a good listener, that he has never lost touch with the 'joys and the hopes, the griefs and anxieties' of his people and that he courageously attempts to have the Church respond as Jesus himself would have done.

As a close friend of Bishop Bill and sharing his vision for the church today, I have been aware for a number of years of his problems with the Holy See. I have admired the way in which he has loyally done everything possible to remain in communion with the pope as the successor of Peter. I admired how step by step he tried to have an honest conversation with Vatican officials and finally with the pope himself. I do not believe that he always felt that there was genuine reciprocity in the dialogue.

Surely in a healthy church we should be able to 'speak the truth in love'. I do not believe that any of us are doing justice to the mission of Jesus when we neglect to name the issues which are haemorrhaging the church at the moment. Our current woes around sexual abuse should provide important lessons here. It is not insignificant that Bishop Morris provided excellent leadership in this domain locally, nationally and internationally.

I note your questions to the Australian Bishops Permanent Committee which met earlier this month. I note from the minutes of that committee that its members are resolved to take up your issues as part of the upcoming *Ad Limina* visit to Rome.

For my part, I wish to express my solidarity with all the people of Toowoomba Diocese in these difficult times. I add my voice to Bishop Morris' plea for you not to walk away from the church as you might be tempted to do. It is your spiritual home as much as it is Pope Benedict's. Like Bishop Bill we all need to act with faith, hope and love and with his passion for truth and justice. More than ever, our world today needs the message of Jesus. You people of Toowoomba are in a unique position to witness to that in the best of the Catholic tradition.

If you consider that it would help your cause, I am happy for this letter to be made public.

Your brother in Christ, (Bishop) Pat Power

Gloria

This reflection and the one that follows honour two noble and much-loved Irish Wolfhounds, 9 July 2005

One of my earliest memories of Gloria was in late 1995, when she was a (rather large) puppy packed into Geraldine's Ford Laser with Molly, her ten-year old mentor, and Cruise, who was a little younger than Gloria. They were on the first leg of their journey to Tasmania where Gloria spent her first few years.

The last time I saw her was just over a month ago, this time in the back of Geraldine's Verada in her own special compartment, heading off to Anglesea to be with Uncle Tony and Jean. Today while I am staying at her old home in Tassie, I got word of her death just short of her tenth birthday. I am told that for a Wolfhound to live to ten, is as great an achievement as a human living to a hundred.

Gloria had a happy life and brought lots of joy to those around her. I never realised I could become so fond of a dog as I was of her. Geraldine tells me that when an eight-week-old puppy is taken from its litter, the new owner becomes its family. Gloria was a beautiful part of Geraldine's life, seemingly knowing all about her, attentive to her every word, movement and feeling. It was more than a rapport which existed between them.

In some ways Gloria was indulged – sleeping inside, fed well, cared for and exercised regularly. She appreciated all the affection she was given and returned it abundantly. In some ways she wasn't particularly sociable towards strangers, even the many admirers she met on her walks. But at home she always liked to be the hostess, enthusiastically greeting people who came to the house.

In her fitter days she ran three km with me around the block, especially when I was training to carry the Olympic Torch in 2000. She enjoyed her walks on Mt Ainslie, with the opportunity to chase kangaroos, (which she never caught). She chased every cat she spotted (except Carolin's) and on her lake walks went after waterfowl (but not other birds) and to her mother's disgust rolled in a dead carp if she spotted it before Geraldine.

Irish Wolfhounds are the tallest domestic dog, which meant that Gloria had to endure comments such as, 'You could put a saddle on him'; 'It must cost a fortune to feed'; 'Can I have a ride on him?' Those comments were more than outweighed by people telling us how beautiful and gracious she was. Of course, we already knew that!

She didn't have puppies of her own but was always nice to others. Little dogs seem to think it is their mission in life to take the mickey out of big dogs, but Gloria responded only with disdain, never with aggression. In fact, I don't recall ever seeing her angry – with canines or humans.

She loved her food and was grateful for the treats given her by Audrey and for all the other care our good neighbour gave her.

Life wasn't quite the same for her when Carolin and her dogs left Canberra a couple of years ago. Gloria was made one of the family among them and had lots of enjoyable stays at Narrabundah. It was her second home. I appreciated Carolin's company and sympathy today when I got news of Gloria's death.

There is much discussion about whether animals have souls. I know that Gloria had a beautiful spirit – she was loyal, understanding, sometimes wilful (obedience was not her strong point), affectionate, long-suffering (especially when she had to have a wash), patient and grateful for what was done for her. I think our world would be a better place if the human population acted like Gloria, and if dogs do go to heaven I'm sure that St Patrick and St Francis would be now welcoming Gloria into their company singing, *Gloria in excelsis.*

Bridey

26 August 2006 – 4 July 2010
A tribute, 26 August 2010

Going through my album recently, there were lots of photos of our beautiful Bridey. One which really touched my heart and said so much to me about Bridey was taken at the 2008 Faith and Light Christmas pageant. Faith and Light caters for handicapped people and Bridey was invited to represent the animals in the re-enactment of the Christmas story. The photo in question had Bridey looking lovingly into the eyes of the lad who was playing Joseph.

That little cameo captured so much of Bridey's gentle and caring nature. She had a special sense of devotion for anyone who was unwell or in need of the attention she instinctively knew they would appreciate. For someone who loved to tear around the place with excitement, she knew when she had to be simply a peaceful presence to people. Geraldine tells of how Bridey would lie at the feet of her mother, Jean, in her 90s, almost as if she were her nurse. I remember another Christmas gathering in 2006 when Bridey showed the same attentiveness to one of my friends who had been diagnosed with cancer and in fact died a few months later.

Maybe her sensitivity arose from her own severe misfortune when she was only a few months old and broke her leg. It was a bad break and she was in plaster for quite a while. However, that did not prevent her from hopping around the place and making the most of whatever opportunities for a bit of fun or adventure.

I still remember vividly the day in October 2006 when Geraldine and I went to Wyee on the Central Coast to pick her up. Geraldine had been up earlier to see her. There were tears all round as we left and Bridey sat on the back seat of my car crying for about 15 minutes. Then she managed to climb over the console on to Geraldine's lap in the front seat. She snuggled up and there was not another whimper. She made herself at home in Campbell and won the hearts of everyone who met her.

For a long time I used to say that Bridey acted just as if she were in the Garden of Eden before the Fall. There was a lovely innocence about her and she believed everyone was as innately good as she was. If another dog snarled at her or had a go at her she just said 'What's your problem?' and went on with life. She loved a run on the beach or in the park, especially where there were other dogs or humans to socialise with. It was heaven for her to be with Carolin and her various canines in Tasmania and latterly with Spirit and Shadow here in Canberra.

It was a treat for me and for her to walk up Mt Ainslie. Of course, she was much admired and even though she had to stay on the lead she loved the exercise even if she was a bit frustrated about not being able chase the kangaroos. In other places, she had the chance to pursue the odd rabbit and loved chasing the galahs who would excite her by leaving it till the last moment before taking to flight.

She was ever so knowing. Geraldine used to say that she knew what we were thinking even though we couldn't always understand what was going on in her head. We never really figured out why she made such a big deal about jumping into the back of Geraldine's wagon. It got to the stage where she would rarely get in for Geraldine solo; if I were there sometimes she would cooperate, but the one thing that always worked was to solicit a perfect stranger walking by and ask for their help. They would be somewhat bemused, but pleased to think they had been of assistance. We weren't able to tell her all the adventures she was missing out on by keeping clear of the car. She confounded a dog whisperer whose professional advice was sought for the problem.

In February 2009, just after we had made the ferry crossing from Melbourne to Devonport, she had her first episode of bloat. With all her Wolfhounds, Geraldine was always careful in guarding against it. But the day before we had had a very hot trip down from Canberra and somehow that may have contributed. In any case, Bridey had to have a big operation and a couple of days in hospital. She recovered but she was restricted in what she could eat and lost a lot of weight. Yet she never lost her beautiful nature. She and Geraldine were extremely close, Bridey being allowed to sleep on her bed from then on. For the next 18 months or more she gave us lots of love but was never quite her old self. When she bloated for the fifth time on 4 July, the lovely female vet said that she could not go on. It was a tearful time for Geraldine and me but we witnessed her die with the dignity we had always recognised in her. That particular day had been a most enjoyable one for her and we thanked God for all the joy she had brought to us and to so many other people in her short life.

As we interred her ashes in our garden under a grevillea plant, Geraldine and I said the Prayer of St Francis, 'Make me an instrument of your peace'. Today would have been Bridey's fourth birthday and Mother Teresa's 100th. The world is a better place for both of them having been part of it. It was my privilege to have known them both.

Carrying the Olympic torch

Recording a great honour, 15 September 2000.

At the end of 1999, when I found out I was to carry the Olympic torch, the implications of the news somewhat escaped me as I was in hospital unable to walk, much less run, following a car accident on 9 December.

Gradually I got better and the torch began its Australian journey at Uluru in early June. My own interest and excitement grew as I witnessed its impact on individuals and large and small communities across Australia.

Nothing really prepared me for the wonderful thrill I experienced on the day itself. A few weeks earlier I learned that I would be carrying the torch from the old parliament house to the new. A great leg to run but a fairly steep climb, so I trained with a two-litre milk container filled with sugar. Four days before the run I was told that I would be lighting the cauldron on the stage in front of parliament house at the end of the torch's first day in Canberra.

Assembling at the old parliament house a few hours before the run, I met my escort runner, Alicia Paul, a delightful 16-year-old student of Merici College. I elected for us to carry the torch together for our 500 metre run and to jointly light the cauldron. We had a little practice, our nervousness being accentuated by the strong wind blowing.

We then set off on the bus with a dozen other runners (including marathon runner Susan Hobson) and two other escorts. As we let our first runner off at the War Memorial, we experienced the emotion as the torch relay made its way up Anzac Parade. Gradually we let off the runners at each stage until I was the only runner left on the bus with our two encouraging coaches.

It was lovely to be enthusiastically greeted by friends and strangers when I got off the bus behind the old parliament house. There was about a ten minute wait which provided an opportunity for photos with the torch and good wishes. Finally the police escorts arrived on Harley Davidsons, with assurances that they would guide us. Then Andrew and Alicia came into view. I lit my torch from Andrew's, shook hands with him and Alicia and I set off up Federation Mall where we heard our arrival being heralded over the loud-speaker.

The television reports said there were 10,000 people present. Maybe that was a bit inflated, but I was overcome by the crowds and their energetic welcome. I recognised a few faces but mostly it was a blur. Just before we reached the stage we were confronted by a group of cadets with rifles in a guard of honour. At first I was unsure whether to run through or around, but straight ahead seemed the only way to go.

Next moment, Alicia and I were on the stage, joyfully holding the torch aloft and then lighting the cauldron. Each of us gave a little speech, then listened to Deputy PM, John Anderson, and torch relay organiser, Di Henry. This was followed by more interviews and lots of photos in a wonderful carnival atmosphere.

We lit the cauldron at about 6.20 pm and left about 7.30, by which time we had gone from light to darkness and from about nine degrees to seven. Yet in all the excitement I hardly felt the cold despite being clad only in the torch relay attire. I don't think the smile left my face until I was leaving for home. I suspect it was similar for Alicia.

At the time of writing, the torch is on the last day of the relay in Sydney. It has continued to be, in the words of the governor-general, 'a unifying force for all Australians'. It was a rich privilege to be part of it, along with cousin Pat Power in Casino, nephew James Summerhays, an escort runner in Sydney, and 11,000 other proud Australians.

South Sydney Rabbitohs

'Keeping the faith' can mean many things, April 2015.

As a ten-year-old in 1952, I became a big fan of Clive Churchill whom some would still say was the greatest ever Australian Rugby League player. Years ahead of his time, full-back for him was not just a defensive position, but he quickly turned defence into attack setting his team mates up for tries and promoting a never-say-die spirit among the rest of the team. Churchill was captain of the Australian team, but not of South Sydney. That honour went to the tough policeman, Jack Raynor.

Although Clive was my idol, I never got to see him play, living in faraway Queanbeyan.

Souths won the premiership in 1953, 54 and 55. Their next golden era was between 1967 and 1971 when they won four premierships, coached by Churchill. By then they had won twenty premierships (including the first in 1908), far more than any other team. At the end of that era, in 1971, the Rabbitohs lost a lot of good players to wealthier clubs and the going was tough for many of the ensuing years. They made the semi-finals a few times and in 1989 were minor premiers under the leadership of the colourful Mario Fenech. Sadly, they did not progress in the finals, being beaten by eventual grand finalists, Balmain and Canberra. I had grand final tickets for that year, but when Souths bombed out, I had no trouble on-selling them to joyful Raiders' supporters.

My old team each year would do enough to keep me interested, but there were many times when I suffered a broken heart. It all came to a head in 1999 when, in the wake of the reconciliation from the Super League days, Rupert Murdoch and News Limited decided there was no place for South Sydney in the competition. In October 1999, I was proud to be part of a 50,000 strong march from Redfern Oval to the Sydney Town Hall, giving voice to our strong support for the Rabbitohs. The driving force was Souths' great George Piggins and his wife Noeline, backed up by Andrew Denton (who was MC on the Town Hall steps), Test cricketer Michael Whitney, politicians Deirdre Grusovin and her brother Laurie Brereton, and a host of former Souths greats, including Bernie Purcell, Jack Raynor, John Sattler, Bobby McCarthy, Michael Cleary, and some of the then current players , including Craig Wing and Craig Coleman.

At the following month's Australian bishops' meeting, another Rabbitoh bishop, Geoffrey Mayne, and I enlisted the help of some our fellow bishops. Geoff used the line that Rugby League without South Sydney would be like the Catholic Church without the Pope.

On the 26 November 1999, the following media release was issued.

BISHOPS SUPPORT SOUTH SYDNEY

Nine Australian Catholic bishops have signed a statement of support for the beleaguered South Sydney Rabbitohs. It is couched in these terms:

'Recognising the important part of sport in the Australian psyche and the grand traditions of South Sydney over 92 years, the under-signed Australian Catholic bishops support the retention of the club in the National Rugby League competition.

In doing so, the bishops seek to be a voice for countless Australians who lament the loss of valued institutions at the hands of corporate giants.

Some of the non-signatories among the bishops were a bit bemused, but in fact our petition attracted more media interest than anything else emerging from the bishops' meeting. In one of the radio interviews I did, I was asked what I thought of Rupert Murdoch being recently made a papal knight. I flippantly replied that it showed how little the pope knew about Rugby League, but added seriously and cynically that the media magnate was given the award for the generous donation he made to the building of a new cathedral in Los Angeles.

Eventually, Souths were kicked out of the competition but after legal battles and lots of popular support were restored two years later. It was a case of the battlers being justly rewarded. George Piggins wrote a moving account of the whole saga in his book, *Never Say Die.* He wrote with appreciation of the bishops' part in the happy outcome.

The rebuilding of the team was difficult, Souths having lost some good talent while they were in the wilderness. But in typical fashion, they battled on without being serious premiership contenders. One year, they landed the dreaded wooden spoon, but even then there was some glory when their popular winger, Nathan Merritt, was the leading try scorer in the comp.

A new surge of interest came with Russell Crowe's association with the club, even though I must admit to being a bit ambivalent about a lot of the hype. But my old team made the semis for the first time since their return to the League and hopes began to rise.

Over the years, I managed to get to a few of the games, but retirement came just in time for me in 2012 which saw a new coach in former St Edmund's Canberra's, Michael Maguire. Over the years, I had persuaded my de Jongh nephews to follow Souths and we were able to enjoy quite a few games. Souths got to the preliminary finals in 2012 and 2013 and were serious contenders for the title before bowing out at the second last hurdle.

The year 2014 wasn't all easy going, and mid-year when Souths had lost three games on the trot my nephew Geoffrey and I went to watch them play St George at the Sydney Cricket Ground. I said to Geoffrey *before* the game, 'If we are to back Souths to win the premiership, this is the time to do it.' The TAB was paying $8 for Souths to win the premiership. We each plunged $50 on the Rabbitohs. My nephews and I agreed that the Grand Final which Souths won 30-6 was the most enthralling sporting event we had ever witnessed, as part of the record crowd of 83,833. It took me weeks to come back to earth. I wrote in my Christmas letter: 'In how many Christmas letters have I made reference to my beloved South Sydney Rabbitohs? You can easily imagine my great joy in them winning the premiership for the first time in 43 years. It was so exciting to be at the grand final with my nephews, Geoffrey, Patrick and Matthew and Matt's son, Harrison. The atmosphere was exhilarating and it was only seven minutes before the end that the tension lifted and we knew that Souths had it in the bag. After the game, I bought a tee shirt with WE BELIEVED emblazoned on the front. I often used to say in the many lean years, that being a Souths' supporter and being a Catholic had a lot in common: we had had many good times as well as tough times, so loyalty was the name of the game.'

A few days after the grand-final, back in Canberra, I was called to the hospice to minister to a man who was dying. I spoke softly to him and prayed with him and it wasn't till I turned around to leave his room that I saw the poster of the Rabbitohs in triumph after their big win. I couldn't help but smile as I walked down the corridor saying to myself, 'Ziggy will die a happy man after what Souths have done for him.'

With injuries and departures from the club, Souths might find it hard going this year, but like Ziggy, I will die happy after what they have achieved in returning to their glory days in recent years, culminating in last year's grand-final victory.

Citizen of the Year

Acceptance speech, Canberra, 12 March 2009.

Thank you all for being here today to share with me the honour of being named 2009 Canberra Citizen of the Year.

This morning I walked up Mount Ainslie, as I try to do most days. From there I am always delighted by the beauty of the bush and the city; added to that, there is a camaraderie among the walkers, rarely without a greeting or a smile. I realise how blessed I am to live in Canberra.

I have always been proud of my origins in Queanbeyan and Canberra. The family of my youngest sister, Pauline de Jongh, who is here today with her daughter, Melissa, still live in the home where we grew up in Queanbeyan.

I am grateful to so many people who have touched my life. Having done all my primary schooling at St Christopher's in Manuka and my early secondary education as a foundation student of St Edmund's College, I still have lots of my childhood friends around me. You friends here today represent a group of people who have had a profound effect on my life.

Living in the suburb of Campbell, I often say that I couldn't have better neighbours and my three immediate neighbours, Audrey, Marion and Vera are here today. Such wonderful neighbourhoods contribute so much to the ethos of Canberra.

One of the most satisfying aspects of my life is the opportunity for ecumenical and inter-faith relations. I am pleased that Dr Kevin Bray, my colleague and dear friend from the ACT Churches Council, is with us, accompanied by his wife, Gwenyth. It has been my privilege to be part of lots community activities in the ACT, many of which have flowed from the ACT Churches Council membership.

Some of the greatest lessons of my life in Canberra have come from the battlers in our community – the people of Causeway in my years as a young priest in the 1960s, the residents of the Narrabundah Longstay Caravan Park, the members of L'Arche community, the refugees who have shown so much tenacity and courage; the people I stand beside in Weston Park, Yarralumla, in October most years, mourning the loss of loved ones from illicit drug use.

In the years to come, I know that one of my most significant memories will be the national apology given by the prime minister in February 2008 to our Indigenous people. I took part in the year 2000 walk over the Sydney Harbour Bridge, while many others did likewise here in Canberra. Many of you people, especially the chief minister, can be proud of what you have done in giving recognition to and seeking justice for the people who have lived on this land for 40,000 years.

In the audience today is my archbishop, Mark Coleridge. I would like to thank Archbishop Mark and his predecessor, Francis Carroll, for allowing me the freedom to spend so much of my time involved in community activities. They have never begrudged the time I have spent out on the fringes and at times they have had to cop a bit of flak when my stances have appeared to be controversial.

Canberra, our city and our home, is also the national capital where we are in a special position of influence in relation to the rest of Australia and the international community. For us, that is an enormous privilege which brings with it the responsibility to help shape a better world.

My favourite ACT numberplate is the one that describes Canberra as the Heart of the Nation. I am deeply conscious of the honour being bestowed on me today by the chief minister on behalf of the people of Canberra. I promise to do all I can during the coming year to promote Canberra as the heart of the nation – a city which cares for its environment and all its people, especially the most vulnerable in our midst.

Thank you and God bless you.

Retirement Mass
St Christopher's

Homily given in the Cathedral Church which has played such an important part in the author's blessed life, 19 June 2012.

Last year, the 25th anniversary of my ordination as bishop, 18 April, fell on the Monday of Holy Week, the day we celebrate the Chrism Mass here in the cathedral. Because of my anniversary, Archbishop Mark kindly invited me to be the principal celebrant. I said on that occasion that when I made my First Holy Communion in St Christopher's, on 24 April 1949, and when I was confirmed here, on 3 May 1953, I never imagined that I would be ordained bishop in this cathedral church on 18 April 1986. I was confirmed by the first archbishop of Canberra and Goulburn, Terence McGuire, ordained priest by his immediate successor, Eris O'Brien, and I was secretary to the next three archbishops, Thomas Cahill, Edward Clancy and Francis Carroll before becoming Auxiliary Bishop to Archbishops Carroll and Coleridge. I think it is a lovely twist of fate that has me serving my last days as Auxiliary Bishop under the diocesan leadership of Monsignor John Woods who was my altar boy when I arrived in this parish as a newly ordained priest early in 1966.

When I became bishop, I took as my motto GOD IS LOVE and I have been alluding to that in my Confirmation homilies in the past few weeks as a way of highlighting the Year of Grace, the observance of which we began on Pentecost Sunday. I first experienced the unconditional love of God through the love of my dear mother. The enduring memory of the countless examples of her love and goodness continues to enable me to see such grace in the lives of people I meet every day. I often say that never a day goes by without me thanking God for the gift of the priesthood which has enabled me to witness such grace in so many ways, in good times and in bad. When we are open to the God of Surprises, we find grace in many unexpected places and in the most unlikely of people. It is when we try to put God into a box, that we fail to see God in the people around us. I have been sharing with the Confirmation children a quotation from Pope John Paul II that I have only recently discovered: 'If we have Jesus in our hearts, we will see his face in every person we meet.'

Professor Manning Clark lived just up the road from here and sometimes dropped in to St Christopher's. He was not a Catholic and sometimes struggled with the whole notion of belief, but he was very much a searcher. He enjoyed a warm friendship with his fellow historian, Archbishop Eris O'Brien, even before the both of them came to Canberra. In 1990, Manning Clark wrote a book called *The Quest for Grace.* I would hope that all of us here this evening are engaged in a quest for grace. Each of our life's journeys and our journeys of faith have been different, but all have been under the influence of God's grace even when we may not have recognised it. As I look into this congregation I see so many of you who have powerfully and heroically witnessed to God's love in your lives and have shared that love with one another. My sisters and brothers of other churches present tonight remind me of the many blessings that have come into my life through their friendship and powerful witness to the values of the Gospel. What I have learnt from you has brought me closer to the heart of Jesus. My brother priests and deacons have been veritable companions on the journey.

The gospel of this evening's Mass speaks to us of Jesus returning to his home town of Nazareth and going into the synagogue where he would have worshipped with Mary and Joseph as he was growing up. He applies to himself the words of the prophet Isaiah: 'The spirit of the Lord has been given to me, for he has anointed me. He has sent me to bring good news to the poor, to proclaim liberty to captives and to the blind new sight, to set the down-trodden free, to proclaim the Lord's year of favour.' At the beginning of his public ministry, Jesus was proclaiming what his vocation was all about. In the three years of his public ministry, he consistently lived up to the promises he made that day. He constantly sought to do the will of his

228 — *Joy and Hope*

Father and continually called his disciples into relationship with the Father under the influence of the Holy Spirit. Through his words and actions he gave comfort, healing, strength and hope to all with whom he came in contact. St Luke's Gospel from which we read this evening in a special way shows the compassionate heart of Jesus.

If my mother taught me the unconditional love of God, it was my father who showed me what it meant to stand up against injustice and to be in solidarity with people who are struggling. Growing up in Quean-beyan, I never objected to it being called Struggletown because I felt that term epitomised many of the most admirable of my home town's qualities. I saw my father, a Justice of the Peace, not just witnessing the signatures on people's documents but particularly in helping them find their way in their search not only for grace but sometimes for survival. He and Mum were particularly welcoming to many of the post-World War II refugees affectionately called New Australians, many of whom were starting a new life in Queanbeyan. Dad had a real heart for the people needing help through the St Vincent de Paul Society. He never had a driver's licence and one time my sister, Maria, was driving him around to do some of his St V de P calls. She sat in the car while Dad went into a house and a lady emerged smoking a cigarette. When Dad came back to the car, Maria said, 'That is a bit rich. Here she is taking charity from the St Vincent de Paul Society yet she can afford to smoke.' Dad replied simply, 'Even poor people are entitled to the little pleasures of life.'

At times, I feel a bit embarrassed when my name goes up in lights for what I have done in the pursuit of justice. So often I have been invited by some group of dedicated people to join in solidarity with them in supporting people at risk in all kinds of situations: our own Indigenous people, refugees and asylum seekers, the Palestinian people, the Tamils, the East Timorese; and, here in Canberra, homeless people, United Voice, the union supporting the cleaners, most of whom are migrant and women, residents of the Long Stay Caravan Park being threatened with eviction in 2006, my friends with whom I pray on World Aids Day each year, and in their annual service at Weston Park those mourning the death of family members and friends from illicit drug use. In those and in many similar instances, I have been humbled to witness the hours of tireless dedication put in by people with extremely generous hearts. I see these people who often make no claim to any religious affiliation and I think of Jesus' words, 'As often as you did this for one of the least of my brothers and sisters you did it to me.'

May I repeat what I said at last year's Chrism Mass. If my joy is in all of you present tonight, my sorrow is in those who no longer feel at home in the life of the Catholic Church. In my ministry as bishop, I have tried to reach out to those who are at the edges, both in the church and in the wider community. I don't think any of us can be comfortable in the family of the church without asking what is causing so many of our sisters and brothers to walk away. So often, I hear the heart-felt plea 'I haven't abandoned the church, the church has abandoned me.'

My hopes for retirement are that, leaving aside the burdens of meetings and bureaucracy, I will be freer to support my brother priests and deacons who are hanging in there for the long haul, to catch up with other friends and family members and to have a special outreach to those on the outer, both in terms of the church and the wider community. I promise to continue to listen to your stories and to be uplifted by your example.

I hope that in this Year of Grace, as we celebrate the fifty years since the beginning of the Second Vatican Council, we may reclaim what it means to be part of the People of God and to help the church be its best self in showing the face of Jesus to every person in our midst. May the Holy Spirit be with us all in our quest for grace.

Pat Power was born in Cooma, NSW, in 1942, grew up in Queanbeyan, and was educated at St Christopher's School and St Edmund's College in Canberra and Chevalier College, Bowral. After leaving school, he trained for the priesthood and was ordained in Queanbeyan in 1965.

He did a doctorate in canon law in Rome, 1972-75, and returned to Canberra to serve as Archbishop's Secretary (to three archbishops) and director of the marriage tribunal. In 1985, he became parish priest of his home parish of Queanbeyan In 1986, he was ordained bishop by Archbishop Francis Carroll in St Christopher's Cathedral, Canberra.

Much of his ministry has been in the field of ecumenical and inter-faith relations, social justice and social welfare. At the 1998 Oceania Synod of Bishops in Rome, he spoke on marginalised people in society and in the church. Much of his efforts have been directed in this area through Catholic Welfare Australia and through local community organisations in Canberra. He has been a strong advocate for the East Timorese and the Palestinian people, for Aboriginal people, for racial respect, for the unemployed, and in opposition to abortion and assisted suicide. In 2000, he chaired a major enquiry into poverty in the Australian Capital Territory.

In December 2006 he was inaugurated into the ACT Honour Walk for being a voice for the disadvantaged in the community, and in 2009 was named Canberra Citizen of the Year

Bishop Pat Power chose to retire at age 70, effective June 2012.

Lightning Source UK Ltd.
Milton Keynes UK
UKHW02f0956231117
313214UK00007B/538/P